Spy and Counterspy

IAN DEAR

Spy and Counterspy

Secret Agents and Double Agents from the Second World War to the Cold War

CANCELLED

Falkirk Council	
Askews & Holts	2013
327.1209	£9.99

First published 2013
by Spellmount, an imprint of
The History Press
The Mill, Brimscombe Port
Stroud, Gloucestershire, GL5 2QG
www.thehistorypress.co.uk

British Library Cataloguing in Publication Data.
A catalogue record for this book is available from the British Library.

ISBN 978 0 7524 5991 2

Typesetting and origination by The History Press
Printed in Great Britain

Contents

Acknowledgements

I would like to thank the following for permission to use extracts from the titles listed below. Other copyright holders have been credited in the chapter notes:

Miranda Carter, *Anthony Blunt: His Lives* (London, 2001). Copyright © Miranda Carter, 2001. Published by Macmillan, 2001

Ewen Montagu, *Beyond Top Secret Ultra* (London, 1977). Extracts reprinted by permission of the Random House Group Ltd, and by the Penguin Group (USA) Inc

Kathryn S. Olmsted, *Red Spy Queen: A Biography of Elizabeth Bentley* (Chapel Hill, NC, 2002). Copyright © the University of North Carolina Press, 2002, www.uncpress.unc.edu

Russell Miller, *Codename Tricycle: The True Story of the Second World War's Most Extraordinary Double Agent* (London 2005). Reprinted by permission of The Random House Group Ltd and Peters Fraser & Dunlop (www.petersfraserdunlop.com) on behalf of Russell Miller

Yuri Modin, *My Five Cambridge Friends* (New York, 1994). Copyright © Editions Robert Laffont S.A. Paris, 1994. Extracts reproduced by permission of the publisher, Headline Publishing Group Ltd and by Farrar Straus & Giroux, New York

Quotes from articles in *Journal of Intelligence and National Security* and *International Journal of Intelligence and Counter-Intelligence*. Reprinted by permission of the publisher (Taylor & Francis Ltd, http://www.tandf.co.uk/journals)

While every effort has been made to contact the copyright holders of all the titles from which I have used extracts, I have not always been successful. These copyright holders are invited to contact the publishers, as are those copyright holders of the photographs I have been unable to trace.

List of Abbreviations

A-A	Anti-Aircraft
ASIO	Australian Security Intelligence Organisation
BBC	British Broadcasting Corporation
CIA	Central Intelligence Agency
COI	Office of Coordination of Information
CPGB	Communist Party of Great Britain
CPUSA	Communist Party of the United States of America
DAK	Deutsches Afrika Korps
DNB	Deutsches Nachtrichten Büro
FBI	Federal Bureau of Investigation
FO	Foreign Office
FUSAG	First United States Army Group
GC&CS	Government Code and Cipher School
GCHQ	Government Communications Headquarters
GRU	Glavnoye Razvedyvatelnoyed Upravleniye: Soviet Military Intelligence
IRA	Irish Republican Army
IRD	Information Research Department
ISOS	Intelligence Services Oliver Strachey
JCS	Joint Chiefs of Staff
KGB	Komitet Gosudarstvennoi Bezopastnosti: Soviet Security and Intelligence Service (1954–91)
LRDG	Long Range Desert Group
MBE	Member of the British Empire
MGB	Ministerstvo Gosudarstvennoi Bezopastnosti: Soviet Ministry of State Security (1946–54)
MI5	British Security Service
MI6	British Secret Intelligence Service
MP	Member of Parliament
NKGB	Narodnyi Kommissariat Gosudarstvennoi Bezopastnosti: Soviet Security and Intelligence Service (1941–46, part of NKVD 1941–43)

NKVD	Narodnyi Kommissariat Vnutrennikh Del: People's Commissariat for Internal Affairs (1922–23, 1934–43)
OBE	Order of the British Empire
OGPU	Obyedinennoye Gosudarstvennoye Politicheskoye Upravleniye: Soviet Security and Intelligence Service (1923–34)
OKW	Oberkommando der Wehrmacht
OSS	Office of Strategic Services
POW	prisoners of war
RNVR	Royal Naval Volunteer Reserve
RSHA	Reichssicherheitshauptamt: Reich Security Main Office, the Nazi Party's umbrella organisation for all its security services
SD	Sicherheitsdienst: Nazi Intelligence Service
SIME	Security Intelligence Middle East
SOE	Special Operations Executive
SSA	Signals Security Agency
USSR	Union of Soviet Socialist Republics

Introduction

This is the final part of a trilogy on clandestine warfare. Like the first two – *Sabotage and Subversion* and *Escape and Evasion* – this book covers events during the Second World War, but it also includes the decades on either side of it. Espionage is often a very long-term business, and it would be no use confining the work of The Cambridge Five, for instance, to the war years when they did as much, if not more, damage to the interests of their country in peacetime. However, the main focus is on the years 1939–45, and the examples I have chosen are but a small cross-section of the espionage both sides employed – even when the countries concerned were supposed to be Allies.

It is commonly acknowledged that more lies have been told about spies and spying than any other subject. A possible exception is sex, and it is not a coincidence that the two subjects are linked by that doubtful distinction. Perhaps someone some day will write on the love life of spies and how it motivated their behaviour. However, the examples of espionage I have chosen are not for any prurient motive, but because more information has become available about each of them. The sources include a short-lived partial access to the KGB archives during the early 1990s; the posting by the United States' National Security Agency of the VENONA signals and related material on the internet during the mid-1990s; and the release into The National Archives at Kew of MI5 and associated files which is still ongoing. The publication of the official histories of MI5 and MI6, in 2009 and 2010 respectively, and the release of certain private diaries and memoirs during the last decade, have also helped me, I hope, edge slightly closer to the truth.

So the fog surrounding espionage during the Second World War is becoming a little less dense. For example, it is now acknowledged that some early post-war tales of espionage were not much more than cover stories for ULTRA intelligence. This is not to belittle the courage of the agent concerned, but shows the extent to which the authorities went to keep ULTRA a secret until it was eventually became public knowledge in the 1970s.

Will the fog ever clear completely? Not a hope. Spying by its very nature is all smoke and mirrors, which is why it remains a subject of such fascination to so many.

Ian Dear
Cottenham, Cambridge, January 2013

1

Pit and Pan and the English Patient

In May 1942 German Military Intelligence (Abwehr) mounted SALAM, the codename for an operation to infiltrate two of its spies across the desert from Axis-held Libya into Egypt. Once this was accomplished, the spies were to implement operation CONDOR, which was to discover British plans to prevent German and Italian forces from capturing the Suez Canal, Britain's lifeline to its Far East Empire. They were also ordered to encourage an incipient Egyptian Army plot to revolt against the British.

Erwin Rommel, the charismatic German general commanding the Axis armies in Libya, already had an excellent, if unwitting, intelligence source in the American military attaché in Cairo, Colonel Fellers. The role of Fellers was to report to Washington on what the British were up to militarily and diplomatically. This he did meticulously, not knowing that the diplomatic cipher (the Black Code) he used to relay his reports was being read by the Italians who had acquired photographs of the code's enciphering tables from the US embassy in Rome.

This Black Code intelligence was invaluable to Rommel for two reasons: it was very detailed and it was extremely reliable, as it was hardly likely that the British would give false information to the United States, which was soon to become their ally. So pleased was Rommel with this intelligence that he called it *die gute Quelle* (the good source), and it was also known to the Germans as 'the little fellows' or 'the little fellers', a play on the US attaché's name. Nevertheless, it was decided that a back-up source was needed should the American one dry up (which it did at the end of June 1942).

Putting agents on the ground would also enable the Germans to encourage the anti-British faction in the Egyptian armed forces – it included two future Egyptian presidents, Gamal Abdel Nasser and Anwar el-Sadat – which was plotting to oust the British from Egypt. In this they faced a formidable task, for

though the country had officially become an independent con-
stitutional monarchy under the Anglo-Egyptian treaty of 1936,
the treaty gave the British certain rights in wartime. These they
invoked when hostilities began that made Egypt virtually an
occupied – though still independent – country.

In February 1941 Rommel and the two divisions of the famous
Deutsches Afrika Korps (DAK) were sent to boost the flagging
Italian Army, whose efforts to conquer Egypt from their Libyan
colony had proved fruitless. In what became known as the Western
Desert Campaign, the two sides fought across the vast expanses of
sand and scrub known as the Libyan Desert, though its eastern part
was in Egypt. The size of the entire Indian sub-continent, it covers
an area of over 1.5 million square miles (3.9 million square kilometres) and dwarfs any of the world's other deserts. Like a rutted
cart track it has a series of parallel escarpments running east to west
down its entire length, some of them as high as 1,000ft (305m). In
places the wind, over millennia, has hollowed out the base of these
ridges so that the underground water table is close enough to the
surface to create oases. Before the advent of the motorcar and the
aeroplane these oases were completely isolated, and the vast distances and the rugged terrain made exploration all but impossible.
The only mode of travel was by camel. This has a maximum range
of about 270 miles (430km) as it needs water after 15 days. So much
of the desert remained unmapped, and early motorised explorers
faced a formidable and dangerous task.

Because of the distances involved, explorers and armies alike
were faced with the problem of supply, particularly fuel. The climate, too, made movement difficult as temperatures in the desert
summer could reach 150°F (65°C) while at night they dropped to
below freezing, and the winds could whip up fierce, blinding sandstorms at a moment's notice. It was an impossibly difficult climate
to fight in where, above all, speed was of the essence. As Rommel
commented, it was the one thing that mattered, and 'territory was
less important than to keep moving until a tactically favourable
position for battle was found, and then to fight'.[1]

Though the British and those allied to them – principally de Gaulle's Free French forces and those from the British
Commonwealth – were sometimes slow in responding to
Rommel's rapier-like thrusts, they did possess a small, highly
mobile, strike force that punched well above its weight. Called the

Long Range Desert Group (LRDG), this was formed in June 1940 by a self-taught geographer, Captain Ralph Bagnold, a Cambridge University-educated regular officer in the Royal Engineers. Its main function was to gather intelligence by keeping a road watch behind Rommel's lines, but it also mounted lightning attacks on enemy fuel dumps, airfields and garrisons, and made a general nuisance of itself.

Between the wars Bagnold had been one of the pioneers of motorised desert exploration using stripped down Model A Fords. An ingenious, mechanically gifted man, he had perfected a method of preventing his car's radiator from boiling dry by using a rubber tube to connect the radiator overflow to a tank half full of water, which was fixed to the car's running board. The steam from the overflow would then condense into water before being sucked back into the radiator.[2] He also learnt how to surmount the 300ft (91m) sand dunes by driving at them full tilt; how to avoid being bogged down in the soft sand by drastically reducing the pressures of his vehicles' tyres; and how, if he did get stuck, to free himself by using steel channels and rope ladders under the front wheels. To navigate across the desert day and night he taught himself to use a theodolite to measure the height of the stars and, knowing how a magnetic compass was affected by the steel in his vehicle, he perfected a sun compass with which to calculate his bearings.

Above all, Bagnold's desert experience taught him never to attempt to venture anywhere with only one vehicle, and if one did break down those in it should never attempt to leave it, however powerful the urge to do so. He later wrote:

> An extraordinary powerful impulse urges one to move, anywhere, in any direction, rather than stay still and think it out. This psychological effect of the true desert has been the cause of nearly every desert disaster of recent years. Always the lost one leaves his broken-down aeroplane or car and begins an unreasoning trudge, somewhere – it does not matter where. The vehicle is found by planes or trackers, but the solitary, half-demented walker is too small to spot.[3]

All this experience Bagnold had accumulated during expeditions with a few companions in the 1920s and 1930s in order to discover and map the most inaccessible parts of the desert. His feats included exploring a vast area of desert between Cairo and Ain Dalla, said to contain the mythical city of Zerzura; and making, in 1932, the first recorded east–west crossing of the Libyan Desert. He always asserted these epic journeys had been made for the fun of it, and there is no reason to disbelieve him, though some suspected him of doing it for military purposes. Certainly when the war came to North Africa he was able to put this knowledge to good effect by forming the LRDG, whose Chevrolet trucks and command cars were manned mainly by New Zealanders. According to Bagnold, they adapted to desert warfare like ducks to water.

* * * * *

Bagnold and his companions were not alone in their early enthusiasm for motorised desert travel. At the same time as they were making their first ventures into the Sahara, a certain putative Hungarian count, Laszlo Almasy, was mounting his own expeditions. The main character in Michael Ondaatje's novel *The English Patient* – later made into a highly successful film – was based on Almasy, who came from what has been described as a dysfunctional and disgruntled family,[4] which lacked a noble title despite its ancient Hungarian lineage.

Almasy was born in 1895 at Castle Borostyanko in western Hungary – renamed Burg Bernstein when the region became part of eastern Austria after the First World War – which belonged to his grandfather, Eduard Almasy. Attached to this forbidding ancient fortress was a large and prestigious estate. Both had been bought by Eduard to increase the family's social standing and the possibility of being ennobled. Eduard had a son, Gyorgy, whose Italian-born wife produced two sons, Janos and Laszlo, and a daughter, Gyorgina. Gyorgy was an ethnographer and explorer, though he preferred to investigate the fleshpots of central Europe. This inevitably brought marital strife and discord and, perhaps, accounted for Almasy's inability in later life to establish long-term relationships. Not surprisingly, the marriage ended in divorce.

Though a gifted linguist – he spoke Hungarian, German, French, Italian, English, and later Arabic – Laszlo Almasy was not interested in academic subjects, at which he proved to be quite hopeless. Instead, from a young age, he became enthralled by two of the new mechanical wonders of the era: the aeroplane and the automobile; at just 14 he built himself a rudimentary glider. Then, in a final attempt to give him a proper education, Almasy's grandfather sent him to an educational establishment in Eastbourne on the English south coast. This also failed, but it did give the budding aviator a chance to join the local flying club, and after only a few hours of instruction Almasy, then aged 17, qualified for a pilot licence. At around this time he also learnt to drive, for his licence records that the following year he was fined for dangerous driving. However, before he could break his neck either on the road or in the air, the First World War broke out and Almasy hastened home to join the army. He then transferred to the recently formed Austro-Hungarian Air Force. In March 1918 he was shot down and wounded, and he spent the rest of the war as a flying instructor.

In 1919 the Austro-Hungarian Empire was broken up and the Hapsburg Emperor Karl IV took refuge in Switzerland. However, there were some, including Almasy, who wanted him back on the throne, even if it was only the Hungarian one, and in 1921 Almasy aided the emperor's two abortive attempts to regain it. As a reward for his support, Karl IV made Almasy a count before retreating to exile in Madeira where he died the following year. However, Almasy could not use the title in Hungary (though he did elsewhere) as it was never ratified by the Hungarian parliament.

In these early post-war years Almasy was employed as secretary and huntsman to a Hungarian bishop, and this brought him many new contacts amongst the rich and powerful, including Egyptian royalty and aristocracy who came to enjoy the hunting on offer. He also pursued his early enthusiasm for the motor car by taking a mechanics course and participating in motor rallies, driving for the Graz-based Steyr Automobile Works. He became something of a star on the rally circuit and this led Steyr to offer him a job in Cairo as their representative for the Middle East and Africa. In the winter of 1926 he began his new career by driving a Steyr touring car from Cairo to Aswan, a distance of some 600 miles (950km) beside the River Nile on what was no more than a desert track. From there he and his companion drove across the Nubian Desert to Khartoum, and then followed the Blue Nile and its tributary the Dinder before returning to Cairo.

This pioneering trek, and the tests Almasy subsequently carried out on other Steyr models, established his reputation as an intrepid motorised explorer. It honed his skills as a mechanic and taught him the techniques of driving in the desert. His method of negotiating a sand dune was a star turn for those he took on desert tours, and he would earn himself extra money by showing them how it was done. Like Bagnold, he drove at top speed up the gradually sloping windward side of the dune. Then, when he reached the top, he would turn sharply so that the car slid sideways down the dune's steep leeward side. So popular did this trick become that the practice was banned on safety grounds, though in fact it was not as dangerous as it sounded.

Taking the rich on desert tours and on hunting safaris soon became a way of life for Almasy, and supplemented his earnings from Steyr as well as giving its products good publicity. An early supporter of his desert forays was Prince Kemal el Din, a fabulously wealthy member of the Egyptian royal family. Kemal, a keen explorer himself, had, in 1926, mapped part of a rocky desert plateau known as Gilf Kebir (The Great Wall), before ill health had overcome him. He gave Almasy a three-year contract to finish the job and, hopefully, to discover the lost city of Zerzura, or the Oasis of the Small Birds as it was called.

Finding Zerzura quickly became an obsession with Almasy – as it had with Bagnold and other desert explorers – as did discovering another of the desert's most enduring legends: the remains of the army of Cambyses, the fifth-century BC Persian conqueror of Egypt, which had allegedly vanished in one of the desert's fearful sandstorms. Such romantic and whimsical destinations caught the fancy of those wealthy enough to indulge their fantasies, and Zerzura in particular became such a magnet to interwar explorers that they formed the 'Zerzura Club'. This had no premises and no rules, beyond the obligation to attend the annual dinner at the Café Royal in London's Regent Street. Both Bagnold and Almasy attended these functions, where Almasy would have met a number of Englishmen who were soon to become his enemies. Doubtless, they exchanged experiences and learnt about each other's desert techniques.

Desert exploration proved to be the ideal life for the young adventurous Hungarian aristocrat. Though he never had any money, he knew everyone and indulged in the good life in Cairo, a city that was more European than it is today. He enjoyed living dangerously and his adventures read like cuttings from *Boy's Own Paper*. However, all this threatened to come to an end when, in 1932, Kemal and another of Almasy's richest backers both died; and, because of the Great Depression, he lost his job with Steyr.

However, in 1933, while exploring part of the Gilf Kebir that Kemal had already mapped, Almasy found some Stone Age cave paintings. Others had come across similar paintings of animals that had inhabited the area before it had gradually turned to sand, but Almasy was the first to discover paintings of the men who must also have lived there, by the side of a long-vanished lake. Those eager to see them paid him well to take them to the caves, but Zerzura remained elusive, and he did not have any luck finding the remains of the vanished army of Cambyses either. Though he continued his desert travels whenever the opportunity arose, he now turned to his other love, flying. He helped found Egypt's Royal Aero Club, became a flight instructor at Cairo airport, and ran the agency for a Hungarian firm that designed and built gliders.

By now there was talk of another war. Not surprisingly, Almasy's desert adventures had attracted the attention of British intelligence in Cairo. One of its tasks was to monitor disputed desert areas, and it had become concerned by the Italian occupation of the larger Libyan oases close to the Egyptian border. Some suspected Almasy was working for the Italians; others thought that he might be in the pay of the Germans; while the Italians were pretty sure he was being funded by the English, as a report by the Italian minister in Cairo indicated. 'It can be taken for granted that he is an agent of the complex English political-military organization in Egypt,' the minister wrote when it became known Almasy had found a way through the Gilf Kebir, which he called the Aqaba Pass. 'This is not tourist information, but indication of military aims. It shows that the English want … to go from Egypt into Italian territory with heavy convoys.[5]

The British Foreign Office, which thought Almasy both eccentric and unpleasant, had its own suspicions about him; for though he had undertaken several desert explorations with Englishmen, it was aware that more recently his travelling companions had come from potentially hostile countries such as Italy, Hungary and Germany. The fact that his elder brother, Janos, now the owner of Burg Bernstein, had taken up with Unity Mitford, a devout admirer of Hitler, must also have caused some suspicions as to where the family's political sympathies lay.

However, the Englishmen who had explored with him found him pleasant enough. Bagnold described him as an amusing,

likeable man, though a secretive loner who would vanish from
Cairo and reappear months later without revealing where he had
been. Mysterious, too, was his sex life. In Cairo he was known
as something of a ladies' man in search of a rich wife, but there
were also rumours of homosexual encounters with small boys
in the backstreets of the Egyptian capital – rather the opposite of the heterosexual English Patient the film portrayed. One
thing was for sure: some English women he met disliked him on
sight; one even refused to shake his hand. What wasn't known
at the time, and only came to light in 1995 when a bundle of
letters was found at Burg Bernstein, was that from the late 1930s
Almasy had been carrying on an intermittent love affair with
a young German actor called Hans Entholt. So smitten was
Almasy with this young man that he made sure he accompanied
him on Operation SALAM.

With war now fast approaching Almasy returned to Hungary
and in 1939 joined the Royal Hungarian Air Force as a reserve
officer and became a flight instructor. The same year his book, *The
Unknown Sahara*, which had been published in Hungary in 1934,
came out in a German edition. This brought him to the attention of the Abwehr's North African desk, which was recruiting
specialists to ferment risings against British rule in the Middle East.
An Abwehr officer from the Balkan desk, Major Nikolaus Ritter,
visited Almasy in Budapest and was suitably impressed. 'A tall, dis-
tinguished-looking man,' he reported back, 'with finely chiselled
features … a cavalier of the old school.'[6]

During one of their talks the name of an Arab nationalist,
General Aziz Masri, cropped up. The British had recently levered
the general out of his position as the Egyptian Army's chief of
staff, and Ritter suggested that Almasy, who was friendly with the
general, might persuade him to defect to Germany. This, Ritter
thought, could inspire the Egyptian Army's officer corps, who
were particularly anti-British and were devoted to Masri, to rebel
against what was virtually a British occupation of their country. Almasy agreed to help, though Ritter suspected he did so
because all he wanted to do was return to Egypt. Rather perceptive of him as it turned out.

With the entry of Rommel into the desert war in February
1941, the plan to suborn Masri, and another to infiltrate agents
into Cairo, was given official Abwehr approval. Ritter was

ordered to form a *Sonderkommando*, or special group, and Almasy, now seconded to the Luftwaffe as a captain, became its second-in-command. Before Almasy left to join it he had lunch with a Hungarian ornithologist and his son. The latter later recalled that when Almasy was asked how he thought working for the Germans could be reconciled with his friendship with the British, Almasy replied that he would not be doing anything that clashed with what he called his military honour.

> Then he stared into space for a long time and slowly added: 'The only thing that really interests me there is to dig out Cambyses! Rommel will supply the petrol ...' I can still vividly recall the almost crazy, obsessed look on his face ... I have always felt he would make a pact with the devil himself to further his voyages of discovery: everything else was of secondary importance.[7]

When Ritter's Commando arrived in Tripoli at the end of March 1941, Rommel's first big offensive was already under way and by the time he ran short of fuel the new front had shifted almost to the Egyptian border. The Commando moved up behind the advancing DAK before setting up its headquarters at Derna on the Mediterranean coast, where Almasy began to organise 'Plan el Masri'. Contact was made with the dissident Egyptian general via a clandestine wireless link, a portable transmitter/receiver that had been smuggled into the still-neutral Hungarian Legation in Cairo, and arrangements were made for him to be picked up inside western Egypt by Almasy flying a German Heinkel light bomber. To avoid being detected by British radar, Almasy was to fly low over the desert to his destination, before touching down near a landmark called the Red Jebel, on a hard strip of sand that would be indicated by a cross. The plan, which seemed foolproof, would never have succeeded as Bletchley Park's Code and Cipher School, which had broken the Abwehr's hand cipher, was monitoring it closely. Anyway, Masri never turned up. He was later betrayed and arrested, though the whole episode was so embarrassing to the British that he was never prosecuted.

The attempt to fulfil the Commando's second task, flying two Abwehr agents into Egypt, was also aborted when the aircraft (which was not piloted by Almasy) ditched in the sea. One of the agents was killed, and Ritter was so badly injured he had to relinquish command of the Commando to Almasy, who now decided that he would execute SALAM by delivering the agents overland. This not only gave cryptographers at Bletchley Park the impression that the Germans had formed a similar unit to Bagnold's LRDG, but alerted one of its intelligence analysts, Jean Alington (later Mrs Howard), to a signal from the German High Command (OKW) about Almasy's intended route. At the time she was acting as a 'long stop', as she described it, for any OKW decodes that had been overlooked, and she immediately realised its importance; for he planned to pass close to a British signals unit, which was transmitting false signals to deceive the Germans that a powerful British army formation was positioned there. She therefore requested she be allowed to search for similar Abwehr and ULTRA intelligence signals about Almasy. This was grudgingly granted, though she was told to do it in her own time, and it enabled her to piece together Almasy's intended journey.

'I thought,' she recalled during a television interview in 1995, 'this man must be caught. It would be terrible if we didn't send someone to catch him before he discovered the truth about our phantom army.'[8] She alerted Cairo to Almasy's route, which was later confirmed by intelligence reports of two mysterious vehicles passing through a British-held oasis, and in due course Operation CLAPTRAP was launched to try and capture him.[9]

* * * * *

As commander of his own special unit, Almasy had the right to choose his own men for the operation. Excluding the two spies, SALAM comprised a seven-man team who were to maintain wireless contact with two of Rommel's signals desert outposts. Six were members of the elite special forces, the Brandenburg Regiment, two of whom were radio operators. The seventh, the unit's medical orderly, was none other than Almasy's officer cadet lover, Hans Entholt, whom Almasy had managed to have transferred from the Eastern Front.

Operation SALAM was launched on 12 May 1942 from the Italian-occupied Gialo Oasis, later described by one of the spies as where 'the springs are brackish and the inhabitants surly. A thousand palm trees and filthy mud huts stand in a hollow in the middle of the desert. The wind howls ceaselessly.'[10] So he couldn't haven't been pleased when, just days after starting out, Almasy was forced to return to Gialo as sand dunes, not marked on any of his Italian maps and impassable to his heavily laden vehicles, barred his progress. Also, his lover and one of the wireless operators were ill with desert colic and were worsening by the hour, obliging Almasy to send them back to Tripoli for treatment (Entholt was later killed in action). He then made an aerial survey of alternative routes, and eventually opted for a longer, but less arduous one. This caused a supply problem as the longer route risked having insufficient fuel and water for the return journey. He solved this, or so he hoped, by reducing his convoy to two 30cwt Bedfords and two Ford V8 station-wagons, and retaining only three of the Brandenburgers.

'During the night everything re-calculated and the trip reorganised,' Almasy wrote in his diary.[11] 'We must go via Kufra! A detour of 500km [310 miles] both on the outwards and return journeys, i.e. increased load for 1000km [620 miles]. Instead of the 2000km [1,240 miles] originally reckoned, it is now about 4200km! [2,600 miles].' This hugely increased the risks.

Driving through the outskirts of the elliptically shaped Kufra Oasis – really a series of smaller oases roughly 30 miles (48km) long and 12 miles (19km) wide – was a dangerous undertaking as it was now in Allied hands after being captured from the Italians the previous year. The two spies, whom Almasy nicknamed Pit and Pan, 'are not overjoyed at driving through Kufra,' Almasy recorded. 'They fear an encounter with the enemy. According to aerial reconnaissance the British post is supposed to be near Bir du Zerreigh ... I shall attempt to turn southwards before then.'

From his comments it is obvious Almasy did not think highly of the two spies. 'Pit and Pan, who are riding in the radio car,' he noted towards the end of the outward journey, 'are the most untidy fellows I've ever had under me. The inside of the radio car looks frightful ... personal effects, weapons and food all mixed up together.' As will be seen, he wasn't particularly impressed with the Brandenburgers either.

However, as all Almasy's vehicles had been captured from the British, there was a good chance they would avoid detection at Kufra. To conform to the rules of war, they bore the markings of the Afrika Korps' 21st Panzer Division, but Almasy partially obscured them with sand. Once through Kufra, Almasy planned to turn eastwards towards the Gilf Kebir, and then north-eastwards to Kharga and its oasis, before reaching his final objective, A͟sͬ͟ the Nile valley. There the two spies would be dropped and would board a train to Cairo.

The reduced convoy passed near a British outpost on the northern outskirts of the Kufra Oasis at about 1230 on 15 May without being detected. 'I drove through it purposely at noon-time,' Almasy wrote; 'that's when Tommy is asleep.' They found an old track that was easy to follow and at 1900 stopped for the night having covered just over 130 miles (210km). Almasy found a good hiding place for the cans of petrol and water that he would need for the return journey, and the next day continued to follow the track across difficult rocky terrain. After 37 miles (60km) he attempted to change course but found the 'moon-landscape' impossible to traverse and returned to the track. This soon became invisible amongst some dunes, but he recognised others from his earlier adventures and in the afternoon reached an open *serir*, or sandy plain, where to his surprise, and probably consternation, he found the fresh tracks of Allied motorised columns. He then turned south, made for a big double *gara* {Russian for hill), and eventually laagered between them at 1830, having covered 156 miles (250km). They hid more petrol, water, and rations for their return journey, and the wireless operator tried to contact one of the two listening posts Rommel had allotted to the operation, but without success.

On 17 May Almasy set out early to try and find the route to Gilf Kebir. 'To the east a large group of high black *garas*, <u>not</u> shown on the Italian map. No mapping was done here outside the Depression and the Gebel Kufra.' Then he queried testily: 'What were they doing from 1931–1939, then?' He also showed his frustration with his companions:

> Through the absence of Entholt I have to see that Woehrmann [the wireless operator] keeps the log-book up to date. He has no initiative and I have to keep on asking and ordering everything. The men still cannot understand, anyway, that, despite experiences in the sea of sand, a long-range expedition through this realm of Death is nothing else than a <u>flight</u> from the desert itself. The terrain is horrible. Dissected plateaus, soft shifting sand … for ever having to change course and check bearings for finding new ways through. Since Woehrmann is not capable of reckoning bearings and distances for me I am continually forced to stop and to check the courses on the useless Italian map. According

to distances in kilometres we should already be on the open *serir*
with which I am familiar but dunes suddenly appear before us.
On the previous occasion I did not sight them N. of my route.
Impassable with the overloaded vehicles so turn about and go
N., to cut across the big enemy L. of C. [lines of communica-
tion] again. A tour of 100km [62 miles]. Frightful!

Later that day plumes of dust were seen ahead which indicated
an enemy convoy of some sort, and Almasy was forced to hide his
vehicles behind a dune. Through his glasses he could make out five
vehicles in front of them – but also, along the eastern horizon, the
great Gilf Kebir escarpment he had been seeking, and he moved
off, making sure the enemy remained well in front of him. At last,
he noted in his diary, he was on familiar territory. The frontier
into Egypt was crossed and the spur of the Gilf Kebir escarpment
rounded. Evidence of the enemy – hundreds of tracks and four
abandoned vehicles – was everywhere, but not a sign of the trucks
they had glimpsed in front of them earlier in the day.

The convoy hugged the wall of rock until a suitable hiding
place was found and Almasy laagered up for the night. 'Day's performance: 240km [150 miles]. 100 of them for nothing.' Another
cache of petrol, water, and rations was hidden for the return journey, as was one of the trucks. Its markings were painted over, and
everything removed that would identify its occupants, before it
was driven deep into a rock-cleft. A note in French was then
struck on the inside of the windscreen to make the 'Tommies',
Almasy noted in his diary, 'think the vehicle belongs to their
Degaullist allies'. It said that the truck had not been abandoned
and that it would be returning to Kufra, and that no part was
to be removed. 'If they catch us they can rack their brains as to
where we have come from.'

Before leaving the area the next morning, 18 May, Almasy drove
to the prehistoric rock paintings he had discovered in 1933, then
continued eastwards to find the cave where, the same year, he had
left eight soldered cans of water. This stash had saved the lives of
Bagnold and his companion in 1935 after breaking the axle of their
only car. Some of the cans were rusted and empty but four were
full. 'I open one cautiously in order not to shake up the water. We
pour it into a cooking pot, it is clear and odourless.' They each to
sip of the 1933 vintage and pronounced it 'excellent'.

They now turned their attention to a group of neatly parked vehicles they had already spotted some 2½ miles (4km) to the south. Positioning a look-out on higher ground, Almasy went to investigate and found six 5-tonners belonging to the Sudan Defence Force. They had not been abandoned because on the windscreen of the front one was the message: 'refuelled for return journey'. In no time at all Almasy had siphoned all the petrol from their tanks. '500 litres of petrol! That changes all my plans. I can carry out the journey to the objective with <u>both</u> cars and probably even take one Commercial with me back home.'

Sand was poured into the oil filters of the parked vehicles and the looted petrol driven some 12 miles (19km) to the north-east where it was 'distributed artistically amongst the black rocks so that none could be seen even from vehicles which might follow our tracks … Today's performance is small, only 120km [75 miles], and about 30 of them back and forth but it was worth it: our return journey is assured.' Just as encouraging was the fact that contact was made with one of Rommel's listening posts, and it was given a progress report. But the other, codenamed *Schildkroete* (tortoise), the mobile unit that would arrange to drop them more supplies if necessary, still couldn't be raised.

The next day was a disaster. Almasy could not find the entrance to the Aqaba Pass through the Gilf Kebir he had found before the war, and a spring in his car had to be replaced. As a result only about 50 miles (80km) was covered, but on 20 May he found the entrance, a dry riverbed called the El Aqaba Wadi that sliced northwards through the Gilf plateau. His old tracks were still visible and the going on the old riverbed was reasonable. A tail dune[12] which blocked the way had to be carefully negotiated, though Almasy remarked:

> Pit drives as usual, like a wild man and instead of following my track drives the "President" [one of the two station-wagons] head over heels down the steep part of the tail-dune. A miracle that the vehicle does not turn over at the bottom. Result: broken track of the shock absorber.

The distance covered that day was 180 miles (290km), 37 of which were spent in a fruitless search to find a shorter route. Almasy's frustration was evident. 'Store [made] of three cans of petrol and two ca

of water. The radio won't work, allegedly the transformer is damaged!'
   The next day proved the 'hardest day so far as regards terrain':

> Low plateaus, and over and over again small hills with the tail dunes
> which are such a nuisance, broad plains with shale stretches and
> only now and again a piece of open *serir*. The vehicles suffer terri-
> bly on this kind of ground, the drivers behind me as well probably.
> I have to keep on stopping and marking the course on the map.
> This time I can't draw in the stretch we have done, but only put in
> tiny points on the map sheet with a sharp pointed pencil: if we get
> caught no surveyor in the world will be able to follow our route
> … my eyes ache terribly from eternal compass-driving.

At noon the remaining truck was hidden with some more petrol
and water, and its load redistributed between the station-wagons.
Camp was made early, 'otherwise the men will go slack on me …
Day's mileage 230km [140 miles].'
   The failure to make contact with *Schildkroete* worried Almasy
greatly as the difficult terrain and the extra kilometres travelled were
consuming their fuel at an alarming rate. 'I have scarcely enough
petrol to get back,' he complained in his diary. 'Everything was discussed and planned in detail. I was only to radio and they drop fuel,
water and food for me in any grid square I liked.' But the radio
still refused to function. 'The men mess around with it for an hour,'
Almasy wrote in exasperation, 'then came in, with the thing still
out of action, to our one-pot supper. Three radio-operators [he
was including Pit and Pan, who had their own wirelesses] and a
mechanic are not in a position to find out what is wrong! In this
undertaking I always have to do absolutely everything myself.'
   The following day, 22 May, they pressed ahead to reach the Kharga
road before night fell, but it was dark before they found it, and they
were forced to camp for the night in the open desert, having covered
250km [155 miles]. Pit used his transmitter, which worked perfectly,
but to Almasy's dismay they still could not raise *Schildkroete*. In his
diary he railed against the mobile signals unit, but curiously does not
mention the other, codenamed *Otter*, as an alternative method of
communication. To save fuel Almasy decided that if,

> I drive through the Kharga Oasis tomorrow <u>by road</u> instead of
> over the dunes, so as to remain unobserved, I shall just be able

to make it. If the worst comes to the worst I shall have to get petrol by cunning or force. My mind is made up: in order to save petrol I shall remain on the road.

In short, at all costs, Almasy was determined to reach his objective, whatever the risks. Before leaving at dawn the next morning, 23 May, he distributed Privistin – one of the amphetamine class of drugs used by the German military during the war – to stimulate the morale and minds of his tired men.

We drive in the first grey of morning towards the north and soon reach the Dachla–Kharga road about 15km [9 miles] before Kharga. Then no halts on the good road to the oasis. I know everything here, the scattered *Barchana* [crescent dunes] of the Abu Moharig dune through which the road snakes in a masterly fashion, the iron tracks of the abandoned railway lines, which were once to have led to Dachla, on the left hand Gebel Ter and on the eastern horizon in the soft red of breaking day the mighty wall of the Egyptian limestone plateau.

Just outside Kharga he stopped and gave his final orders, drumming into the men in the rear car that they were 'not to get left behind under any circumstances, to halt when I halt and to start off when I start off. The sub-machine guns are held at the ready, but arms should not be resorted to unless I myself have started it.'

As they drove into the town square they saw two Egyptian *Chaffire* (night-watchmen) standing in the road. Almasy stopped, and one of them greeted him respectfully in Arabic, regretting that he didn't speak English. Almasy replied in Arabic, and the man told him that anyone passing through had to report to the local commanding officer at the *Markaz*, or seat of local government. Almasy, showing just how quick-witted he was, even after several exhausting days in the desert – perhaps he had taken some Privistin, too – immediately replied that of course his *Bimbashi* (major) would report, but that he was only driving the major's luggage to the station and had to get to there without delay.

'Where is the *Bimbashi*?'

'In the fourth car.'

The *Chaffire*, puzzled, looked down the road behind the two vehicles.

'How many cars are there behind me?' Almasy asked quickly.

'Only a second one.'

'Good,' Almasy replied, and pointed to the other night-watchmen. 'You stay here, and wait for the other two cars. The *Bimbashi* [major] is travelling in the fourth car. You will show him to the *Markaz*.' Then, only interested in getting the two night-watchmen parted quickly before they had time to think about what was happening, he ordered the other to get on the running board, and show him the way to the turning which led to the station.

The night-watchman saluted: '*Hadr Effendi*.'

When they came to the turning the *Chaffire* stepped off the running board, Almasy thanked him and both vehicles drove on and out of Kharga. The road was now excellent, which to Almasy's great joy had a positive effect on their petrol consumption. About 29km [18 miles] from their destination one of the vehicles with two of the Brandenburgers was parked out of sight to await the return of the others. If Almasy did not come back after three hours their orders were to return on their own. 'At 2 p.m. we reach the edge of the plateau. Scarcely 4km [2.5 miles] below us lies the huge green valley with the silver glittering river, the large white city, the countless *esbahs* [farms] and country houses.' Pit and Pan were deposited on to the road with their suitcases, and after changing into civilian clothes, began their walk over the crest and down the road to the railway station on of the edge of Assiut. If anyone asked, they were to pose as travellers whose car had broken down in the desert. 'Not many words are said,' Almasy recorded, 'a few handshakes, one last photograph, a short farewell', and then he turned round and motored back the way he had come.

Despite some close calls with British patrols, and a great deal of anxiety at missing the dumps left on the outward journey, Almasy and his men arrived safely back at Gialo on 29 May. The prearranged three white flares were fired and the Italian tricolour was hoisted on the car's aerial mast. It had been an epic journey, a truly remarkable accomplishment.

Operation CLAPTRAP to capture the Commando was launched two days later, but ended, as one writer remarked, 'with nobody caught in the trap and little to clap about'.[13]

* * * * *

So who exactly were Pit and Pan, who were left plodding along a desert road with their suitcases containing two transmitters and, according to some commentators, £50,000 (it was in fact £3,000 in sterling notes and £600 in Egyptian pound notes)? Well, Pit, the madcap driver and wireless operator, was Heinrich 'Sandy' Sanstede (sometimes Sandstede), a German national born in Oldenberg in 1913, the son of a chemistry professor. Educated in Germany, he continued to live there until he emigrated to West Africa in 1930, realising by then that he was a natural adventurer who was quite unable to fit in with the aspirations of his middle-class professional family background. He subsequently travelled widely and worked in South West and South Africa, and by 1938 was office manager for the Texas Oil Company, first in Dar-es-Salaam and then in Kampala, Nairobi and Mombassa.

When war broke out Sanstede was interned in Dar-es-Salaam, but in January 1940 he was repatriated to Germany as part of an exchange. He then worked in the topographical department of the German High Command in Berlin, correcting and translating maps of those parts of Africa with which he was familiar. He spoke perfect English (with a slight American accent) and before joining the operation had been issued with a false British passport by the Abwehr in Berlin under the name of a businessman, Peter Muncaster.[14]

But the main protagonist was Pan, alias Johannes, or John, Eppler. According to one British report he was born illegitimately to a German woman in Alexandria in April 1914 who later married an Egyptian named Gaafar. He was brought up in Germany between 1915 and 1931, when he returned to Egypt, and attended the French *Lycée* in Cairo. He went back to Germany in 1937, married a Danish woman, and ran a fur-farm for his father-in-law until September 1940 when he was conscripted into the army. Another report confirms his year of birth and that his mother was German, and adds that his father was probably British, a Lt Webb. It also confirms that in 1915 the mother took Eppler back to her home town, Backnang, and that around this time she married Salah Gaafar.[15]

Eppler's version of events is somewhat different. He says in his memoirs that his German mother had run a hotel in Alexandria inherited from an uncle, and that his father was an investment adviser for European mining and oil companies. When he died suddenly, Eppler's mother married Salah Gaafar, who kept a suite in her hotel. Gaafar was a prosperous pro-British Egyptian magistrate of Arab origin. He adopted Eppler, and treated him as the eldest son – even though the marriage produced a second boy, Hassein Gaafar, who later became embroiled in Eppler's espionage.

At a young age Eppler says he was converted from Roman Catholicism to Islam and was introduced to the traditional Moslem customs that ruled his extended family. He also spent time with the family's Bedouin tribe based at the Ajun-Musa Oasis in the Sinai Desert, and wrote evocatively about his first contact with them:

> In the shade of a plane tree, sat two Bedouins, awaiting my arrival. They were swathed from head to foot in cloth, except for a small slit to look through. Europeans are no use at waiting. They are always in a hurry. These two men of the desert, however, were sitting motionless in the shade, like the camels lying on the ground next to them, chewing their cuds and gazing into the void.[16]

How truthful Eppler is about his early life is anyone's guess, but his book is full of such nice touches. His description of his stepfather's house in Cairo is equally evocative. It was there, he wrote, that the breath of adventure 'first brushed my cheek, and I knew that as long as I lived it would never let me go'. Day and night a huge Nubian, his ebony skin glistening in the blistering sun, guarded the gate of the large, walled building situated on the eastern bank of the Nile. On its top floor Eppler had a self-contained apartment where no woman was ever allowed to enter, while outside it lay a dark-skinned Sudanese *Bisharin*[17] ready to defend his master with his life.

He described how, beyond the gate, lay a dark passage that led into a wide sunlit courtyard ablaze with roses and surrounded by a shady arcade. At its southern end were two doors, one leading to the harem, guarded by a fat eunuch, the other leading to the men's quarters known as the *salamlik*. Long cushioned divans lined the courtyards walls on which the men of the family reclined, discussing the ways of the world, drinking coffee, or drawing on their hubble-bubbles, while a black Berber carrying a copper brazier walked slowly round the four sides, gently chanting an Arab song and leaving a trail of sandalwood-scented smoke. At precisely the same time each morning, small boys carrying cups and copper jugs hurried to and fro across the courtyard from the huge kitchen to serve coffee to the women in the harem, while every morning and night an ancient, sightless *Ulema*,[18] supported by a knotted stick, appeared in the eastern colonnade and sat on a stool halfway along it. Then, in a sing-song voice, he recited a chapter from the Koran before leaving through a little door made in the big gate and disappearing into the palm grove beyond.

Eppler says that at 16 he undertook a pilgrimage to Mecca, the wish of every devout Moslem. By then it held no religious meaning for him as he already knew the ways of his desert family were not for him, nor was their religion. But the pilgrimage released within him his sense of adventure and two years later, bored with the playboy life that seemed to be all Cairo and Alexandria had to offer, he went gold prospecting in the Lupa goldfields in what is now south-western Tanzania. But he failed to make his fortune and his memoirs then fast-forward to Beirut in May 1937 where, at the Hotel Saint George, he waited for an unknown German who had come all the way from Istanbul to meet him. The meeting had been arranged by the German embassy in Cairo, which had been ordered by the Abwehr to provide a list of all those with German blood living in Egypt. Eppler was high on the list for he was a member of an important Arab family – though hardly anyone was aware his mother was German – and he was already known in Cairo for seeking out adventure. It therefore wasn't surprising that it didn't take him long to decide that what the Germans proposed – to join the Abwehr – might provide just the kind of excitement he was seeking, as well as giving him the excuse he needed to avoid the dull career trajectory his family had planned for him.

His terms of employment were successfully negotiated and in August 1937 he arrived in Berlin to start his induction into military intelligence, which included basic army training, courses in parachuting and operating a portable wireless, and coding and decoding signals. By October he was back in the Middle East and in his memoirs he describes his involvement as an Abwehr agent in such diverse anti-British activities as preparing the way for a German–Russian attack on India; finding a method of infiltrating a commando unit into Turkey, where it could lie low until it was needed to aid the Wehrmacht secure the Romanian oilfields of Baku; helping the leader of the failed 1941 Iraqi revolt against the British to reach Germany; and working with members of the Egyptian military (the PYRAMID organisation[19]) who were planning a revolt against the British. On his various visits to Berlin he says he met the head of the Abwehr, Admiral Canaris, and even had a chat with Hitler. Like Sanstede, he was employed in the German High Command's cartographic department in Berlin, and he also worked for the Military Geographical Department, where he assisted in bringing out a new book on Egypt. He seems to have crammed a lot into a short time.

After his capture Eppler betrayed the PYRAMID organisation, but in the reports of his interrogation there is no mention of his Abwehr activities. This is not surprising, as revealing this while apparently under imminent threat of execution would only have further incriminated him in the eyes of his captors. More surprising is that during his interrogation Eppler claimed to have travelled extensively in the Egyptian and Sudanese deserts during the 1930s. With one exception his memoirs give no details of his desert adventures between the wars, so he may well have invented them for his interrogators as unverifiable cover for his activities as an Abwehr agent. However, he does mention one desert journey with Almasy:

> The assurance of this man Almasy was truly enviable. He had not changed since that day in 1935 we had broken down with engine trouble near the great Mohariq Barkan Dune. We had been searching for a lost oasis and were resigned to awaiting the end, but he quite calmly repeated: 'The last moment has not yet come. Someone will turn up and get us out of this.' And right enough, someone did just about at curtain time. It was Robert Clayton, who took us back to the Nile Valley.[20]

* * * * *

The luck of the two spies held – at first. The original plan had been for Sanstede to stay in Assiut, to relay any information Eppler transmitted to him from Cairo. However, at some point both of them decided to go to Cairo, and they buried one of the transmitters with their desert clothing before walking into Assiut. After rounding a bend, they came upon a British army camp that straddled the road. After showing their identities, they explained how they had come to be there. They were hospitably received in the officers' mess, given lunch, and then driven to the station, having been told in no uncertain terms how insane they had been to drive into the desert with only one vehicle.

Before boarding the late afternoon Luxor–Cairo express, Eppler solved the possibility of their suitcases being inspected by field security when they reached the capital by hiring a young Nubian who was propping up a nearby wall. Nubians were known to be totally honest and reliable, and that no one would bother to stop a native with a couple of old suitcases, so the boy was given the suitcases, and a meeting place in Cairo was agreed.

The facts about what happened after they reached Cairo on the evening of 24 May differ widely. Eppler's memoirs say that when he and Sandy, as he called Sanstede, arrived there they immediately went to the villa Eppler had rented when previously visiting the city. However, contemporary official reports based on their interrogations say they rented rooms, first in the Pension Nadia in the Rue Taufik, where they stayed two nights, then at an apartment in the Sharia Borsa el Gedida owned by a Mme Therese Guillermet (the name varies), which turned out to be a brothel. Some reports say she remained with them in the flat; others say she moved out soon after their arrival and was given a hefty premium for doing so.

Wherever it was they stayed, one can accept that they were soon absorbed into the atmosphere of the great city which was Eppler's home; and with money in their pockets they set out to enjoy themselves, and to make contacts with those who were well disposed towards them and were prepared to help them achieve their clandestine objectives. 'It was the pleasantest time of day to be in Cairo,' Eppler wrote of that first evening.

> The population sat chattering outside the cafes and restaurants, drinking *zibib* or beer and eating vast quantities of *meze*, smoking their *nargilehs*,[21] sipping coffee, and laughing. The city was brightly lit. Groups of people were loitering on the banks of the river, and those aboard the graceful *feluccas* on the water were enjoying the river breeze. At Guezira[22] we could at last spend a night in civilized surroundings after our murderous journey through the desert.

After a slap-up meal Eppler says their next port of call was the Kit-Kat club – a favourite watering hole for British staff officers as well as those on leave from the front – as Eppler wanted to recruit someone there who would be of use to them in their quest for intelligence. This was the beautiful, supple belly-dancer, Hekmat Fahmi, whom Eppler knew well from his days as a playboy.

Fahmi agreed to help and they returned to her *Dahabia* (house-boat) where she lived and where her alleged lover, an English Army major, kept some of his belongings when on duty in the desert.

At this stage it is difficult to know which of the various sources to believe, if any of them. However, they all seem to point to the fact that this was the only time the two spies got their hands on any military intelligence at all, even if it was of no operational value whatsoever. According to one source, the two spies examined the major's belongings and found an out-of-date map of Tobruk's defences. However, as the major never existed, it seems more likely that Hekmat obtained it and showed it to the two spies, as their interrogation report seems to confirm:

> When told of the discovery of secret plans of Tobruk in Hegmet's [Hekmat's] possession, both PW expressed great surprise and they denied any connection with it. Eppler stressed the fact that Hegmet is a very ignorant girl who knows nothing outside of dancing, drinking and the etc., who speaks no other language but Arabic and cannot possibly understand any conversation relating to military matters. Eppler said they had no instructions to get the plans of Tobruk but Rommel's chief of intelligence had ordered them to obtain plans for the fortifications of Mersa Matruh.[23]

Both the spies had kept diaries, the purpose being to document for their German masters, when they arrived in Cairo, how usefully the Abwehr's money had been spent. When the houseboat was raided in July, Sanstede threw Eppler's diary in the Nile, but his own was found. One of the entries, on 25 June, seems to confirm the origin of the map, though it was almost certainly written to justify the money being spent on the belly-dancer: 'Hegmet [*sic*] has rendered us valuable services. Today I received the plans and dug-outs and fortifications of Tobruk. This pile of material will have to be destroyed ... I dare not keep too much – the diary is enough of a worry.'[24]

From all this it seems reasonable to assume that the map probably did exist, though the British authorities judged it of such little consequence that Hekmat was not even punished with internment, but merely given a severe ticking off. But around this map was subsequently woven a beguiling, but totally fictional, story by those who wrote about Operation CONDOR after the war. According to them, when Hekmat's putative lover returned for his next leave, he realised the spies had found the highly secret information Rommel needed to make his vital breakthrough, which he had carelessly left in his belongings. Knowing he had unwittingly betrayed his country, the mythical major took the only honourable course. He had a map incorrectly marked out that showed where the Germans could best attack the British positions, buttoned it into his tunic and then committed suicide by driving straight into a minefield in front of the German lines. The Germans found the fake map on his body and were duped into making a fatal attack on the British defences.

Added to this fabrication there were, during the six weeks or so that the spies were at liberty, stories of secret encounters with a pro-Axis priest who kept a transmitter under his altar; frantic efforts by Eppler, aided by dissident Egyptians, to return to the German lines to discover why the Germans had abandoned them; and the interesting appearance of a beautiful young Jewess who was alleged to be working for SIME (Security Intelligence Middle East, MI5's Middle East equivalent). A few of these stories may have been at least partly based on true events; most of them were not.

In fact, the truth – so far as it can be ascertained – was much more mundane. Visiting Hekmat did give the two spies the idea of renting a houseboat themselves, as the brothel was badly situated for transmitting signals. Sanstede had rigged the transmitter's aerial to look like the one for an ordinary radio he had bought, but they were getting no response and concluded that the apartment was in the wrong location. The houseboat, on the other hand, offered more seclusion and, more importantly, they could run the aerial up the mast, making it both more efficient and more difficult for the casual eye to detect, while the transmitter and its operator were ingeniously concealed below. Hekmat, who seems to have been an obliging sort of girl as well as being strongly anti-British, agreed to find them a houseboat near hers. This she did, though the spies were still renting their rooms in the brothel when they were arrested.

Despite the improved aerial, they were still unable to make contact with *Schildkroete*,[25] and began to wonder if their transmitter was faulty. So they contacted the Egyptian armed forces resistance movement and enlisted the aid of the virulently anti-British Anwar el-Sadat. Despite an earlier acrimonious encounter with Eppler, when the German laughed off the possibility of the Egyptian Army staging an effective uprising, Sadat agreed to help.

'As a signals officer I knew something about radio,' he later wrote,[26] 'and I said I would do it for them.' According to him the two spies and their transmitter were aboard Hekmat's houseboat, but this is contradicted by all other accounts, though his description of what he found was probably fairly accurate. 'I was quickly enlightened about the sort of life which these young Nazis were living. The place was furnished like something out of the Arabian Nights.' He looked around for the transmitter:

The room seemed to be full of bottles of perfume and whisky. Appler [sic] took me out into the hall and showed me a radiogram, with a lid of carved wood. Under the lid there was the usual pick-up and turntable, but by pressing a catch the whole top of the radiogram opened up to reveal space big enough to contain transmitter and operator. A small lamp illuminated the space, and the operator, once inside, could be hidden from view by closing the lid on top of him. While he worked, the radiogram played dance music … It would need a clever investigator to guess that inside this commonplace article of furniture there was a secret transmitter sending messages to the Wehrmacht. I got inside the space to examine the transmitter. It was a solid piece of work and it had been carefully installed. I could not find out where the fault was.

Having seen how the two spies lived, he began to suspect that with lots of money to spend on girls and easy living, they were trying to spin out their stay in Egypt for as long as possible, and had probably deliberately put their transmitter out of action. 'But I stumbled across their game too late. The second time I went to the houseboat I found the pair of them dead drunk with two Jewesses. They were arrested the following day.'

Apart from not being able to make contact with Rommel's listening post, the two spies also found that the bulk of their money – the £3,000 in sterling notes – was not common tender in Egypt, a fact their Abwehr masters seemed to have overlooked. So Eppler's error of using sterling notes to pay for a round of drinks at the Turf Club alerted a certain Major Sansom of British Field Security. 'Under the currency regulations in Egypt at that time,' Sansom later wrote, 'English money was not changed by banks, but had to be taken personally to the British Army Paymaster. So I went to the Paymaster's office to find out how much sterling had been coming in.' The answer was not much more than normal, but enough for Sansom to request being told where the notes were being exchanged. He then charted the places on a map of Cairo, and soon discovered they came from the usual haunts of British service officers out to have a good time. Then he had samples of the sterling notes flown to London to be inspected by the Bank of England. The Bank reported that the genuine ones originated from deposits in neutral countries, making it more likely they were being used for clandestine purposes. But the Bank also reported that the £5 notes were excellent forgeries, far too good for any individual to produce. 'Almost certainly forged by the German Government' was its conclusion.[27]

* * * * *

While Sansom was attempting to track down the source of the sterling notes, the spies fumbled and bumbled their way round Cairo, first living the high life and then from hand to mouth as their money ran out, and committing the most elementary breaches of security in their desperate search for a way out of their predicament. It seemed to them that the Germans had sent them on a pretty hopeless mission and had then abandoned them.

The British were equally in the dark. They knew something was up, and suspected there was a connection between those using the fake sterling currency, Almasy's journey across the desert, to which they would now have been alerted by Jean Alington, and the signals of a clandestine wireless set in Cairo which they had so far not been able to locate. Then, quite suddenly, they had the breakthrough they needed. As later recorded in a memo by the District Security Officer, 'an interned escapee called Kurt Siegel was recaptured. He told his interrogators that a German employed by the Swedish consulate – one of Eppler's contacts – had talked about a houseboat.' This information fitted with previous reports about mysterious happenings on a certain houseboat, and was the result of watching the movements of a car driven by a chauffeur called Mohammed. It was decided to round up the occupants of the houseboat and everyone at whose house or apartment Mohammed's car had been known to call. 'This was done and as a result the two Germans above mentioned [Eppler and 'Sandy'], the half-brother of Eppler, one Hassan Gafaar [*sic*]; a lady doctor Amer, and a large collection of people mostly of doubtful antecedents were caught.'[28]

Like so much written about CONDOR this obscures more than it reveals, as no doubt it was intended to do to protect the informer concerned; for 'Kurt Siegel' didn't exist, and the intelligence supplied by him actually came from one Victor Hauer. Employed by the Swedish consulate, Hauer was an Austrian by birth, but German by nationality, who had been permitted by the Egyptians to work in the Swedish legation, looking after German interests. 'In July 1942,' noted a post-war SIME report to MI5 in London, 'Hauer got in touch with (name withheld) and told him that he had been approached by two German agents with the request for a W/T set and passports. It was clear that Hauer would be able to lead the security authorities to these two men, and indeed under interrogation gave full details of the case. Following this confession he was interned for his own protection.' But as another SIME report makes clear, Hauer had been working for SIME before the war had even started. So it is not surprising that immediately after it London was cabled that, as a matter of urgency, Hauer needed to be repatriated to Austria as soon as possible, doubtless to keep him out of the hands of the members of the PYRAMID organisation who had aided the two spies and whom Hauer had also helped uncover.[29]

A more dramatic conclusion to Operation CONDOR would have been if the two spies had fought it out when their houseboat was boarded by Sansom and the Egyptian authorities on the night of 25 July. However, about all they managed to do was scuttle the vessel, though Eppler gave Sansom a scare by lobbing what looked like a hand grenade at him. In fact, it was a pair of rolled-up socks, an appropriately soft and woolly end to an absurd episode in the history of espionage, redeemed only by Almasy's truly remarkable drive across the desert.

In his book on Eppler's adventures,[30] published in 1958, the war correspondent Leonard Mosley wrote that the two men were spared execution because Eppler's stepfather 'had been a good friend of Britain in Egypt', and this was why they were treated as prisoners-of-war. This seems highly unlikely. It is much more probable that Jean Alington, who had retained her interest in Almasy and his epic journey, hit upon the truth. She wrote to

Bagnold in the late 1970s that she had recently met Eppler for lunch in Paris, and had concluded he had probably been a double agent, perhaps even a triple one.[31] He was certainly a witness for the British at the secret military tribunals convened to prosecute PYRAMID members.

NOTES

1. Quoted in 'Western Desert Campaigns', Dear, I.C.B. (ed.), *Oxford Companion to World War II* (revised edn, 2005).

2. In *Operation Condor: Rommel's Spy* (Little, Brown Book Group, 1977), p. 22 Eppler describes the same device when he visited what is now Tanzania in 1933. So its popularity, like all good inventions, must have spread quickly.

3. Bagnold, R., *Libyan Sands: Travels in a Dead World* (Eland, London, 2010), p. 80.

4. Bierman, J., *The Secret Life of Laszlo Almasy* (London, 2004), p. 11. The author is indebted to Bierman for the details that follow of Almasy's life before the war

5. *Ibid.*, pp. 108–09.

6. *Ibid.*, p. 137.

7. *Ibid.*, p. 139.

8. *Ibid.*, p. 169.

9. TNA KV3/74 contains Bletchley Park's decrypted Abwehr signals that alerted the British to Almasy's journey and gives details of CLAPTRAP. Almasy's new route must have taken him away from the British signals unit.

10. Eppler, J., *op. cit.*, p. 202.

11. There is a translation of Almasy's diary in the Lloyd-Owen papers, Imperial War Museum. All Almasy's quotes in the text come from this source.

12. 'A tail dune forms when an obstacle such as a small bush or hill checks the velocity of the wind, causing it to deposit its sandy load.' *Encyclopedia of World Geography*, vol. 8, edited by Peter Haggett (London, 2001), p. 2203.

13. Dovey, H.O., 'Operation Condor', *Journal of Intelligence and National Security* (vol. 4, no. 2, 1989), p. 371, n. 27.

14. Consolidated report on Operations SALAM and CONDOR in TNA KV2/1468 written on 5 January 1943 by E.B. Stamp, an MI5 officer.

15. Both reports are in TNA WO208/5520.

16. Eppler *op. cit.*, p. 5. Eppler's descriptions of his life and adventures all come from this source unless stated otherwise.

17. A tribe of the Beja nomadic ethnic group who are mostly Sufi Moslems.

18. A Moslem scholar.

19. TNA KV2/1463: Letter of 20 June 1943 from the head of SIME to Colonel Dick White of MI5 in London: 'I enclose herewith copy no. 1 of a report on the PYRAMID organisation. This is a Germano-Egyptian espionage organisation (probably SD not Abwehr) which we have been observing since last autumn in the hope of using it for Special Section purposes. The organisation proved, however, to be so ineffectual as to be useless for such purposes, and we therefore decided to arrest those members of it who were in our territory.' Special Section was the SIME cover name for the XXX-Committee which ran a similar operation to the XX-Committee in London (see Chapter 6). Almasy

was involved in recruiting the leading member of PYRAMID, Mohsen Fadl, as a German agent in Paris in Nov. 1941.

20. Eppler, *op. cit.*, p. 199. He may have meant Pat Clayton, though a rich baronet, Sir Robert Clayton-East-Clayton, was also a desert explorer. He and his wife Dorothy were probably the models for the fictional Geoffrey and Katharine Clifton, in *The English Patient*.

21. A kind of hookah, or water pipe.

22. Literally 'island', a prosperous island district of Cairo.

23. TNA WO208/5520.

24. *Ibid.*

25. The spies were not to know that on the night of 28 May, during a New Zealand attack on Rommel's desert headquarters in the area of Hacheim, all but two of *Schildkroete*'s personnel had been killed. The 8th Army War Diary, in TNA WO169/3936, records that the remaining two were captured, along with documentation relating to Almasy's commando. The two survivors refused to say what their duties were, but once the material found with them had been examined British intelligence weren't slow to reach the right conclusions. Also found amongst the Germans' possessions was a copy of Daphne du Maurier's novel *Rebecca*, though neither German could speak or read English. On closer examination a pencilled price of 50 escudos was discernible on the inside front flap, and further investigations revealed that in April the Germans in Lisbon had purchased six copies of the novel for encoding and decoding signals. Many years later, in 1980, the novelist Ken Follett published his best-selling novel *The Key to Rebecca* which was based on Eppler's exploits.

26. Sadat, A., *Revolt on the Nile* (London, 1947), pp. 47–48.

27. Sansom, A., *I Spied Spies* (London, 1965), pp. 113–15. By 1942 the Germans were indeed producing forged sterling notes, as part of Operation BERNARD, their plan to flood Britain with counterfeit currency. This was never implemented, and the Bank of England has no record of Sansom's request, but an open file in its archives (file reference PW17/5) does confirm that by 1942 it had become aware that the Germans were producing high-quality counterfeit notes.

28. TNA FO141/852. The memo is dated 2 August 1942.

29. TNA KV2/1467–8.

30. Mosley, L., *The Cat and the Mice* (London, 1958), pp. 152–53. After the war, Mosley was only able to trace Eppler when Anwar el-Sadat, accompanied by his private secretary, visited Europe in 1956. Mosley met them and found that the private secretary was Eppler's half-brother, Hassein Gaafar. A curious coincidence, indeed.

31. Correspondence (C.31) in the Churchill Archives Centre. In the same correspondence Bagnold mentions he met Almasy after the war when the Hungarian told him that during it he had landed a light aircraft with a motorbike aboard behind the Pyramids. He had then driven into Cairo, had a drink at a nightclub, and used its telephone to contact some agents before returning to his aircraft. This seems far-fetched, but in Almasy's case perfectly possible. Bagnold did not say if he had done this before or after SALAM.

2

Stalin's Master Spy

'His work was impeccable.' (Kim Philby)

'The spies in history who can say from their graves, the information I supplied to my masters, for better or worse, altered the history of our planet, can be counted on the fingers of one hand. Richard Sorge was in that group.' (Frederick Forsyth)

'The most formidable spy in history.' (Ian Fleming)

'The spy to end spies!' (John Le Carré)

So how did this extraordinary man come to command such respect from those who know the murky world of espionage inside out, and what exactly did he do to gain such admiration? Part of the answer was that Richard Sorge, and the spy ring he ran in Tokyo between 1933 and 1941, worked at a higher political level than practically any other espionage network operating during the Second World War; and the intelligence he provided was so important that it is no exaggeration to say that it altered the course, and maybe outcome, of this global conflict.

Born in October 1895 on the outskirts of Baku, the capital of Azerbaijan, then part of the Russian empire, Richard Sorge was the youngest of nine children of a German mining engineer contracted to the Caucasian Oil Company. However, his mother was Russian, potentially a huge stumbling block for anyone needing to cloak his avid Communist ideals behind a Nazi persona, as Sorge was obliged to. He therefore went to great lengths to disguise his mother's origins when he joined the Nazi Party in 1934, and the Nazi Press Association the following year. He would never have been allowed to belong to either if it had been known he was the son of a Slav.

Sorge's father's contract ended when Sorge was 2 years old and the family returned to Berlin. At the start of the First World War, Sorge joined the army as a volunteer, by which time he was well on the way to becoming one of those rare individuals who combined being a man of action with an outstanding intellect. He was wounded three times and twice he returned to the front line. On the third occasion shrapnel shattered both his legs and he was medically discharged. His bravery earned him the Iron Cross, 2nd class, but his wounds were so severe they left him with a permanent and pronounced limp.

Sorge's experience of war, both at the front and in a Berlin wracked by poverty and profiteering, politicised him. He spent his convalescences there studying and reading Marx; and encouraged by a nurse and her family, who took him under their wing after his third stay in hospital, he became a fervent Communist. The Russian Revolution of November 1917 proved a turning point for him. When the German fleet mutinied at Kiel in October 1918, he urged the mutineers to join the struggle against capitalism, and conducted secret lectures on socialism to groups of sailors and dockworkers.

In August 1919, after studying economics, Sorge was awarded a doctorate in political science from Hamburg University, became an assistant lecturer at a technical college in Aachen, and joined the Communist Party, becoming a coal miner for a time to find recruits for it. He also embarked on his remarkably prolific love life by having an affair with the wife of a professor of economics who had befriended the militant, charismatic young lecturer. Rather reluctantly, as he regarded marriage as a bourgeois institution, Sorge married her in May 1921, and they moved to Frankfurt where the obliging professor had found Sorge a job – it is one of the extraordinary aspects of Sorge's life that he rarely seems to have offended the husbands of the women he seduced, and even sometimes managed to retain their friendship and loyalty. The stories of his conquests are numerous. One of them described how a Tokyo bargirl called Keiko threatened to throw herself into a volcano when Sorge entered the bar one evening with a glamorous European woman on his arm. The police rescued her in time and, resigned to living, she continued her habit of hovering close to Sorge at the gaming table, spitting into his dice cup for luck.

In 1924 Sorge was chosen to be a bodyguard for some important Soviet politicians attending the Communist Party's Ninth

Congress in Frankfurt, and his efficiency and charm impressed them. When the Congress finished he accepted their offer to work at the Moscow headquarters of the Comintern, the international organisation Lenin had formed in 1919 to overthrow the established capitalist order in non-Communist countries. His job was to assemble reports on the political and working conditions of other countries, particularly Germany, and he also began to write articles for the Communist Party and the Comintern, thus kick-starting a distinguished career in journalism. His wife did not take to the life, and she slowly grew apart from her self-contained and sometimes remote husband. 'No one, ever,' she wrote many years later, 'could violate the inner solitude, it was this which gave him his complete independence – and perhaps explained the hold he had over people.'[1]

They soon went their own ways, but they met at least once more when she accompanied Sorge to England in the spring of 1929. Ostensibly, Sorge went to gather information about the trade unions and the British Communist Party. However, his real mission, so he later said, was to meet a Soviet agent within MI6 who passed on to him some important military intelligence, a story confirmed by Sorge's wife who went with him to the assignation.[2] On his return to Moscow, Sorge joined the Fourth Department of Soviet Military Intelligence (GRU), the department that operated agent networks in other countries. He was given the necessary training, including the use of ciphers, allotted the codename RAMSAY, and was sent to Shanghai to work with a GRU intelligence network already established there. His principal mission was to investigate which of two revolutionary factions – and former allies – the Soviet Union should support, those led by Chiang Kai-shek or those supporting Mao Tse-tung; but he also persuaded the head of the Fourth Department, General Jan Berzin, to allow him to report on the political and social situation in China.

Before leaving for Shanghai, he went to Berlin in November 1929 to establish his legal cover as a journalist, and was commissioned to write a number of articles for specialist journals and newspapers. He also arranged to write regular briefs to the head of the official German News Service, the DNB (Deutsches Nachtrichten Büro), which during the Nazi era were passed to German intelligence.[3]

* * * * *

Carrying a valid German passport in his own name, Sorge sailed from Marseille for Shanghai where he arrived in January 1930. Sociable and astute, he was not slow to make acquaintances in the thriving metropolis. One of them was an American, Agnes Smedley, who worked for the German newspaper *Frankfurter Zeitung*, to which Sorge had arranged to contribute articles. She was quickly smitten by the charismatic young German, and they became lovers. Though she was older than Sorge, it was nevertheless a meeting of minds as Smedley was a devoted Communist and a talented journalist. 'I'm married, child, so to speak,' she wrote to a friend, proving the old adage that intellect is the best aphrodisiac:

> just sort of married, you know; but he's a he-man also, and it's 50-50 all along the line, with he helping me and I him and we working together or bust, and so on; a big, broad, all-sided friendship and comradeship. I do not know how long it will last; that does not depend on us, I fear not long. But these days will be the best in my life. Never have I known such good days, never have I known such a healthy life, mentally, physically, psychically.[4]

Agnes gave Sorge the important press contacts he needed, and also helped him with his espionage. Indeed, he regarded her as part of the GRU network to which he now belonged, though Smedley was far too independent to think of herself as part of any organisation. This network, which Sorge soon took charge of when his superior was forced to flee Shanghai, mostly comprised local Chinese agents. They knew him as an American journalist, Mr Johnson, while the German community in Shanghai knew him as the respected academic, Dr Sorge, who wrote esoteric articles for German journals.

Among the Germans living in Shanghai were a number of officers who advised Chiang Kai-shek's armed forces. As an army veteran, Sorge soon gained their confidence and procured much valuable intelligence from them about the political and military situation in China. The GRU was particularly alarmed by the expansionist policies of the semi-autonomous Japanese Kwantung Army stationed in Manchuria to guard its country's interests there. In September 1931, it faked a sabotage attack on the South Manchurian railway, then controlled by the Japanese under the peace agreement that had ended the Russo-Japanese war of 1905–06. China was blamed for this outrage, known as the 'Manchurian Incident' by the Japanese, who used it as an excuse to occupy the region's capital, Mukden, and then most of Manchuria, which they renamed Manchukuo. Once firmly installed along the Soviet border with China, the Kwantung Army posed a constant threat to the Soviet Union that was to have an enormous impact on Sorge's espionage activities when he began working in Tokyo.

Among Smedley's influential friends was a young Japanese journalist, Ozaki Hotsumi, who worked for Japan's most important newspaper, the *Osaka Asahi*. Ozaki, a dedicated and idealistic Communist, came from a wealthy Japanese family with close ties to the Japanese establishment. The two men soon found they had much in common and took an immediate liking to one another, and it was not long before Ozaki joined Sorge's Shanghai network. One commentator wrote:

> [They] were possibly the most intellectually overqualified spies in modern history. Neither was a spy for financial gain; their motivations were political, and of the two, Ozaki's were the more sophisticated and more daring. Ozaki became a traitor to Japan because Japan failed to fulfill its destiny in East Asia. He was an intellectual whose background, experiences, and knowledge compelled him to political action.[5]

It also compelled him to become an accomplished spy and he later summarised his skills – probably very similar to the ones used by Sorge – as follows: most importantly – and this certainly applied to Sorge as well – it helped to have specialist knowledge that people knew about, and that he, Ozaki, had often extracted intelligence from those who wanted him to answer questions relating to his area of expertise. He also recommended that: one should not give an impression of being eager to obtain news; if one succeeded in giving others the impression that one already knew more than they did, they would give what information they had more freely; at drinking parties and the like, before they got too wild, it was often possible to extract important news by just making hints; getting to know personally those who were important sources of information was sometimes the best way of acquiring that information; and, finally, the greatest secret was to win the confidence of others and to create an atmosphere where information could be exchanged quite naturally. He also made the point that, like Sorge, he was well connected in the world of journalism and this often helped him obtain his information direct.

In Shanghai, Sorge also met the man who was to become his radio operator in Tokyo, Max Clausen. Clausen was part of the Fourth Department's technical department and had just established a radio link between Shanghai and Vladivostok. He was therefore an accomplished radio technician, but his loyalty to Communism, as will be seen, left a lot to be desired. Another member of the Shanghai ring was Ruth Kuczynski, alias Werner, who was later to play a part in the Soviet effort to acquire the West's atomic secrets. She was talent-spotted by Sorge who trained her initially, and, codenamed SONIA, she later served the GRU in Britain. Besides SONIA and Smedley, Sorge recruited at least two Chinese women, so it is surprising that he later stated that women lacked the aptitude for espionage. 'They have no understanding of political and other affairs and I have never received satisfactory information from them. Since they were useless to me, I did not employ them in my group [in Tokyo].'[6]

In January 1933 Sorge returned to Moscow where he was warmly praised for his work in China. He quickly re-established his relationship with Katya, the girl he had left behind, and settled down to write a book on Chinese agriculture. However, within months he was dispatched to Tokyo, with the mission to discover whether Japan was plotting to invade the USSR from Manchukuo; and he was also to keep Moscow informed about the trends in Japanese domestic and foreign policies, particularly its attitude to China.

Sorge left Moscow for Berlin in May 1933, en route to his new posting. He knew the risks involved in entering a country which was now a Fascist state, but he needed to broaden his journalistic credentials, and gambled that the new police apparatus had no record of him being a member of the now banned Communist Party. By now he had influential contacts in the newspaper world and his name was sufficiently well known for him to be commissioned to write articles for several journals.

More usefully, the highly respected *Frankfurter Zeitung* made him their accredited representative in Tokyo and several other newspapers decided to appoint him their Tokyo correspondent. He was also given letters of introduction to several German contacts in the Japanese capital and may have made his first tentative enquiries to join the Nazi Party, though he eventually applied after his return to Japan. He certainly had influential contacts within the party, as the Nazi propaganda minister, Josef Goebbels, attended his farewell dinner before he left in early July for Tokyo, via the USA. He travelled on a valid Third Reich passport in the name of 'Mr. R. Sorge', but he would be working as an 'illegal' as he had no diplomatic or other form of legal protection.

Sorge soon found that Japan was, like Nazi Germany, a police state. Apart from the ordinary police, there was the *Tokko* (Special Higher Police) and the *Kempei* (Military Police), both of which routinely used torture and beatings in pursuit of what was known as *chian iji*, or the maintenance of order. The *Tokko*, also known as the 'Thought Police', were especially brutal, the oriental equivalent of the Gestapo, who specialised in tracking down Communists and other political dissidents.

> Its main legal weapon was the Peace Preservation Law of 1925, which after the 1928 revision made it a capital crime to attempt to form any organisation aimed at destroying the *kokutai*, Japan's unique national polity centred on the emperor ... In their zeal, *Tokko* officers, who numbered about 2,000, frequently violated the procedural rights of suspects and became notorious for brutality and torture.[7]

The military also completely dominated the civilian politicians, and assassinated several of them, and there were stringent laws to control anyone attempting to subvert authority. Foreigners were treated with great suspicion and were closely watched. It was hardly an exaggeration to say that every Japanese abroad considered himself a spy, and in his own country assumed the role of spy-catcher. There was even a 'National Spy Prevention Week' when loyal citizens were urged to actively seek out any spies lurking in their neighbourhood.

Knowing how successfully he had obtained intelligence from Germans living in Shanghai, both military and diplomatic, Sorge set out to penetrate the German embassy in Tokyo and establish himself in the local German community. A promising early contact was Lieutenant-Colonel Eugen Ott, a liaison officer with a Japanese artillery regiment in Nagoya. Ott was delighted to meet the charming journalist, who shared his wartime experiences and relieved the boredom of his provincial surroundings. They got along splendidly, and Sorge soon gained Ott's trust completely, particularly after he had read the letter of recommendation Sorge had brought with him. 'You can rely on Sorge in all respects,' wrote the chief editorial writer of one German magazine. How untrue that proved to be.

Moscow had given Sorge two years to see if he could establish an effective spy ring and gradually its core, provided by the Fourth Department, began to assemble in Tokyo. But for over a year the spymaster concentrated entirely on making sure his operatives were well placed, well informed and perfectly trained. All of them were idealists who worked because they believed in what they were doing. Once the ring became operational, in the spring of 1935, Sorge ran it firmly but without excessive discipline. According to one of his inner circle, the only time Sorge ever threw his weight around was the once or twice that he lost his temper – 'even when he was angry he simply appealed to our political conscience or friendship toward him, never to other motives'.[8]

When Sorge's radio operator, Bruno Wendt, arrived with his wife in October 1933 he set up as a businessman, and assembled a radio powerful enough to reach Vladivostok. Despite this Sorge found him technically inadequate and so excessively timid that he had to resort to using the skills of another member of the ring, an exiled 29-year-old Yugoslav called Branko Vukelic. As a trained photo technician it was Vukelic's job to microfilm documents that could not be sent by radio, and the microfilm was then smuggled to Shanghai where it was delivered to Fourth Department couriers. Of course, this method took much longer than sending the reports by radio, and caused unacceptable delays, but for the time being there was nothing Sorge could do about it.

Vukelic, it turned out, was under-funded, and though he managed to earn some money as a journalist, he soon found himself nearly destitute. Sorge stepped in to help but he was never overimpressed with the raw recruit Moscow had sent him. However, Vukelic must have had his uses once he began working for the French News Agency, Havas, as it gave him access to the Japanese Domei News Agency. This handled news items banned from publication because of the strict Japanese censorship laws, and must have been a useful source of information.

More promising for Sorge was Miyagi Yotoku, a 30-year-old bilingual artist recruited from the large Californian Japanese community, whose job, apart from espionage, was to undertake any translating that was needed.

The American historian, Gordon W. Prange, wrote[9] that Miyagi's paintings combined sensitivity with technical ability, while his character was an unusual mixture of everyday pragmatism and political naivety. His literary taste, which gave him a wide vocabulary, embraced Tolstoy and Gorky, and his knowledge of Oriental art made him an ideal companion for Sorge who was also keenly interested in Japanese and Chinese painters.

Though a devoted Communist, Miyagi was nevertheless very nervous about working as a spy in his country of origin, as he reasoned that in wartime he would be shot if discovered. This also applied to Ozaki Hotsumi, of course. But when Sorge asked him to join his spy ring, after Ozaki returned to Japan in 1934, he seemed to have no qualms in accepting, though it eventually cost him his life. Sorge needed Ozaki to supply information on Japanese politics and economics, as well as the country's military capacity. Ozaki accepted immediately, explaining after his arrest that he thought one of the network's most important roles was the defence of the Soviet Union, and 'for that defence, our most important mission was to provide accurate information'.[10]

The inner members of the ring had their own informants who were unknown to the others, though one of them, Gunther Stein, the Tokyo correspondent for the London *News Chronicle* between 1935 and 1938, knew all the main conspirators. An expert on Japan's foreign trade and economic problems, he was immensely helpful to Sorge, feeding him intelligence acquired from the British ambassador and several other members of his staff. Though Sorge told his interrogators after his arrest that Stein had co-operated with him 'only as a sympathiser', Stein was more than that as he allowed his house to be used as one of the transmitting locations for the network's radio. In fact, the first contact with 'Wiesbaden', the codename for the Soviet radio station at Vladivostok, was in February 1936 from Stein's house.

Transmitting was an especially risky undertaking, but though the Japanese did detect the signals they could not trace their source and, apparently with one exception, were unable to decrypt the messages. These were put into English before being encoded by using numbers from the German *Statistical Yearbook* for 1933 and 1935, and were transmitted in five-digit word groups.

Once the ring became operational the main source of Sorge's intelligence came from his contacts within the German embassy, particularly Lieutenant-Colonel Eugen Ott, who had recently been appointed the senior military attaché. It was a relationship both found agreeable on a personal level and of inestimable use on the professional one. Via his Japanese contacts, Sorge, despite having only a basic knowledge of the language, had an entrée into Japanese society that Ott could never acquire; while Ott gave Sorge insights into German military thinking and strategy.

So closely did the two work together that within a year Ott had come to trust his charismatic, brilliant friend implicitly. He particularly relied on Sorge's advice and his knowledge of China and Japan; and when Sorge accurately predicted the consequences of Japan's full-scale assault on China in July 1937 (known as the China Incident), Ott's trust in his friend's judgement was complete. He even took Sorge with him on a tour of the new Japanese territory of Manchukuo to assess the military situation there. When he returned Sorge wrote a detailed appreciation of their investigations, which was well received, not only in the German embassy, but by Ott's superiors in Berlin. Not surprising, therefore, that an MI6 agent, who escaped from Japan in 1942, said that he knew Sorge and had always regarded him as 'a hot Nazi'.[11]

Sorge particularly impressed German officials and his Soviet masters with his report on an army mutiny that occurred in Tokyo in February 1936. Several politicians were hunted down and killed, and the Prime Minister, Admiral Okada, only escaped with his life when the assassins mistook his brother-in-law for him. He hid in a lavatory for two days, and only escaped when his enterprising family smuggled him out of the house by adding him, dressed as a mourner, to his own funeral procession. At the height of the mutiny, Sorge toured the streets to assess the situation, while Miyagi translated the pamphlets and the manifesto issued by the mutineers. Sorge's report on this bloody affair, supported by the information Miyagi and Ozaki had collected, was well received by the German ambassador. It also impressed General Georg Thomas, the head of the Wehrmacht's economic department in Berlin, who requested Sorge write a special report on the mutiny for him. Then, after he became ambassador in April 1938, Ott appointed his friend to a part-time post in the embassy's press section. He even allowed him to read confidential documents on the Japanese Army, documents Sorge was able to photograph surreptitiously.

By such means did the Soviet spy burrow his way into the very heart of the German power structure. It was espionage conducted at the very highest level.

* * * * *

In May 1935 Sorge returned to Moscow to consult with the Fourth Department prior to the ring becoming operational. He went home via the United States, and in New York he was handed a genuine passport in the 'long and outlandish' name of an Austrian national with Sorge's photograph and description on it. He used this to enter and leave the Soviet Union, so when he returned to Japan there was no evidence in his own passport that he had been in the country he was spying for.

On his arrival in Moscow he found that Berzin had been replaced. Though Sorge did not know it, his former chief had become yet another victim of Stalin's purges. The department's new head, General Semion Uritskii, agreed that Bruno Wendt, Sorge's useless wireless operator, could be replaced, and Sorge chose Max Clausen, his operator from Shanghai. Later Clausen said how proud he was that he had been put in charge of the RAMSAY network's wireless operations and that he went to Japan 'as an enemy of the Japanese government and, as I thought, as a friend of the Japanese people'.[12] However, under the pressures of transmitting in an enemy country, his dedication flagged. He also came to dislike Sorge, saying he was capable of destroying his closest friend for Communism, an accurate assessment of Sorge's ruthless personality.

Once Sorge had made clear the RAMSAY network was in place and could provide useful intelligence, Uritskii gave him his orders. He outlined the strategy he wanted Sorge to follow in seven paragraphs. These amounted to discovering whether Japan, either by itself or with another power, was plotting to invade the Soviet Union, and was it sufficiently well armed to achieve this?[13] Though during his interrogations after his arrest Sorge played down his military espionage, three of the paragraphs related directly to the Japanese Army. So his protestations, that he was not a spy at all but was merely working for peaceful relations between the Soviet Union and Japan, are not convincing.

There is evidence that Sorge found Moscow disillusioning. Stalin's purges had everyone fearing for their lives, and several of Sorge's acquaintances and friends had already been executed or sent to the Gulag. His only consolation was that Katya was eagerly awaiting his return; for a few months they were able to enjoy each other's company, and in August they were married. But this did not stop Sorge, on his return to Japan, from starting a long-term affair with an attractive 25-year-old Japanese bar girl, Miyake Hanako. Sorge remained attached to Hanako for the rest of his life, though he was no more faithful to her than he was to Katya. At the same time as he began sleeping with Hanako, he was already having an affair with Ott's wife, Helma, though his growing passion for the young Japanese eventually terminated his relationship with the older woman. Ott knew about Helma and Sorge, but apparently did not let it affect his friendship with the latter, whom he now regarded, as did Ott's two children, as part of the family.

So completely did Ott trust Sorge that one day he confided to him details of the highly secret negotiations between Japan and Germany that were to culminate in the Anti-Comintern Pact of November 1936. As the negotiations for the pact were far too confidential for the embassy staff, Ott asked Sorge's help to encode a message about the negotiations to the German General Staff in Berlin. Sorge therefore not only knew every detail of the pact – including the secret protocol which made it practically a military alliance between Germany and Japan against the USSR – but must have had access to the keys of the German Wehrmacht code in which the message was sent. It was a coup that any spy dreams about, and it is therefore not surprising that Soviet code-breakers were amongst the most successful of the war.

* * * * *

Throughout this period Sorge was writing affectionate letters to Katya. Some of these survive in the Russian archives as they were included in the microfilm Vukelic regularly assembled, and they tell of his longing to return to Moscow to see her. But, at the same time, he was refusing orders to return there, saying that the contacts he had carefully built up would be largely wasted if he did so. Probably the true reason for him remaining in Tokyo was his fear of being liquidated.

In April 1938 Ott became the German ambassador in Tokyo, and this could well have spelt the end of the close relationship between the Soviet spy and his main, unwitting, informant. However, Ott continued to regard the German journalist as a friend, confidant and close adviser, and even suggested he act as the German embassy's courier when Sorge told him he was about to visit Hong Kong. Sorge agreed and was issued with a temporary diplomatic pass that protected him from customs' searches and any potentially awkward questions by the Japanese police. As Sorge's true purpose in visiting Hong Kong was to make contact with Fourth Department messengers, he later described himself as being a double courier carrying documents from both sides, a situation which must have given him some amusement.

However, by June 1939 Sorge was finding it harder to remain at Ott's side, and pessimism began to seep into his reports to Moscow, as one sent to the Director of the Fourth Department that month shows. '*Ott has at last become a figure of importance. As a result, he has much less time to go around with me and discuss things one to one. So the future looks dark to me.*'[14] He also reported that the Japanese were making even more stringent rules about foreigners and that two of his best contacts in the embassy, the assistant military attaché, a particular friend of his, and the naval attaché, had been transferred out of Japan. '*I have the impression that the best time for our activities here is completely finished, or at least will be soon,*' he added, and ended his report by requesting he be allowed to return home, for remaining any longer '*really seems too much to endure*'. His request was ignored.

So Sorge, having earlier refused to return to Moscow, was now desperate to be recalled. This *volte face* could have been at least partially caused by the motorcycle accident he had had in April 1938, which may have upset his mental balance. He had gone on a drinking binge, which he did more and more to relieve the terrible stress of operating a double life in a hostile country, and had been badly injured. A series of cosmetic operations had to be carried out on his face, but the accident transformed not only how he looked, but how he behaved. Ott for one was convinced that it had affected his friend mentally. Sorge's recovery was long, slow and painful, and was not made any easier by trying to fend off the unwanted care Helma tried to lavish on him. Because of the injuries he sustained he got Moscow to agree that Clausen should have access to the ring's top-secret code so that he could take over the task of enciphering and deciphering its messages. It was an error of judgement Sorge was soon to regret.

* * * * *

Sorge was still recovering from his motorcycle injuries when, in September 1938, the Soviet officer in charge of the NKVD in the Far East, General G.S. Lyushkov, defected. He was brought to Tokyo for interrogation and gave valuable information about the disposition of Soviet forces on the Soviet–Japanese borders and their low morale caused by Stalin's purges. On hearing of the defection, Admiral Canaris, head of the Abwehr (the German Military Intelligence service), sent a senior officer to question Lyushkov. Soviet intelligence was seriously alarmed by the affair, and on 5 September 1938 the Fourth Department cabled Sorge: 'Ramsay. Make maximum effort to obtain copy of report which Canaris' courier received from Green Box or result of his direct interview with Lyushkov. Cable all you know about it at once.'[15]

This was a tough assignment, but Sorge was now so completely accepted in the German embassy that he had little difficulty in persuading his friend, the assistant military attaché Erwin von Scholl, to tell him what he knew about the interrogation, and Scholl even allowed him to read the Abwehr officer's report, which Sorge promptly photographed. This was untold treasure for Moscow as it detailed how the Japanese and Germans viewed Soviet military capacity in the Far East; what its weaknesses were; and how these could be exploited.

Sorge's coup was later assessed by the spy's principal Japanese prosecutor as being 'one of the most important tasks that Sorge accomplished for Moscow during his eight years in Japan'.[16] It paid almost immediate dividends, for a few months later, in May 1939, the Soviet and Japanese armies clashed on the Mongolian/ Manchukuo borders at Nomon-Han (the Battle of Khalkhyn Gol). There had been border skirmishes before, and one the previous year had developed into a battle that had lasted a month. But the Nomon-Han Incident was more like an undeclared war. It lasted several months, and during this time the Japanese Army suffered a series of devastating defeats which established the reputation of one of the Second World War's most accomplished Soviet generals, Georgy Zhukov. 'It produced the Far East's first evenly matched aircraft and tank regiments,' wrote one historian.

'The undefined border between Manchukuo and the Mongolian People's Republic was the immediate cause of the dispute, but in a larger context Nomon-Han was a major probing operation by the Kwantung Army's military adventurers.'[17]

The Nomon-Han Incident was a good example of how efficiently Sorge organised his ring. His right-hand man, Ozaki Hotsumi, questioned Japanese journalists when they returned from the front line, and he reported discussions about the incident in the Breakfast Society, an informal but influential government think-tank in which Ozaki played an important role, coming to the conclusion that the Japanese Prime Minister wanted to avoid war with Russia at all costs. Ozaki's other principle source of intelligence, personnel in the South Manchurian Railroad, confirmed that the reinforcements being sent to the front were not large enough to indicate anything other than a limited offensive. Vukelic came to the same conclusion when, as a representative of Havas, the Japanese Army invited him in July to visit the Nomon-Han battlefield.

However, it was Miyagi who gave Sorge the most valuable intelligence on the fighting. He had more sub-agents than any other member of the ring, the most important among them being an ex-soldier, Odai Yoshinobu.[18] Odai had fought in China and Inner Mongolia before being sent on garrison duty in Korea. He therefore knew a lot about the army, and many of his colleagues were still serving in it. In the spring of 1939 he and Miyagi investigated the Japanese order of battle in Manchukuo in depth, and whether the Kwantung Army's attack was the precursor of a full-scale invasion of Soviet territory. They concluded it was not, but Moscow chose to reject this intelligence and, on 1 September 1939, Sorge was informed that 'your information on current military and political situations has deteriorated during the summer. Green [Japan] has begun important moves lately to prepare for war against Red [Soviet Union] but we are not getting the valuable information which you must be fully aware of through Anna [Ott's GRU codename].'[19] It was an early indication of Stalin's blind refusal to believe anything that contradicted his own paranoid conclusions.

In fact, the fighting did not last long and a peace was signed on 15 September 1939. It left the Kwantung Army humiliated, and the Japanese government trying to keep the magnitude of the defeat from its people. To avoid comments in Japan on the large numbers killed, it used the ruse of bringing home the dead in small batches, and on 24 January 1940 Sorge sent a long dispatch to the Fourth Department that pointed out how events had swung in favour of the Soviet Union:

> *Difficulties with the economy, the fact that the war in China is dragging on, the defeat at Nomonhan, and finally German–Soviet co-operation* [Sorge is referring to the Nazi–Soviet Pact of August 1939] – *all these factors have shaken the position of the army within the leadership of Japan, and in the eyes of the Japanese people. The Army has lost its prestige not only in domestic and foreign policy, but even in military affairs. Currently, the leadership is in the process of shifting to court circles and a group of big capitalists. The recent trend is for political parties and the navy to become more active, in the hope of gaining the upper hand.*

However, Moscow remained unconvinced that a Japanese invasion was not imminent and during the first half of 1940 Sorge was pestered with demands for more details on Japan's armaments and military capabilities. This was no easy task either, as even the production of bicycles was kept secret. Luckily for Sorge General Georg Thomas, who had been so impressed by the Soviet spy's 1936 report on the Japanese Army mutiny, now asked him to provide one on Japan's manufacturing industries and how these were being prepared for war. This gave Sorge unrestricted access to the embassy's extensive resources on the subject – which he promptly photographed and sent to Moscow.

* * * * *

The August 1939 Nazi–Soviet Pact, whereby the two deadly enemies agreed a treaty of non-aggression, caused a severe rift between Japan and Germany, so much so that flags bearing the Nazi swastika, which had decorated some Tokyo shops and streets, completely disappeared. But by July 1940, with almost all of Europe in German hands and Britain apparently on the verge of defeat, the Japanese government recognised the opportunities that were opening up to acquire the rich Asian colonies belonging to Britain, the Netherlands, and France. Rich in the resources that Japan lacked, such as oil and rubber, they must have proved an irresistible lure, and one that gradually replaced Japanese ambitions on China's mainland.

Under such circumstances an alliance with the all-conquering Nazis not only made sense but seemed essential, and in the autumn of 1940 a special envoy, Heinrich Stahmer, arrived from Berlin to initiate discussions on a pact between the two countries. Held in the utmost secrecy, they lasted three weeks. Their outcome, of course, was of the utmost importance to Moscow and Sorge saw to it that he kept in close touch with Stahmer, whom he had previously met in 1938 when the German had visited Tokyo for similar talks. 'A splendid fellow with a first-rate mind' was how Stahmer had described Sorge to Ott in 1938, and now he was so well disposed towards him that Sorge had access to the daily telegrams Stahmer sent to Berlin on the progress of the talks.

Moscow, therefore, knew every detail of what became known as the Tripartite Pact[20] long before it was signed in Berlin in September 1940. In it both parties agreed to work for a new world order that would oust British and American supremacy in the world and replace it with an Axis one. Germany and Italy (a co-signatory to the pact), would create a 'new order' in Europe while Japan would form the 'Greater East Asia Co-Prosperity Sphere', signalling a war of liberation in south-east Asia against the western colonial powers.

Monitoring the progress of these talks, and then the signing of the pact, was another coup of the highest order for the Soviet spy. However, by now he was having trouble with Clausen. On his arrival in Japan in November 1935 Clausen had had a 'strong Communist spirit', and had been eager to help overthrow the capitalist system in Japan. To help establish a cover for him, the Fourth Department, ironically, had financed him to start a business. The first had failed but a second, which manufactured and sold presses for making industrial blueprints, prospered, and by 1940 the company, 'M. Clausen Shokai', had made the wireless operator a rich man. As his wealth increased so did his disenchantment with Communism, and when in the autumn of 1940 he read a message from Moscow his disenchantment was complete. It said that because of the war there was a problem obtaining the right currencies and it was also becoming difficult to send money. 'So from now on remittances will be limited to 2,000 yen a month,' Sorge was instructed, 'and what is needed over and above this you should take out of Clausen's operating profits.'[21]

This was too much for Clausen to swallow. He reported to Moscow that all was not as it seemed. In fact the business was not doing well and that it cost money to keep up appearances amongst the German community as he was required to do. Sorge said nothing when he read Clausen's message, though he must have known Clausen was lying. From that time Clausen's already erratic behaviour towards his work deteriorated further. He altered the contents of Sorge's messages, or abbreviated them, and sometimes failed to send them at all.[22] He presumably began shortening them, to lessen the danger of being tracked down. Perhaps his nerve had gone, though when interrogated after his arrest, he jauntily asserted he always managed to divert suspicion, 'by acting cheerfully in public, and looking stupid'. This sounds like bravado.

* * * * *

By the end of 1940 Sorge had begun to hear rumours from visiting German officers that Hitler might abandon the expected invasion of Britain. Instead, the Führer was considering the destruction of the arch-enemy in the east, the USSR, which, to his fury, had recently invaded Bukovina, threatening the Romanian oil that Germany largely relied upon for its war machine.

In December 1940 a new German military attaché, Colonel Alfred Kretschmer, was appointed to the Tokyo embassy and Sorge, who had been warmly recommended to Kretschmer by the previous attaché, quickly struck up a friendship with him. Kretschmer confirmed what Sorge had heard, that operation BARBAROSSA, the codename for the invasion of the Soviet Union, was indeed being planned. On 28 December, Sorge passed these rumours onto Moscow, the first of many on the subject. He also kept Moscow informed of the diplomatic moves the Germans were making to entice Japan into the war on their side. However, on 13 April 1941, Japan rebuffed Germany by signing a Neutrality Pact with the Soviet Union. In it the parties agreed that if either side were attacked, the other would remain neutral. Another important factor in the diplomatic roundabout was the United States, whose relationship with Japan had deteriorated after the China Incident, and there were secret talks between them to lower the diplomatic temperature. It was a time of intrigue and murky diplomatic moves, and Sorge and his ring were hard put to follow each twist and turn, with Sorge passing intelligence on the talks not only to Moscow but to the DNB in Berlin as well.

So far as the standoff between Japan and the United States was concerned, it was Ozaki's belief that whatever the outcome it would benefit the Soviet Union:

> If Japan and the US reach an accord, this will distance Japan from Germany. And then Japan will be careful not to antagonise the Soviet Union. On the other hand, if the talks break down, it follows as a matter of course that Japanese forces will advance towards the South. And if this brings Japan into conflict with America and Britain, then the Soviet Union will be spared from a Japanese attack.[23]

* * * * *

In early May 1941 Sorge sent the first of a series of urgent messages to Moscow on which his reputation as a spy of the highest calibre has since been built:

> *I discussed the German–USSR relationship with German Ambassador Ott and the naval attaché. Ott said that Hitler is absolutely determined to crush USSR and get hold of the European part of the Soviet Union and use it as a grain and raw materials base to put the whole of Europe under German control.*
>
> *Ambassador and attaché both agreed that two critical dates are approaching as regards German–USSR relationship. The first date is on the completion of sowing [crops] in USSR. After end of sowing, war against USSR can start at any moment, as Germany has to gather the harvest.*
>
> *The second crucial moment concerns the negotiations between Germany and Turkey. War will be inevitable if USSR creates difficulties concerning Turkey's acceptance of German demands.*
>
> *Possibility of outbreak of war at any moment is very high, because Hitler and his generals are confident that a war with the USSR will not hamper conduct of war against Britain in the least.*
>
> *German generals estimate the Red Army's fighting capacity is so low that they believe the Red Army will be destroyed in the course of a few weeks. They believe the defence system in the German–Soviet border zone is extremely weak.*

Decision on start of war against USSR will be taken by Hitler alone either as early as May, or following the war with England.

However, Ott, who is personally against such a war, feels so sceptical at the present time that he already advised Prince Urach[24] to leave for Germany in May.

Before Urach left for Germany, Ott asked if he would persuade Sorge, with whom Urach had become firm friends, to return with him as Ott was becoming seriously concerned about Sorge's erratic behaviour. Certainly, the years of extreme stress had altered Sorge's personality, and his latest bed companion noticed how his fits of rage alternated with acute depression. The endless drinking bouts were also taking their toll and Ott wanted his friend out of the way before he created a serious incident. But Sorge refused to go and Ott, instead of distancing himself from Sorge as he should have done, did the opposite by requesting his friend to undertake an unofficial mission to Shanghai to sound out the reactions of Japanese circles there to the United States' offer to be mediators in their country's ongoing conflict with China. This was another espionage coup for Sorge, but at around the same time Hanako found him curled up on a sofa sobbing. After calming him down she asked what was troubling him. Lonely, Sorge told her, he had no friends. The truth was, as he must have realised, spies don't have friends, not real ones.

Then, prior to his departure for Shanghai, Sorge sent Moscow two messages, dated 19 May. One read:

According to Otto [Ozaki's GRU codename] *and German Ambassador Ott's sources, USA proposed, through Grew* [the US Ambassador to Japan]*, to Japan that they establish a new friendly relationship. USA offered to mediate between Japan and Chungking* [Chiang Kai-shek's capital] *on basis of Japan's troop withdrawal, to recognise Japan's special position in China, and grant favoured commercial status. USA also offered to give special treatment to Japanese economic demands in South Pacific. However USA demanded Japan stop encroachment in South Pacific* [it had occupied part of French Indo-China in September 1940] *and effectively renounce Three Powers Pact* [Tripartite Pact] *… Ott learnt that Japan will remain neutral for first few weeks in case of German–Soviet war. However, Japan is likely to begin military action against Vladivostok in case of*

Soviet defeat. Japanese and German military attachés are maintaining watch on westward transfer of Soviet troops from the Far East.

The other message emphasised the continuing danger of a German invasion of the Soviet Union:

New representatives who arrived here from Berlin said the war between Germany and USSR may start at the end of May, because they are under orders to return to Berlin by then. However, they also said that it is possible the danger may blow over in this year. They reported that Germany has nine army corps composed of 150 divisions.

The Fourth Department had ignored Sorge's warnings about a possible German invasion before, and it responded to this second message by bluntly saying it doubted Sorge's information was true. The same message also evoked an angry tirade from Stalin, who called Sorge 'a shit who has set himself up with some small factories and brothels in Japan'.[25]

* * * * *

In Shanghai, Sorge soon gauged the attitudes of the Japanese armed forces and the Japanese business community based there: both strongly opposed any attempt by their government to impose a peace plan. Employing the German embassy code, which, as the ambassador's emissary, he was entitled to do, Sorge sent his findings to Ott, who forwarded them to Berlin unchanged. As with the army code Sorge had used in 1936, there seems little doubt that the key to the embassy code quickly found its way to Moscow.[26]

While Sorge was in Shanghai, his friend Erwin von Scholl arrived in Tokyo from Germany to brief Ott on the looming military confrontation between Germany and the USSR. On Sorge's return, probably on 27 May, Ott told him about Scholl's mission. Though Ott did not know the exact date of the invasion, it was certainly enough for the spy to draft yet another urgent message to Moscow on 30 May:

Berlin informed Ott that German attack will commence in latter part of June. Ott 95% certain war will commence. Following is indirect evidence which I see at the present time:

The technical department of German Air Force in my city [Tokyo]
received orders to return home without delay.

*Ott instructed military attaché not to send any important reports
via USSR.*

Shipment of rubber through USSR reduced to minimum.

*The motives for the German action: because of existence of power-
ful Red Army, Germany has no possibility to widen the sphere of war
in Africa, and has to maintain large army in eastern Europe. In order
to eliminate all dangers from USSR side, Germany has to drive off
the Red Army as soon as possible. This is what Ott said.*

Sorge then sought out Scholl at the Imperial Hotel and they had
dinner together. What Scholl told him made Sorge draft a further
message:

*Expected start of German–Soviet war around 15 June is based
exclusively on information which Lieutenant-Colonel Scholl
brought with him from Berlin, which he left on 6 May heading for
Bangkok. He is taking up post of attaché in Bangkok.*

*Ott stated that he could not receive information on this subject
directly from Berlin, and only has Scholl's information.*

This warning message could not have been clearer, yet the original
signal in the Russian archives had scribbled over it: 'Suspicious. To
be listed with telegrams intended as provocations.' [27]

When all his warnings fell on deaf ears Sorge contacted the *New
York Herald Tribune*, but only the paper's Tokyo correspondent was
interested in what he had to say. However, the article he wrote, 'Tokyo
expects Hitler to Move Against Russia', was buried deep in the paper
and evoked little interest. Nevertheless, the author of it must have
been pleased at the prescience of his informant when, in the early
hours of 22 June 1941, German forces launched BARBAROSSA
and attacked the Soviet Union with overwhelming force.

* * * * *

BARBAROSSA obliged Stalin to change his attitude to the
'shit', for only Sorge and his ring were in a position to report if
the German invasion was going to prompt a Japanese one from
Manchukuo. As Stalin could not afford to transfer divisions in
the east to the Western Front, where they were urgently needed,

without first knowing Japan's intentions, any intelligence Sorge transmitted was now beginning to receive attention in Moscow.

When Sorge lunched with Ott on 28 June, the ambassador told him how Japan was responding to continuing pressure from Germany to join its war against the USSR. This information, and what Sorge acquired from Ozaki on the same subject, was contained in a telegram to the Fourth Department:

> *The decision to send troops to Saigon* [Japan's continuation of its occupation of French Indo-China] *was adopted under pressure from radical elements who demand action, but with the condition first, that conflict with America is to be avoided and, second, that Japan will play for time while the German–Soviet war is being fought.*
>
> *Invest* [the GRU's new codename for Ozaki] *maintains that Japan will attack to the North* [into the Soviet Union] *as soon as the Red Army is defeated, and also pointed out that Japan intends to purchase Sakhalin* [only the northern two-thirds of the island was then Soviet territory] *in a peaceful manner …*
>
> *German Ambassador Ott corroborated first part of the above. But with respect to the second part, Matsuoka* [the pro-German Japanese foreign minister], *queried by Ott, replied that Japan will fight against the USSR, as he had always assured him she would.*
>
> *Matsuoka told Ott that the Emperor* [Hirohito] *has given his approval to the movement to Saigon some time ago, and this cannot be changed at the present time Thus Ott understood that Japan will not attack to the north for the time being.*

On 10 July, a week after an imperial conference had taken place to decide on Japan's policy towards the German–Soviet war, Sorge prepared a further message for the Fourth Department:

> *Invest said that at the conference in the presence of the Emperor it was decided not to alter the plan for action against Saigon* [Indo-China], *but it was decided at the same time to prepare for action against the USSR in case of the defeat of the Red Army.*
>
> *German Ambassador Ott said, in similar vein, that Japan would begin the attack if the Germans reach Sverdlovsk.*
>
> *The German military attaché telegraphed to Berlin that he is convinced that Japan will enter the war by the end of July or the beginning of August, and as soon as she had completed preparations.*

Sorge also mentioned Matsuoka's fear the Soviet Union would bomb Japan if the latter went to war against it, and that Ott had replied that the Soviet Air Force only had 1,500 first-class aircraft in the Far East, and only 300 of these were heavy bombers capable of reaching Japan.

Japan's mobilisation was closely monitored by Sorge's network, particularly by Miyagi and Ozaki. The latter's important sources of information were the usual ones, personnel running the South Manchurian Railway, the Breakfast Society, and the business community. Following his own precepts on spying, Ozaki casually mentioned to one businessman connected with shipping that it seemed to him the Japanese Army was intending to attack northwards. The businessman immediately replied that from what he had heard more units were going south than were being dispatched north, and then quoted what must have been highly secret numbers: '250,000 [troops] to the north, 350,000 to the south, 400,000 remaining in Japan.'[28]

Miyagi, aided by one of his sub-agents on Hokkaido Island, had already supplied Sorge with a map of the island and of another, Karafuto, both of which were situated close to the Soviet mainland. Anything of military importance had been marked on the maps, and notes made about them. With the help of his soldier informant, Odai Yoshinobu, who had been called up again, Miyagi also collected intelligence on the mobilisation. They discovered, for example, that only inexperienced units were being shipped to Manchuria, and they were not of the right calibre to launch an attack on the Soviet Union. They also noted the types of uniform being issued, to help calculate the numbers being sent north and south, winter clothing for the former, tropical kit for the latter, and on 30 July Sorge cabled Moscow details of the intelligence the two spies had gathered:

Invest and Intari [Miyagi's new GRU codename] *said more than 200,000 men will be called up under the new mobilization in Japan. Thus about two million men will be under arms in Japan by the middle of August.*

Japan will be able to begin war from the second half of August, but will only do so should the Red Army actually be defeated by the Germans, resulting in a weakening of defence capabilities in the Far East.

> *This is the viewpoint of the Konoye group* [supporters of the Prime Minister Prince Konoye Fumimaro], *but how long the Japanese General Staff will bide their time is difficult to say at the moment.*
>
> *Invest is convinced that if the Red Army stops the Germans in front of Moscow, Japan will not make a move.*

These and similar cables were closely scrutinised by the Soviet hierarchy. The one of 28 June was read both by Stalin and the foreign minister, Vyacheslav Molotov, and the one of 10 July was signed by Stalin and by other members of the Politburo. There is also a note at the end of the latter message written by the deputy head of the Soviet Army's General Staff Intelligence: 'In consideration of the high reliability and accuracy of previous information and the competence of the information sources, this information can be trusted.' At last Sorge's intelligence was receiving the attention it deserved, though Clausen's treachery was diluting its effectiveness.

Clausen confessed after he had been arrested that he had only transmitted about a third of the messages that Sorge had drafted, saying it would have been too much hard work to send them and that he had no wish to ruin his health (he apparently had heart problems). He had also 'become sick of spy work. Recently my belief in Communism began to waver, and I lost the will to pursue spy work really seriously.'[29] Clausen, of course, was pleading for his life, and desperate to show he was not the Communist spy he was accused of being. This makes his evidence unreliable, and there is no way of knowing how much of Sorge's intelligence he altered, destroyed, or failed to send, and how important it was.

A cable Sorge dispatched to the Fourth Department on 11 August 1941 showed how uncertain he still was about where the Japanese would strike, north or south:

> *During the first days of the Germany–USSR war, the Japanese government and General Staff decided on major mobilization to prepare for war. But after six weeks of war, Japanese leaders are watching the German offensive being held up, and significant German forces being destroyed, by the Red Army.*
>
> *The American position is becoming more anti-Japanese, the economic blockade against Japan is intensifying* [both the British

and Americans were now employing sanctions, freezing Japanese foreign assets and throttling their supplies of oil and other vital commodities] *and the Japanese General Staff has no intention of terminating mobilization. There is a firm belief in the General Staff that they should take the final decision in the immediate future, especially as winter is already approaching. In the coming two to three weeks, Japan's decision will be finally made. It is possible that the General Staff will take the decision to intervene without prior consultation.*

As August progressed it became increasingly evident that the Germans may have bitten off more than they could chew, and Japanese enthusiasm for joining the war, and taking a large bite out of the Soviet empire, began to diminish. On 22 August, the German naval attaché told Sorge that he had concluded Japan had decided not to move against the Soviet Union in 1941, though Ott continued to believe it might still be persuaded to attack. However, the attaché's conclusions were reinforced when Ozaki told Sorge that a recent top army conference, which had included the chiefs of the Kwantung Army, had decided against any immediate attack on the USSR.

On 23 August, Sorge drafted two more messages to Moscow. The first covered Miyagi's and Odai's intelligence where they had calculated, by counting the different uniforms being issued, the numbers of troops being sent north and south:

> *In the first and second mobilizations, 200,000 soldiers were shipped to Manchuria and Northern Korea.*
>
> *There are now altogether 25 to 30 infantry divisions including 14 old divisions in Manchuria, 350,000 soldiers will be dispatched to China, 400,000 remain in the islands* [Japan].
>
> *Many soldiers have been issued shorts – short sharovary [wide trousers] especially for the tropics – and from this it can be assumed that large numbers will be shipped to the south.*

The other message read:

> *Invest* [Ozaki] *reported that* [Inspector-General of Aviation] *Doihara and* [war minister] *Tojo believe the time is still not ripe for Japan to enter the war.*

The Germans are very dissatisfied with this attitude of the Japanese. Konoye ordered Umezu [commander-in-chief of the Kwantung Army] *to avoid all provocative acts. At the same time, government circles are discussing the question of occupying Thailand and Borneo more seriously than before.*

Though the evidence was building that Japan would not move against the Soviet Union that year – the weather alone would virtually rule out such a move once August had passed – the Fourth Department remained unconvinced that the Kwantung Army, always a law unto itself, would not defy orders and launch an offensive of some kind. It was critical to Soviet strategy that the Eastern Front was secure so that reinforcements could be transferred from there to fight the Germans approaching Moscow, and it continued to urge Sorge to find out everything possible about Japanese intentions. Sorge responded by informing the Fourth Department that he was sending Ozaki to Manchukuo to investigate, though actually Ozaki was going anyway to take part in a conference at the South Manchurian Headquarters in Dairen, where he would meet experts on logistics who would know exactly what was happening.

Before he left, Ozaki provided Sorge with another vital piece of intelligence that the Fourth Department required: the highly secret statistics on the oil reserves held by Japan. The answer must have given Moscow further reassurance, for the figures revealed that the Japanese reserves were so low they had only two alternatives: they could either strike south as soon as possible to capture the oil-rich Dutch and British possessions – this would inevitably lead to war with Britain and the USA – or capitulate to American demands to withdraw from China and French Indo-China, so that the oil sanctions could be lifted. Either way the Soviet Union would benefit.

On 14 September, Clausen dispatched a cable to the Fourth Department that Sorge had written soon after Ozaki had left for Dairen on 4 September: '*Invest left for Manchuria. He said that the Japanese government had decided not to go to war against the USSR, but that armed forces will stay in Manchuria for a possible offensive next spring in case USSR is defeated by that time.*'

The second paragraph was garbled in transmission but the meaning of the message was clear: '*Invest noted the USSR will be absolutely freed* [word illegible] *after 15 September.*'

This was good news indeed and must have boosted Sorge's sagging morale. If it did, the euphoria did not last long, for at the end of the month the dreaded moment of discovery, so long anticipated and so long averted, arrived.

As was standard practice amongst Soviet agents everywhere, Sorge's spy ring would have known not to have anything to do with local Communists, as they would have been closely watched by the 'thought police'. However, finding political sympathisers for even the most outer periphery of the organisation was hard; and it was inevitable that some of Sorge's companions were forced to enlist the help of those who had once been connected to the illegal Japanese Communist Party. It was a weak link that was to be the undoing of Sorge and the RAMSAY network, for on 28 September a Miyagi sub-agent was arrested by the *Tokko* on suspicion of having Communist sympathies, and she implicated Miyagi. Miyagi was arrested and brutally handled. He refused to talk, and when he had the chance jumped out of the second-floor window of the police station. He survived the fall and was hauled back into the police station. Bleeding badly, he eventually broke down, and named both Sorge and Ozaki as fellow conspirators, and by 18 October every important member of the ring had been taken into custody. Eventually hundreds were arrested.

Miyagi died in prison in 1943 before he had been convicted; Vukelic and Clausen received life sentences. Vukelic died in prison in January 1945, but Clausen survived and was released by the Americans in October 1945, shortly after Japan surrendered. After a series of lengthy interrogations, Sorge and Ozaki were sentenced to death and hanged in November 1944. Sorge's faithful Hanako visited his grave regularly until her death in 2000.

* * * * *

For many years the Soviet Union refused to acknowledge Sorge's existence, but in 1961 a French film, *Qui êtes-vous, Monsieur Sorge?*, was made of his life and achievements, and proved very popular in Europe including the Soviet Union. The Soviet leader at that time, Nikita Khrushchev, saw it and enquired if the story was true. When he was told that it was, articles on Sorge began to appear in Soviet journals and newspapers,[30] and in November 1961 the Soviet spy was posthumously awarded the Supreme Soviet's highest honour, 'Hero of the Soviet Union'. Other honours followed, and streets were named after him, postage stamps bearing his lined features were issued, and an opera based on his feats was performed. Soviet honours were also awarded to Clausen (Order of the Red Banner), who died in 1979, and to his wife Anna (Order of the Red Star), who died in 1978; and posthumously to Branko Vukelic (Order of the Patriotic War).[31]

Exactly how much the RAMSAY network contributed to the defeat of the Germans outside Moscow – a defeat that arguably led to an Allied victory against the Axis – cannot be known until all the Russian archives are finally opened. However, according to one estimate, by the end of 1941, when Moscow was still under siege, Stalin had been sufficiently confident to move about half the divisional strength of his Far Eastern forces to fight in the west.[32]

NOTES

1. From an article, 'Mein Mann – Richard Sorge' which Christiane Sorge wrote for the Swiss weekly magazine *Weltwoche* in 1964.

2. See Peter Wright's book, *Spycatcher* (New York, 1987), pp. 327–29. Wright was on the track of a suspected double agent in MI6, William ('Dick') Ellis. Ellis is mentioned in Keith Jeffery's official history, *MI6: The History of the Secret Intelligence Service, 1909–1949* (2010), which describes Ellis as having strong Russian connections, but there is nothing about him being a double agent

3. In his book, *The Schellenberg Memoirs* (London, 1956), pp. 175–76) Walter Schellenberg, head of the Nazis' foreign intelligence service (Amt VI of the Sicherheitsdienst) from 1943, wrote that by 1940 certain elements of the Nazi Party were creating difficulties because of Sorge's Communist past. But Schellenberg, aware of the importance of the information Sorge was sending to the DNB, agreed to protect Sorge, provided he also supplied intelligence reports on China, the USSR and Japan. Thus did Sorge reinforce his image of being a trusted and respected agent of the Fascists he secretly reviled.

4. See MacKinnon, J. and MacKinnon, S., *Agnes Smedley: The Life and Times of an American Radical* (Little, Brown, 1988) p. 147.

5. Johnson, C., *An Instance of Treason: Ozaki Hotsumi and the Sorge Spy Ring* (expanded edn, Stanford University Press, CA, 1990) p. 4. Anthony Blunt, a member of The Cambridge Five (see Chapter 3), is possibly the only other spy who had as distinguished an academic record as Sorge and Ozaki.

6. Sorge's remarks are recorded in Vol. 1, p. 123, of the four-volume *Gendai-shi Shiryo, Zoruge Jiken* (*Collection of Source Materials Relating to Modern Japanese History: The Sorge Incident*) edited by Obi Toshito (Tokyo, 1962). These volumes could be said to be the bible on Sorge's spy ring for they contain, *inter alia*, the police interrogations of those arrested; the evidence collected against them; and those parts of Sorge's memoirs he wrote in prison which survived destruction from an air raid.

7. Dr Elise Tipton in Dear, I.C.B. (ed.), *The Oxford Companion to World War II* (2005), p. 873.

8. Obi Toshito (ed.), *Collection of Source Materials Relating to Modern Japanese History: The Sorge Incident* (Tokyo, 1962, Vol. 3), p. 631.

9. Prange, G.W., *Target Tokyo* (New York, 1985) p. 67.

10. Obi, *op. cit.*, Vol. 2, p. 131.

11. West, N. (ed.), *The Guy Liddell Diaries, Vol. II: 1942–45* (Taylor & Francis, 2005, p. 23).

12. Obi, *op. cit.*, Vol. 3, p. 64.

13. Prange, *op. cit.* p. 94.

14. Whymant, R., *Stalin's Spy: Richard Sorge and the Tokyo Espionage Ring* (I.B. Tauris, 1996) p.333. The quote is annotated as coming from 'The Russian Archives' as are the other quotes printed in italics in this chapter. In his foreword the author describes them as being 'hitherto unpublished material from Russian Defence Ministry and KGB files', but as he died in the Indonesian tsunami of 2005 it is not possible to verify how he obtained them, or to give them a more accurate reference. They are given prominence here because it is known that Moscow received them, and that they are authentic, and not loose interpretations of them which were published in articles and books in the 1960s when Moscow at last acknowledged Sorge's achievements. It is therefore possible to judge the potential importance of them to Stalin.

15. 'Green box' was the codename the GRU used for the Japanese Army. Apparently, the message was intercepted by Japanese radio monitors. See Whymant, *op. cit.*, p. 333, n. 61.

16. Interview with Yoshikawa Mitsusada, quoted in Whymant, *op. cit.*, p. 105.

17. Johnson, *op. cit.*, pp. 149–50.

18. In Johnson, *op. cit.*, the author spells the name Kodai Yoshinobu.

19. Obi, *op. cit.*, Vol. 4, p. 76.

20. The primary intention of the Tripartite Pact was to forestall the United States from entering the war on the side of the Allies. It failed in its objective as the United States became a belligerent when the Japanese attacked Pearl Harbor on 7 December 1941.

21. Obi, *op. cit.*, Vol. 4, pp. 101–02.

22. It is known Clausen did this because the Japanese police found both the messages Sorge had given him to send, and the text of the ones he actually sent.

23. Obi, *op. cit.*, Vol. 2, p. 188. By 'south' the message implied attacking the colonies of the western powers, rich in the resources Japan urgently needed. But neither Ozaki nor Sorge knew about any plan to strike Pearl Harbor, and the myth that Sorge informed Moscow of the proposed date of this attack is destroyed by Gordon Prange in *Target Tokyo*, pp. 449–51.

24. Prince Albrecht von Urach (1903–69), a German aristocrat whose family, between 1911 and 1918, were the legitimate heirs to the throne of Monaco. A painter and journalist, he joined the German foreign office in 1939, and in May 1941 was sent to Japan, ostensibly to improve the co-operation of the German and Japanese press services. However, his real, highly secret mission was to persuade the Japanese to attack British possessions in Asia immediately, particularly Singapore. In this he failed and, as advised by Ott, returned to Germany in June 1941, shortly before the German–Soviet war broke out.

25. Andrew, C. and Gordievsky, O., *KGB: The Inside Story of Its Foreign Operations from Lenin to Gorbachev* (London, 1990), p. 213.

26. *Ibid.*, p. 139. The authors suggest that the Soviet lauding of Sorge since the 1960s, and the intelligence he sent to Moscow, might really have been a method of concealing the success of Soviet SIGINT (Signals Intelligence), and that SIGINT might well have played an even more important role in providing Japanese intelligence than Sorge. The authors do not mention the possibility that Sorge provided Soviet codebreakers with the keys to certain German ciphers, presumably because there is no absolute proof that he did so.

27. Wymant, R. *Stalin's Spy: Richard Sorge and the Tokyo Espionage Ring* (I.B. Tauris, 1996). This quote is annotated as coming from 'The Russian Archives'. (See n. 14).

28. Obi, *op. cit.*, Vol. 2, p. 238.

29. *Ibid.*, Vol. 3, p. 109.

30. In 1965, after the Soviet Union finally recognised Sorge's achievements, a biography called *Tovarischch Sorge* was published in Moscow. This claimed Sorge gave the exact date of the invasion (22 June 1941), but there is no proof that he did so from the evidence available.

31. The Soviet name for the German–Soviet War of 1941–45 was the Great Patriotic War, but the decoration was called the Order of the Patriotic War.

32. Prange, *op. cit.*, p. 448. Prange based his estimate on a US Army intelligence report, dated 27 November 1941, that said 'it has been reported on good authority, that between 18 and 24 infantry divisions and 8 armored brigades from the Russian Far Eastern Army have been identified on the Western Front'.

3

The Cambridge Five and Their Soviet Handlers

The Cambridge Five were known to their Moscow spymasters as 'The Five', and later – after the success of the 1960 film *The Magnificent Seven* – as the 'Magnificent Five'. They were Kim Philby, Anthony Blunt, Guy Burgess, Donald Maclean and John Cairncross. The Soviet foreign intelligence service (First Chief Directorate) that controlled them was part of a security organisation that had various names before it was renamed the KGB (Committee for State Security) in 1954. Here, for the sake of simplicity, the NKVD (People's Commissariat for Internal Affairs) will be used throughout.

In the decades following the defection to Moscow of Burgess and Maclean in 1951, a number of books were published about the exploits of The Five, and others appeared after the head of the KGB, in September 1990, ordered its archives be used to create a more positive image of the agency by publicising 'its more celebrated cases'. These later publications included summaries of documents selected from the archives of the First Chief Directorate, though the archives themselves remained closed. After the collapse of the Soviet Union in December 1991, these summaries were made available to certain ex-KGB officers who collaborated with western authors to produce books that contained new information about The Five, or about Soviet agents connected with them whose names had not been previously published.[1] One of the latter was the English-born Kitty Harris – previously known only by her codenames (ADA, NORMA, GYPSY) – which made public new revelations about her relationship with Donald Maclean.[2]

These publications made it clear that it had not been the outstanding organisational skills of Soviet intelligence that had protected the Cambridge spies from discovery for so long. In fact, for much of the 1930s and the early 1940s the Russian secret services were thrown into turmoil by Stalin's purges, which badly affected their efficiency. One commentator has calculated that between 1937 and 1951 the Cambridge ring were out of touch with Moscow for about seventy-two months, or nearly 50 per cent of the time, mostly because their Soviet controllers in London had severed contact with them for one reason or another.[3] So badly was the organisation affected that figures published in 1999 showed that of the NKVD's staff of about 24,500 in 1936, by January 1938 nearly 6,000 had been dismissed, arrested, transferred – or executed.[4]

While the purges were under way The Centre – the colloquial term used for the Foreign Intelligence Service based in the former Lubyanka prison in Moscow – became almost paralysed. Equally vulnerable to the blood-letting were those NKVD employees who worked abroad, known as either 'legals' or 'illegals'. The former worked under diplomatic cover in Soviet embassies and legations overseas, or lived legitimately in the countries in which they were working; the latter were based in secret *rezidentura* under false identities and nationalities. The Russian journalist, Genrikh Borovik, while researching his book[5] on Kim Philby, found in Philby's KGB file (no. 5881) a list of his one-time handlers who had been shot as spies, or had defected to avoid certain execution or the Gulag. Borovik says it is cursory and incomplete, but shows how impossible it became at times for The Five to continue communicating with The Centre. That they remained determined to do so shows just how dedicated they were.

Of the five men, Philby is generally considered the most dangerous, the most able, and perhaps the hardest to assess. Born Harold Adrian Russell Philby in the Indian city of Ambala on 1 January 1912, he was the son of Harry St John Philby, an Indian civil servant with a maverick disposition. During and after the First World War, Philby senior worked in the Middle East in various capacities, and became well known as an Arabist, explorer and Moslem convert. It was the elder Philby who gave his son the nickname Kim after the eponymous hero of the Kipling novel, saying he was a carbon copy of the character. They did not get on; perhaps their personalities were too similar. 'Politics begin in the nursery,' the journalist Cyril Connolly wrote after the defection of Burgess and Maclean in 1951, 'before we can hurt the Fatherland, we must hate the father.'[6] The diplomat and former intelligence officer, Nicholas Elliott, who knew Kim Philby well, said of him: 'Outwardly, he was a kindly man. Inwardly he must have been cold, calculating and cruel – traits which he cleverly concealed from his friends.'[7]

It was generally agreed that Philby possessed great charm and an easy-going disposition which hid an acute intelligence and a dedicated mind. However, his disarming manner, helped rather than hindered by a stutter, became dissipated in later life, as his drinking and womanising took its toll. Also, the sheer deceit of his double life – a source of amusement to him when young – must eventually have corroded his personality. Like his father he went to Westminster School and then, in 1929, to Trinity College, Cambridge, a typically British upper-class education, as it still is. But Philby and his fellow students lived in a very different world to the one we know today, overshadowed as it was by the Great Depression, the rise of Fascism, and the immense social and economic chasm between the rich and the poor. As Robert Cecil, who was at Cambridge at that time, wrote in his biography of Maclean:

> I was not myself converted to Communism, but I could read the minds of those who were impatient with Baldwin's [the British Prime Minister] lethargy in the face of the imperative need to tackle unemployment and rearmament. Russia, by contrast, was *terra incognita*, land of mystery and, for some, infinite promise, where dreams would come true and the evils of contemporary society be corrected. If old men insisted that the dawn in the East was a false dawn, that made it all the more likely that young men would run to meet it.[8]

Though already a committed Socialist, and well known for it at Cambridge, Philby did not become fully radicalised until he left university and went to Vienna to improve his German. There he met a dedicated young Communist called Litzi who involved him in the political violence then causing turmoil in the city's streets. They fell in love, had a passionate affair, and in February 1934 married before returning to London together. Despite their common interest in Communism, the marriage didn't last and in September 1939 Philby met Aileen Furse who bore him three children. They married in 1946.

Soon after the pair had returned to London, a Communist friend of Litzi's from Vienna, the photographer Edith Tudor Hart, recommended Philby to a Soviet intelligence recruiter, an illegal named Arnold Deutsch, codenamed OTTO. Deutsch, an Austrian Jew by birth and a lecturer by profession, was a follower of the

Austrian psychologist and sexologist, Wilhelm Reich, whose theories attacked Fascism and supported sexual freedom, an attitude Philby would have been attracted to. Deutsch had just arrived in London with his wife – a trained NKVD wireless operator – to initiate his plan to recruit suitable individuals from Oxford and Cambridge universities, knowing they would find careers in influential parts of the British establishment. Once recruited they would drop their Communist connections and adopt a political disguise more suitable for the careers they would follow to help The Cause.

One day Edith asked Philby if he wanted to meet someone of importance who might be of interest to him, and he immediately agreed. To avoid the possibility of being followed, she took him to Regent's Park by a circuitous route, and then walked up to a man sitting on a bench, introduced him as the man she had mentioned, and walked quickly on. The young idealist's impression of Deutsch remained with him throughout his life. 'It was an amazing conversation,' he told Genrikh Borovik in the 1980s, 'and he was a marvelous man. Simply marvelous … I felt that immediately. And it never left me.'[9] And in a previously unpublished memoir, he commented that Deutsch soon became a sort of substitute father and a kind of elder brother. 'A father for guidance, advice and authority,' he wrote, 'an elder brother for fun and companionship. An ideal relationship.'[10]

Other meetings followed and Deutsch began moving the young Philby's life into an entirely new direction. Philby, given the impression that he was being recruited by a secret anti-Fascist organisation connected with the Comintern – the organisation founded by the Soviets in 1919 to spread Communism worldwide – responded eagerly, though taken aback by some of Deutsch's suggestions. He was told, for instance, to avoid the Communist Party of Great Britain (CPGB), which, on his return to London, he had applied to join. He was also told to drop all connections with any individual or organisation tainted by left-wing politics, destroy any evidence in his possession (like books) that he had ever had left-wing inclinations, and was quietly to assume a cloak of traditional conservatism. His tentative thoughts of joining the Indian Civil Service were also quickly vetoed. Instead, Deutsch suggested he studied at the London School of Oriental Studies, perhaps as a preliminary to joining the Diplomatic Service, though he and Deutsch soon decided he would have to choose a more circuitous route to reach the centres of power. He was also initiated into the elaborate precautions necessary to avoid being followed, just one aspect of what was known as *konspiratsiya*, the rules that The Centre imposed upon its agents and handlers. In short he was expertly groomed for his future as a Soviet agent at the heart of the British establishment.

The question of money was tentatively raised and quickly rejected by Philby, though it was agreed he should be paid his travel expenses as his security routine involved taking expensive taxis as well as public transport. Deutsch then extracted a promise from his new recruit that if he ever got into financial difficulty, for whatever reason, he must contact him, not for his good but for the good of The Cause. In fact, all The Cambridge Five were motivated by ideology, though later, when The Centre sent them the occasional bonus as a reward for services rendered, they did not refuse them. Both Burgess and Cairncross were also given money to buy cars to facilitate their espionage; and at the end of the war all of them were offered lump-sum pensions, though these were refused on the grounds it would have been impossible to hide the source of such large sums of money.

The meetings with Philby progressed so favourably that in June Deutsch and another illegal called Teodore Maly (codenamed THEO), who was working with Deutsch at that time, decided to recruit him without obtaining The Centre's approval first. This type of independent action was strictly forbidden but perhaps Deutsch wanted to pre-empt Philby from approaching the CPGB. Anyway, The Centre accepted this *fait accompli* without demur. This was possibly because many people at that time thought, incorrectly, that the elder Philby was an important member of the British intelligence community, and that his son would therefore have a good chance of penetrating the British secret services. In fact, one of Philby's first tasks as an agent was to search his father's flat in case he might find information of use to The Centre.

On 22 June, Maly followed the cable with a more detailed letter, saying Philby would be given the codename SONNY, or SOHNCHEN in German, and that Deutsch had been very impressed by the new recruit. Then, in July, Philby was sent to Cambridge as a talent spotter and to draw up a list of likely recruits amongst his friends and acquaintances. His list comprised seven names, and after writing everything he knew about his chosen candidates Philby arranged a meeting with Deutsch to hand it over. It was then that he first met Maly, who was soon to become his handler. A man of formidable intelligence, who had studied theology and philosophy in a Catholic seminary, Maly had later trained at a military academy and served as an officer in the Austro-Hungarian Army. He, too, made a great impression on the young Philby, who later wrote that he remembered Maly as a man of wisdom and great kindness.

Top of Philby's list of possible recruits was Donald Maclean, a dedicated Communist. Born in 1913, Maclean had arrived at Trinity Hall, Cambridge, in 1931, having won an open exhibition (minor scholarship) in languages from his East Anglian public school, Gresham's. The son of a Labour politician and a high-minded mother, Maclean had the right connections in the highest places and in October 1935 was to embark on his chosen career in the Foreign Office. To Philby he seemed to have the right temperament and was a man destined to reach the highest echelons of the service. The Centre agreed, and a meeting was arranged with Deutsch – and perhaps Maly was there, too. The meeting went well and by December 1934 the budding diplomat had become the second member of the ring.

Maly subsequently wrote to The Centre:

> I like the new people very much. They are very different, very individual ... WAISE [Maclean's codename, which meant 'orphan' in German]: the first thing to be said is that he is certainly very good looking. There is something feminine about him not only in his facial expression but also in his body language. But he is half a head taller than me. He is modest, clever, looks at everything from the Comintern point of view, disciplined but still very young, inexperienced and therefore frightened ... We meet somewhere way out in one of the suburbs in a little restaurant but when we get on to ticklish subjects and name names he shivers in fright in case someone might hear us. He is an idealist and we need to be very careful how we deal with him so as not to destroy his idealism. He regards us as Gods.[11]

Guy Burgess was also on Philby's list, though probably right at the bottom of it, for Philby had strong reservations about him. He did not doubt Burgess's commitment to Communism but strongly questioned the suitability of his character for a life of subterfuge. A brilliant conversationalist and a flamboyant homosexual, Burgess came from a rich naval family. Educated at Dartmouth Naval College and Eton, in 1930 he won an open scholarship to Trinity College, Cambridge where he read history. Illness prevented him from taking his finals,[12] but his outstanding ability was well recognised and he was offered a two-year postgraduate teaching fellowship at Trinity. He knew both Maclean and Philby from their common devotion to Communism, and when they began to disassociate themselves from their former left-wing friends and interests Burgess was far too bright not to guess that things were not what they appeared. He started to badger them, and no one, Philby commented, was able to badger more effectively.

Eventually, it was agreed that Burgess would be less dangerous in the fold than out of it, so at the end of 1934 he was also recruited. Deutsch was favourably impressed. 'His ability to get to know anyone,' he wrote in a psychological study of Burgess, made him a potentially valuable agent. But he was 'a very temperamental and emotional man and he is easily subject to mood swings. The party was for him a saviour. It gave him above all an opportunity to satisfy his intellectual needs',[13] though one gets the impression that nothing could have saved Burgess from himself and the drunken, sad conclusion to his life in a foreign city he loathed. He must have been, as Philby commented, one of the few people to have forced themselves into the Soviet intelligence community. He was certainly persuasive, and as one of his friends, Goronwy Rees, a fellow Communist, commented: 'It used to amuse me to observe Guy's power of manipulating his friends, and it was clear to me that on the whole they were chosen precisely because they were willing victims for it.'[14]

Burgess also received orders from Deutsch to distance himself from Communism and anyone connected with it. Being Burgess, he did this in a spectacular manner by taking a job with a right-wing Conservative MP called Macnamara. Like Burgess, Macnamara was a homosexual. The two took to each other and went on several 'fact-finding' missions to Germany, the true object of which was apparently to have as much sex as possible with young boys. In mid-1936 Burgess moved to the BBC, where The Centre thought he would be well placed to cultivate good contacts and make influential acquaintances. After an initial stint at Bristol he worked for the talks department in London on a programme called *How Things are Made*. He also arranged for David Footman – whom Maclean knew and rightly suspected as being on the payroll of MI6 – to give a series of talks on the Balkans, and this collaboration led to Footman giving him freelance missions for MI6.

* * * * *

In July 1936 the Spanish Civil War broke out between the democratically elected Republican government and the Fascist army rebel, General Franco. It was during these dramatic summer months that Burgess first approached his friend, Anthony Blunt, a young Cambridge don who was to become the fourth member of the ring. One of Blunt's biographers, Miranda Carter, is convinced that 'Without Burgess, Blunt would never have become a spy.'[15] Certainly, the two were very close, and remained so, but not, apparently, lovers. Certainly, the academic, aesthetic and nervously inclined Blunt was not an obvious choice for clandestine work.

For some months Blunt dithered, months in which the gulf between democracy and Fascism became ever clearer on the European scene. Then in January 1937 he decided that, in the words of his only public interview after his exposure in 1979, he would best serve the cause of anti-Fascism by joining Burgess, as the Communist Party and Russia were the only firm barrier against Fascism. This was all too true as Britain and France, in one of their worst acts of appeasement, had turned their backs on the democratically elected Spanish government. In Britain it was even made illegal to fight in Spain; only the Soviet Union officially sent help to the beleaguered Republicans; and Germany and Italy flouted a non-intervention agreement by dispatching both arms and men to support the rebel Franco. It was a tipping point for democracy, as well as for Blunt, whose Marxist theories on art now took a more practical turn.

Blunt, born in Bournemouth in 1907, was the son of a vicar who became the chaplain of the British embassy in Paris in 1912. So by the time Blunt arrived at his public school, Marlborough College, in January 1921 he was fluent in French, an art connoisseur beyond his tender years, and a budding intellectual and aesthete. He read mathematics at Trinity College, Cambridge, before graduating with a first-class degree in modern languages. It was the beginning of a distinguished career as an art historian, and in 1936 he moved to London to lecture at the Warburg and Courtauld Institutes, becoming deputy director of the latter in 1939. This led him, after the war, to be appointed the Surveyor of the King's Pictures, and in 1956 he was appointed a Knight Commander of the Victorian Order. It was the perfect cover for a spy, or so he must have thought. Recollections of Blunt vary considerably. The chairman of the wartime Joint Intelligence Committee found him 'a dull dog', but Blunt at Cambridge was far from that according to those who knew him then. 'He used to have a party every two weeks,' the poet Gavin Ewart told Miranda Carter. 'The gin and tonic flowed like water'; and the philosopher Isaiah Berlin thought him 'handsome, agreeable, civilised, charming and distinguished. What more could you want?'[16]

What is generally agreed is that Blunt at Cambridge was someone of note. Deutsch needed a talent spotter there, and Blunt's reputation as a don who sought out bright young left-wing students fitted Deutsch's requirements exactly. Blunt was given the code name TONY, and Deutsch wrote of him that he was a typical English intellectual: very clever, and spoke very high-flown English. He looked very feminine, and was a pederast. Communism for him was based on theory, and he possessed several books on Marxism in the history of art. 'He would hardly give up his career for the sake of our work,' Deutsch concluded, but he understood the tasks he had 'to do for us and is ready to help us. He has a large influence on students.'[17]

Blunt proved to be a shrewd talent-spotter. The first name he put forward was a rich young American, Michael Straight, who had arrived at Trinity College, Cambridge, in 1934 to read economics. Straight was later to write in his memoir *After Long Silence* (1983) that he was never really a Communist at all, but that Blunt had emotionally browbeaten him into meeting Deutsch. Straight's friend, the Communist poet John Cornford, had recently been killed in Spain and Blunt reminded him that Cornford had died for The Cause.

Straight is just one of the many minor characters who stray in and out of the strange story of The Cambridge Five. But Blunt's second recruit, John Cairncross, was a major player and became its fifth and final member. It has already been mentioned that Cairncross was different from the others. One of the differences

was social. Born in Glasgow in 1913 of lower-middle-class parents, Cairncross never attempted to disguise, or even minimise,
his strong Glaswegian accent; and although he met all the other
members of the ring at one time or another, he only knew that
the ubiquitous Burgess was working for the NKVD. He comes
across in his autobiography, *The Enigma Spy* (1997) – published
two years after his death – as being a very spiky individual indeed.
Unfortunately for him, his adamant denials in this book that he
had never been a long-term Soviet agent, and certainly not a traitor, were finally and definitively exposed for the lies and half-truths
that they were when summaries of his files in Moscow were made
available to researchers.

In his book Cairncross says he took an instant dislike to Blunt
at Cambridge and clashed with him on a number of occasions.
Curious, then, that the philosopher Stuart Hampshire told Miranda
Carter that he remembered Cairncross being starry-eyed when
talking about Blunt, and that Blunt gave him a highly favourable
reference when he applied to join the Foreign Office. Whatever his
temperament, and the size of the chip on his shoulder, Cairncross
was undoubtedly one of the cleverest and most able men of his
generation: that he came top in both the Home Office and Foreign
Office exams, a previously unknown achievement, is certainly
proof of that. He started work in the American Department in
October 1936, but the following February moved to the Western
Department where Maclean was already working. They had known
each other slightly at Cambridge and without becoming close
friends got on tolerably well. At one point Maclean gave him the
friendliest of warnings, saying the trouble was that Cairncross took
no notice of what was regarded as conventional behaviour and that
his spontaneity was equally suspect. It wasn't, Maclean had added,
just a matter of Cairncross holding incorrect views, though this
had not passed unnoticed, but that he came from the wrong background. If Maclean was correct, this was far more a condemnation
of the Foreign Office than it was of Cairncross.

The same month that Cairncross moved to the Western
Department, Blunt invited him to Cambridge for the weekend, where he was introduced to Burgess who was there to start
the process of recruiting the young Scot. On 1 March, Burgess
reported his impressions to The Centre. He considered him 'a
typical petit bourgeois' who believed he could achieve a lot in his

department and in society, and was full of his own achievements. His recruitment, Burgess said, would be difficult but not impossible. 'It seems to me that if we say to him that he can have the one and the other, i.e. both the party and the Foreign Office, he would start working for us ... He feels no respect for the British Foreign Office or his colleagues.'[18] However, Burgess considered it dangerous for either Blunt or himself to make the next step with Cairncross and suggested that it would be best if a trusted open party member approached him, who would be used only on this one occasion.

The person chosen for this delicate task was another peripheral personality in the history of The Cambridge Five, a CPGB member called James Klugmann, who, like Maclean, had been educated at Gresham's and Cambridge University. Klugmann's report to The Centre on the recruitment of Cairncross is not in the KGB archives, but on 9 April 1937 Maly told The Centre the young Scot had been recruited and that he was to be given the codename MOLIERE.[19] The honeymoon did not last long, for Cairncross disliked his job, and on 24 June Deutsch was reporting that he thought the Foreign Office would not keep him for long, and that he would soon have to start looking for another post. For this reason, Deutsch wrote to The Centre, Cairncross was being kept back and was not being asked to pass any documents. However, he had urged the Scot to stay where he was and adapt to his new environment. But, as Cairncross himself remarked, one either belonged or one did not, and in October 1938 he was moved to the Treasury, which he found more amenable.

* * * * *

By the time Cairncross had moved, both Deutsch and Maly had left the country as neither had been able to arrange to stay on a permanent basis. Maly left in the summer of 1937 and was summoned to Moscow. He never returned, and his name is on the list of putative traitors that Borovik found in Philby's Moscow file, with the remark: 'Resident of OGPU in London 1936–37. Shot in 1938. German spy.'[20] Deutsch left for Moscow in the autumn, probably fearing the worst. However, he was only sacked from his NKVD post, and managed to find a job at the Academy of Sciences.[21]

Up to the time the two illegals had departed, Maclean had been the most productive of The Cambridge Five, but with both

Maly and Deutsch no longer in London all contact with Moscow ceased. This was possibly a precautionary measure on the part of The Centre, as another Russian spy ring had just been broken up by British counter-intelligence. In any case, the hiatus did not last long and in April 1938 Deutsch and Maly were replaced by Grigory Grafpen. He was given diplomatic cover working from the Soviet embassy in Kensington, and was ordered to re-establish contact with Maclean as The Centre feared the young English diplomat might have given up. If he was found, Grafpen was told, Maclean was to be cherished and given the highest priority.

The Centre need not have worried, for Maclean was much too dedicated just to abandon spying, and he continued to go to the regular rendezvous where he met his handlers. One day, to his surprise, who should turn up but Kitty Harris, whom he had last met in a London safe-house she ran for the illegals. A British-born Canadian, Kitty was in her late thirties, attractive, a committed Communist, and the estranged wife of Earl Browder, the head of the American Communist Party. Now she became Maclean's handler, and then his lover, and when he was posted to the Paris embassy in September 1938 Kitty was ordered to Paris to continue working with him.

Unfortunately for Kitty, Maclean's new post did not give him much access to secret documents and he rarely had anything for Kitty to microfilm. Then he fell in love with an American student, Melinda Marling, and the affair with Kitty petered out, though they continued to work together. Melinda became pregnant, and Maclean married her in June 1940, just as the British embassy was being evacuated to escape the invading Germans. Melinda apparently knew about her lover's true loyalties, for in a drunken moment Maclean told Kitty that he had confessed to Melinda he was a Soviet agent. However, it is unlikely that Melinda was ever an active member of the ring.

With the departure of Maly and Deutsch, Cairncross was also left in limbo and Burgess, who had his own contact with Moscow via the *rezidentura* in Paris, warned The Centre that Cairncross, now isolated from any contact with Moscow, might abandon his espionage work. In this he underestimated the young Scot who, before moving to the Treasury, had managed to copy high-level documents concerning the September 1938 Munich Crisis. Not being in touch with Grafpen, he had passed them on to Klugmann for transmission to Moscow.

Grafpen did not last long, for in December 1938 he was also recalled to Moscow, and became another victim of the purges.[22] His replacement was Anatoli Gorsky (codenamed VADIM). When Cairncross met him, in April 1939, he found him unlike the sophisticated and empathetic Deutsch, and thought him distant and suspicious. As by then the purges had eliminated quite a high percentage of NKVD personnel, Gorsky's behaviour was, perhaps, not surprising. Blunt, who called Gorsky 'flat-footed', was not impressed either. However, Maclean got on with him so well that when the young diplomat was posted to the United States in 1944 Gorsky went, too, so he could remain Maclean's NKVD contact.

Gorsky reported that Cairncross was working in the Treasury section that supervised the Post Office and other government departments – an unpromising position for a spy, one would have thought. However, the Treasury had to be kept informed about many of the government's secrets and, according to one source, in the summer of 1939, Cairncross passed 'some fascinating documents on the establishment and offices of the Security Service [MI5]; on the construction of a chain of secret radio interception stations; and details of the Government Code and Cipher School'.[23]

* * * * *

In what was certainly a fit of paranoia by Stalin, the London *rezidentura* was closed in February 1940 and Gorsky was ordered back to Moscow, once more leaving Cairncross and the others in limbo. Again the hiatus did not last long, and when Gorsky returned in December he must have been delighted to find how The Cambridge Five had managed to manoeuvre themselves into wartime positions where they could be of use to Moscow.

Donald Maclean, The Centre's most prized possession at the time, had managed to escape from France with his new wife. Promoted to second secretary, he was now ensconced back in the Foreign Office working in the General Department and remained there until March 1944 when he was posted to Washington. His new post in London was not particularly prestigious, but did give him oversight of a variety of documents that included the Foreign Office's liaisons with the Admiralty, and with the Supply and War Ministries, most of which one can assume ended up in Moscow. He also passed to Gorsky some Foreign Office correspondence with Washington which Yuri Modin, the handler of some of The

Five in London after the war, wrote was 'of huge interest to us',[24] though he does not say why.

If Maclean was highly regarded by The Centre, its other civil servant mole, John Cairncross, was somewhat out on a limb in the Treasury. But encouraged by Gorsky, the two of them worked out a scheme for Cairncross to fill the vacant position of private secretary to Lord Hankey, a minister without portfolio in Churchill's cabinet. There was nothing unusual in a lowly Assistant Principal, which is what Cairncross was at the time, being appointed to such a post, but the method the Scot employed to obtain it certainly was.

Hankey was an enthusiastic vegetarian who, with his family, often frequented a vegetarian restaurant off Leicester Square. As Cairncross knew one of Hankey's sons from his time in the Foreign Office, he was instructed by Gorsky to become a devoted vegetarian and go there too. This ruse paid off, and one evening the son introduced Cairncross to his father. Hankey, who approved of modern young men who had embraced vegetarianism, was impressed, and in September 1940 Cairncross started work in his office where, as one of Cairncross's obituarists later noted, 'he sensed not only the anti-Soviet atmosphere but also the continuing pro-German policies espoused by some government ministers'.[25]

Hankey was no fan of Churchill, but as a member of the cabinet he was entitled to receive all cabinet papers, and also oversaw the workings of the intelligence services. He also often chaired secret committees, including the Scientific Advisory Committee that played a key role in the early development of the atomic bomb programme. The post suited Cairncross, for he not only enjoyed working for Hankey, whom he admired, but was soon passing to Gorsky many classified documents, so many in fact that at the end of May 1941 Gorsky informed The Centre that sixty rolls of film containing his material were being sent. It included weekly bulletins from MI6 and the Foreign Office; two reports from a commission that Hankey had set up to investigate MI5; reports on radio measures against night bombers and on bacteriological warfare; 'and documents from the Y committee (a special committee on cipher security).'[26] An impressive haul indeed.

During 1941 alone, Cairncross provided over 3,000 items of intelligence with Gorsky informing The Centre that the Scot had passed a 'most secret report of the government committee on the development of uranium atomic energy to produce explosive material which was submitted on 24 September 1941 to the War Cabinet'.[27] Cairncross's involvement in passing this high-grade intelligence was summed up in a 1945 report by the NKVD's chief of intelligence, who wrote that the first intelligence on ENORMOZ (NKVD codename for the development of the atom bomb) had come from LISZT (Cairncross) and that the material he had provided:

> contained valuable and highly secret documentation, both on the essence of the ENORMOZ problem and on the measures taken by the British government to organise and develop the work on atomic energy. This material formed the point of departure for building the basis of and organizing the work on the problem of atomic energy in our country.[28]

While Cairncross was filching what was possibly the most important documents any of The Five ever passed, Philby had also manoeuvred himself into a useful position for Moscow. While working as a war correspondent for *The Times*, he had already proved his worth to The Centre by providing it with intelligence on the Spanish Civil War, though he did not attempt its suggestion that he assassinate Franco. When hostilities against Germany broke out in September 1939, *The Times* sent him as their accredited correspondent to the British Army HQ at Arras. In June 1940 he was evacuated to England, with a group of journalists. According to his memoirs,[29] one of them worked for MI6's Section D (sabotage and propaganda), and she recommended him to MI6. Burgess who, thanks to Footman, had joined the section in December 1938, also naturally recommended Philby, and Philby ended up working for him. Philby later wrote that he was surprised how easily he was accepted, and that the only investigation into his past was an enquiry to MI5, which reported that there was nothing recorded against him. A true Nirvana, Philby thought, compared to the later intensive scrutiny employed by 'positive vetting'.

Section D did not last long, for it was soon merged with the newly formed Special Operations Executive (SOE), a sabotage and subversion organisation whose objective, in Churchill's phrase, was to set Europe alight. Burgess, to his intense annoyance, was sacked, but Philby transferred to SOE as a political instructor. This proved too far from the action for his liking and the following year he rejoined MI6 to work in Section V's Iberian sub-section. Section V was responsible for countering any German espionage that might be mounted from abroad against British territory, so its intelligence was of direct interest to MI5. It was, as it were, the other side of the same coin. The Germans were very active in the area, and they used Portugal as a springboard for dispatching agents to Britain and the United States.

This post appealed much more to Philby. He was even more pleased when he found that the Central Registry, the heart of MI6's secrets, was stored next to Section V's offices in St Albans, and he quickly began cultivating its archivist, who was particularly fond of pink gin. This paid off and before long Philby, under the pretence that he was getting to know his job, was able to ransack the Registry almost at leisure. Over time he passed to Gorsky a lot of highly classified material to be photographed, including the complete internal structure of MI6. He also passed on what gossip he heard. For instance, at the end of October 1941 he related the bizarre story of Lieutenant-Colonel Dudley Clarke, the Middle East expert on deception who had been arrested ten days previously in Madrid, wearing women's clothes.

* * * * *

By early 1941 Burgess was back at the BBC as a producer to work in the BBC talks section on the programme *This Week in Westminster*, which involved contact with MPs, many of them influential. By then, as MI5's official historian records, Blunt had recruited him as an agent with the codename VAUXHALL; and though the BBC had previously agreed that Burgess should be available for military service, Blunt successfully argued with the authorities in 1941 to cancel his call-up: 'Burgess has been working for us for some time and has done extremely valuable work,' he explained, 'principally the running of two very important agents whom he discovered and took on.'[30]

Blunt's statement was somewhat overblown as one of the agents was Burgess's current boyfriend, who picked up scraps of information while working as a telephone operator in a London hotel. Blunt also attempted to have Burgess recruited as an MI5 officer. Guy Liddell, who liked both of them and trusted them absolutely, was enthusiastic. However, the idea was eventually vetoed, and it is a sad fact that Liddell's highly promising career was blighted by his friendship with the two spies. He died, quite forgotten, in 1958, some six years before a cornered Blunt was forced to confess his treachery to his MI5 interrogators.

While working as a producer, Burgess met the Labour politician Hector McNeil, and it may have been McNeil who found Burgess a job with the Foreign Office's press department, which he joined in June 1944. This immediately gave him access to more interesting intelligence. From August 1944, he was permitted to take documents home at night, and within weeks his new controller, Boris Kreshin (MAX), was reporting that Burgess had brought with him a large number of documents, including six decrypted telegrams, which had been photographed on ten rolls of film. The contents of the telegrams might not have had much intelligence value in themselves. However, being able to compare them with the intercepted originals would have been of enormous help to Soviet cryptographers when breaking the cipher in which the telegrams were originally sent.

Kreshin also noted that Burgess had become noticeably nervous, which is not surprising considering the risks the latter knew he was taking. This did not escape the notice of The Centre either and in October it warned Kreshin that the practice was endangering Burgess. It was right to do so as Burgess was an unstable character at the best of times, always drinking heavily and often behaving outrageously. That he managed to avoid being caught with incriminating documents seems miraculous. On one occasion, he was stopped by a police patrol that suspected his bag contained stolen goods or housebreaking equipment, though they quickly apologised when they saw that it only contained papers. On another, when he met Kreshin to hand over material to be photographed, he dropped his briefcase in a pub, scattering Foreign Office documents all over the floor. Then, after Kreshin had returned the documents to him later that evening, he dropped them all over the floor of the public lavatory where they had agreed to meet. 'It was good that there was no one else in the lavatory,' Kreshin commented phlegmatically, 'and the floor was clean.'[31]

* * * * *

Even before war broke out in September 1939, Blunt was eagerly seeking advice from The Centre on how he could be most useful to Moscow. He suggested he could either enlist as an officer in the

Territorial Army, or attempt to join Military Intelligence. The latter was deemed preferable, and by the end of the year he was a captain in charge of a Field Security Section in France. When he returned to England in May 1940, MI5 was beginning to recruit, contrary to its traditional dislike of intellectuals, from academics of standing such as the historians John Masterman (see Chapter 6) and Hugh Trevor-Roper. Blunt, with his languages and experience in security, must have seemed an ideal candidate. The details of his recruitment in June 1940 have not survived in the files of MI5 but a later MI5 document stated that 'the exact circumstances in which he joined MI5 are obscure, but do not appear to be unusual or sinister'.[32]

One version is that on Blunt's return to London, Victor Rothschild asked him if he would like to meet a 'Captain Black of the War Office'. Having been at Cambridge with him, Rothschild knew Blunt well – perhaps too well for Rothschild's good, as he was to come under suspicion of being a spy himself after Blunt was eventually exposed. A scion of the wealthy banking family, who had become the third Lord Rothschild in 1937, he was already a member of MI5, working under Guy Liddell, at that time head of 'B' Division, which was responsible for sabotage and counter-espionage. The meeting went well and when 'Captain Black' revealed himself to be Liddell, Blunt was offered a job.

One of Blunt's early tasks was to investigate the communications of neutral embassies in London, as there was no systematic method of monitoring them. Blunt quickly established a rapport with MI6 on the tapping of telephones and on the illegal extraction of material from the diplomatic bags belonging to neutral countries – an operation codenamed XXX or TRIPLEX that was kept secret for decades. He soon found that by using the MI5 resources he could obtain material not available to MI6. With the diplomatic bags, a technique had been devised which made it impossible to detect if the sealed bag had been opened. So by employing the officers MI5 had in British ports, it was possible, through various ruses, to obtain the diplomatic bags being carried out of the country by couriers, and to photograph anything of interest found in them. This worked particularly well with the Spaniards and Portuguese who usually departed for Lisbon from Poole or Bristol. He also arranged that when certain Allied couriers were obliged to pass through the Wandsworth Patriotic Schools, a screening centre for any alien entering the country, they had to relinquish their diplomatic bags for safe keeping, giving MI5 the opportunity to open and read the contents, and photograph them if necessary.

Blunt also started recruiting agents in neutral embassies. One of the best was a secretary in the Spanish embassy (Spain, though neutral, was pro-Nazi), who provided drafts of the ambassador's reports, correspondence and general gossip, including visitors to the embassy and the dinner parties held there. This secretary, code-named DUCK, proved very useful in other ways, too. In January 1942, and on at least two subsequent occasions, she 'was able to walk out of the embassy with the current Spanish diplomatic cipher tape in a bag to hand over to an MI5 car waiting around the corner'.[33] As the tapes continued to be used for some months, Bletchley Park was able to decrypt the embassy's communications with Madrid.

All this intelligence doubtless found its way to Moscow. Of greater importance to The Centre was the British debriefing of the GRU (Soviet Military Intelligence) agent, Walter Krivitsky, who had defected in 1937, the details of which Blunt passed to his handler in January 1941. And as Blunt helped compile the monthly reports of MI5's activities for the Prime Minister, 'it is highly probable they went to Soviet intelligence as well – and quite possibly to Stalin personally. Indeed, Moscow may well also have received the longer version before it was condensed by Blunt and thus have seen more detailed reports than Churchill.'[34]

* * * * *

In the spring of 1942, The Centre made an analysis of what Philby had passed the previous year. Though it praised him for sending a lot of interesting material, it raised the question that was to plague the ring for some time to come: what was MI6's network in the Soviet Union? Since MI6 had recruited numerous agents in Europe over the past few years, principally from countries now occupied by the Germans, The Centre reasoned that the Soviet Union was receiving the same kind of attention. Assurances that no such network existed – had in fact been specifically banned – was received with disbelief. 'SOHNCHEN'S (Philby's) and TONY'S (Blunt's) suspicious understatement of the work of British Intelligence against us,' the London *rezidentura* was told, 'MADCHEN'S (Burgess) offer to recruit Johnson [a senior member of MI5], and "the existence of communication and contact between SOHNCHEN, TONY and

MADCHEN"'[35] was sure evidence of a deeply laid plot to deceive The Centre.

That Burgess and Blunt shared a London flat belonging to Victor Rothschild was certainly in flagrant breach of *konspiratsiya*. But Blunt at least had surely proved his loyalty by providing The Centre with information regarding the surveillance of the Soviet Union's London embassy, which had enabled it to take appropriate counter-measures; and he had also reported that the CPGB's London headquarters was being bugged by MI5. Nevertheless, The Centre remained unconvinced, and the head of its British desk went so far as to denounce them outright as double agents. This crisis of confidence only started to dissipate in the autumn of 1943 when Moscow and the London *rezidentura* began comparing the intelligence the ring had provided with identical material acquired from other sources, and found they matched exactly. Also, in May 1944, Blunt proved his *bona fides* by passing the entire deception plan (codenamed FORTITUDE) for the Normandy Landings that took place the following month. However, the suspicions never went entirely away, and there were KGB officers, still serving when the Soviet Union disintegrated in 1991, who believed that at least some of The Cambridge Five had been double agents. How else, they asked, had they been able to acquire such a vast amount of material?

The figures are indeed extraordinary. According to one source,[36] between 1941 and 1945 Blunt supplied 1,771 documents, Maclean 4,593, Cairncross 5,832, Philby 914 and Burgess 4,605. Some of these, particularly those concerning the development of the atomic bomb, must have been priceless intelligence for Stalin. But until the Moscow archives are made available to western researchers, it is impossible to know the importance of these documents, or the Soviet reaction to them, though surely a large percentage must have been routine paperwork.

Much of the intelligence passed by Blunt and Cairncross originated from the government Code and Cipher School at Bletchley Park, which deciphered German signals, including those encoded by the German Enigma cipher machine that produced the vital ULTRA intelligence. In the spring of 1942 Blunt told Kreshin – in what seems a rather confused and contradictory message – that he now had access to Abwehr (German intelligence) decrypts, hand ciphers known as ISOS (Intelligence Services Oliver Strachey, who headed the section that broke the cipher). But he warned that:

ISOS and diplomatic intercepted documents can't be taken out [presumably of the building for photographing]. However, as to diplomatic documents, sometimes I take them out, but ISOS, never. ISOS could be taken out, but with a certain risk. I often keep ISOS for the night, but then it is necessary to arrange regular photographing.[37]

Cairncross was called up in June 1942 but was demobbed almost immediately and in August 1942 was posted to Bletchley Park – without any kind of vetting. He says he soon suspected that the complete ULTRA intelligence signals relating to the Eastern Front were not being passed to Moscow. This is true as only summaries of German signals were sent to Moscow. Their origins were carefully disguised in case the Soviet codes might be vulnerable to German cryptographers, thus revealing to the Germans that their ciphers were vulnerable, too. However, it is highly unlikely that Cairncross would have known anything about such matters, though he may well have picked up that the Eastern Front did not have a high priority at Bletchley. Since at the time the Soviet Union was bearing the brunt of the fighting against Hitler, he, understandably, would have thought it unforgivable that it should be deprived of potentially vital intelligence. To his mind this totally outweighed the risk that the Germans might discover that their ciphers were being broken.

One wonders if Moscow ever took this disguised ULTRA material seriously, such was the suspicion with which the Western Allies were regarded. For instance, when Churchill, forewarned by ULTRA, alerted Stalin to the imminent German invasion of the USSR in June 1941, Stalin simply suspected the British Prime Minister of duplicity. It was therefore not surprising if Cairncross, well aware of the suspicions with which Britain was regarded, might, in some twisted way, have rationalised that the risks he was taking were worthwhile. If the intelligence came from a source that was regarded in Moscow as being more trustworthy, it might, he could have reasoned, be taken at face value, though we know now The Cambridge Five were certainly not trusted by Moscow either.

Cairncross says he discussed his dilemma with Gorsky when they next met. His handler convinced him that any ULTRA intercepts the Scot obtained would be sent by courier to Moscow and not by radio. Reassured, he began passing decrypts to Gorsky, sometimes copied by hand from the original signals but also purloining original decrypts from a disposal box before they were destroyed. In 1942 he passed 1,454 documents and decrypts. But the work was affecting his eyesight and in the summer of 1943 he was transferred to MI6's counter-intelligence branch at St Albans. However, before he did so he was able to pass original Luftwaffe decrypts that were to influence, perhaps crucially, what was to be the largest tank battle ever fought. These revealed, before the German counter-attack around Kursk in July 1943, the position of certain German airfields, which enabled the Red Air Force to mount pre-emptive attacks that destroyed over 500 German aircraft on the ground. Though the British also provided intelligence about the German build-up around Kursk, this was, as usual, only in summary form and not as detailed as the original German texts that Cairncross provided.

Though, surprisingly, he does not mention it in his autobiography, Cairncross apparently also passed decrypts concerning vital technical information about the new German Tiger tank, which gave the Red Army the opportunity to develop an anti-tank shell that could pierce the armour of this fearsome new weapon. For his contribution to the Kursk battle, Cairncross was awarded the Order of the Red Banner. The medal, in its velvet-lined box, was sent to London and Cairncross held it in his hands for a moment before returning it to his handler at the time, Yuri Modin, who later remarked how obviously happy he was at receiving it.

Blunt always insisted that he had 'retired' from spying when the war finished, but this is not true, though he left MI5 in October 1945, and returned to his job at the Courtauld. The Centre agreed that he should do so, for his nerves were shot and he was drinking heavily, and had recently been quite ill. He remained in touch with the London *rezidentura*, making himself useful as a go-between with other members of the ring and passing snippets of intelligence he gleaned from his wartime MI5 contacts. He even photographed documents – something he had refused to do during the war – that Burgess passed him for delivery to the London *rezidentura*, using a camera he kept at the Courtauld. He also visited Germany several times to collect intelligence from Leo Long (codenamed ELLI and RALPH), who was with the British Control Commission there. Blunt had recruited Long at Cambridge before the war and ran him during it when Long was in MI14. This War Office department analysed the German order of battle, and allowed Long access to some ULTRA intelligence.

During the latter part of the war, Philby's work with MI6 brought him the approval of not only his Soviet bosses but his English ones as well, and between 1942 and 1943 his responsibilities were extended beyond the Iberian Peninsula to North Africa and then to Italy. In May 1943 a new section (IX) was created, whose remit was Communism and Soviet espionage, and Philby was told by The Centre that he had to do everything, but *everything*, to ensure that he became head of it. As it was planned that the section would merge with the counter-intelligence section (Section V) after the war, and would inevitably become the major player within it, this meant Philby ousting his immediate superior, Felix Cowgill, to whom he had become a close and trusted adviser. This Philby did without a qualm, and he was appointed head of Section IX in 1944 and the head of the combined sections when the war ended.

Philby's coup, and his subsequent postings, put him right at the heart of the West's intelligence activities against the Soviet Union, and this cost lives. In one incident an NKVD officer, Colonel Konstantin Volkov, turned up at the British consulate in Istanbul in September 1945 and requested asylum for himself and his wife. In return for this, and a large sum of money, he offered to reveal the penetration of the British intelligence services and the Foreign Office by Soviet agents. He wrote that there were probably about nine agents, including one who 'fulfils the duties of the chief of an *otdel* (department) of the English counter-intelligence Directorate in London'.[38]

When Philby received the report on Volkov's proposal from Istanbul, he immediately informed Kreshin. He then sought, and received, permission from his MI6 superiors to fly to Istanbul to negotiate with Volkov, who had not yet been given sanctuary. However, by the time he arrived, Volkov and his wife had been spirited away to Moscow, where Volkov was later executed. In his memoir Philby wrote, with a cynicism that takes the breath away, that one of the theories about what had happened to Volkov – that someone had tipped off the Russians about his approach to the British – had not been worth including in his report of the affair, as it had no solid evidence to support it. It had been a close call for the ring, and more narrow escapes were to follow.

* * * * *

Though the Second World War in Europe officially ended on 8 May 1945, with Germany utterly defeated and the Red Army occupying the eastern part of the country, including Berlin, The Five continued their fight for the triumph of Communism in the West. However, in September 1945 the defection of a GRU cipher clerk in Ottowa, Igor Gouzenko, and then news of the intended defection of Konstantin Volkov, again led to the suspension of contact between the London *rezidentura* and its agents. In January 1946 Kreshin was in touch with Philby, who advised that the situation was not yet right for resuming communications with The Five. Blunt may not have minded, might even have been relieved, but Burgess must have been distraught, for he now found himself in a position to supply The Centre with high-grade material: in December 1946, Hector McNeil, now the under-secretary of state for Foreign Affairs, had appointed him his personal secretary. This put Burgess at the centre of British policy making in defence and foreign affairs.

Burgess's appointment led to contact with The Centre being resumed in early 1947, as it required intelligence on a forthcoming four-power conference of foreign ministers in the Soviet capital. The documents that Burgess handed over were received with such pleasure in Moscow that the minister of state security personally authorised that Burgess should receive £500 as a gift. Then, at the end of 1947, when the four great powers met in London to discuss the future shape of Germany, Burgess supplied some 300 Foreign Office documents about these proceedings. This earned him a bonus of £200 and the praise of the Soviet foreign minister, Vyacheslav Molotov.

Around this time Burgess was introduced to his new NKVD handler, Yuri Modin, known to the ring by the codename PETER. Modin wrote of him that 'what I knew about Burgess boiled down to this: he was a rogue, but a phenomenally brilliant one; he was ready to die for the cause; he was reliable in a tight corner; and he was the only member of the group who could bring all the others together in one place'.[39] Almost despite himself, it seems, Modin, could not but admire Burgess, especially his brilliantly shiny shoes (he always had them polished at the Reform Club), though he also noticed that at closer quarters his impeccably cut suits were not always clean.

The truth is that Burgess was entering the final phase of his descent into being a shambolic and outrageous drunk – when the head of the Foreign Office's security branch encountered him in 1947, he noted he was dishevelled and unshaven, and smelt strongly of alcohol. By the end of the year McNeil had probably had enough of him, for he recommended him to Christopher Mayhew, the parliamentary under-secretary at the Foreign Office. Mayhew was in charge of a new organisation, the Information Research Department (IRD), formed to combat Soviet propaganda. With his knowledge of Communism and propaganda techniques Burgess seemed just the man, and Mayhew willingly took him on, thus, almost certainly, enabling Burgess to give The Centre a detailed report on the new organisation. Moscow must have been delighted, but Mayhew was not amused by Burgess's indiscretions while visiting European embassies on IRD business, and in November 1948 he again found himself moved, this time to the Foreign Office's Far Eastern Department.

Perhaps his new position suited Burgess better, for colleagues were to remember, with respect, how he cleverly and passionately argued for the recognition of Mao Tse-tung's new Communist government in China that had been established in October 1949. He also managed, according to notes made by Vasili Mitrokhin from the KGB files,[40] to pass 168 documents to Modin in December 1949, and to create friction in the Anglo-American alliance by highlighting their policy differences over China.

This posting, too, was short-lived when rumours of his behaviour while on holiday in Tangiers – which included singing 'Little boys are cheap today, cheaper than yesterday' in local bars – reached the ears of his superiors. He was severely reprimanded, but somehow escaped being sacked. By this time even Modin had had enough of him and was using Blunt as an intermediary whenever possible. Probably much to Modin's relief, and certainly to the relief of his superiors in the Far Eastern Department, in August 1950 Burgess was appointed a second secretary to the British embassy in Washington. This appointment was almost certainly viewed as Burgess's last chance to salvage his career. If it was, the United States was an unfortunate choice, for Burgess loathed the country.

While Burgess's career was steadily disintegrating, Philby's continued to flourish. 'You know as well as I do the valuable work which Philby is doing for me,' the head of MI6, Stuart Menzies, wrote in March 1943, refusing a request to return him to the Foreign Office, adding that he did not wish to interfere 'with the career of so able a man as Philby is'.[41] By 1946, when Philby was appointed an OBE (Order of the British Empire), it was generally agreed that it was only a matter of time before he reached the top of MI6 and received a knighthood.

He was equally well thought of within the NKVD, where his reputation, according to Modin, was treated with almost religious awe. A few months before he received his OBE he was awarded the Order of the Red Banner, as his successful intrigues against Cowgill had led to his appointment as the head of R.5 (counter-intelligence). This was the new post-war designation for the combined Sections V and IX, a position of critical importance to his Moscow superiors. It was a masterstroke that Maclean's biographer, Robert Cecil, thought had few equals in the history of espionage, as it allowed Philby to pass every last detail of Britain's strategy to combat Communism. To give him wider experience, in February 1947 he was posted to Istanbul as MI6's head of station. While there he was directly responsible for the deaths of two agents – and probably of their families and contacts, too – who were infiltrated into the Soviet Union from Turkey. According to the official MI6 history, the operation was 'designed to infiltrate two Georgians "with an intelligence brief" into Soviet Georgia, but the unfortunate men had died on the frontier in obscure circumstances'.[42]

When, many years later, Genrikh Borovik asked Philby how he felt about sending the young men concerned to their deaths, he replied: 'It's an unpleasant story, of course. The boys weren't bad. Not at all. I knew very well that they would be caught and that a tragic fate awaited them. But on the other hand, it was the only way of driving a stake through the plans of future operations.'[43]

If Philby thought their deaths would be a sufficient deterrent, he was wrong, for another operation was mounted the following year. One agent dropped out before the operation began and the other, on returning to the border after two weeks in Soviet Georgia, had a shoot-out with a Soviet patrol, quite possibly positioned there from information Philby had supplied. The agent returned safely with what the official MI6 history describes as being 'relatively modest' intelligence, which included contact with anti-Soviet resistance groups. Though judged a success, there were various security concerns about these operations, unrelated to what had happened to the agents involved, and they were suspended.

Philby also betrayed another, larger, operation to infiltrate Communist Albania in 1949, though the official MI6 history does not mention him in connection with it. What it does describe is the planning for the operation, codenamed VALUABLE, and its execution when twenty-nine émigré Albanians, divided into six groups, were landed by sea on the Albanian shore close to Corfu. If the operation went well it was to be a prelude to landing armed guerrillas the following year to stimulate an armed rising. However, one group was obliterated, another disappeared, and the other four had to retreat into Greece, though one managed to remain operational for over two months. Again, lack of security precluded any further operations because what MI6 were up to seems to have been common gossip in the eastern Mediterranean and certainly in the émigré groups involved.

At around the same time as VALUABLE was launched, Philby was recalled to London prior to being posted to Washington as MI6's liaison officer with the CIA and the FBI. It was another big step up the ladder, for now Philby was positioned to pass intelligence not only on MI6 but on the American intelligence services as well. He did not hesitate to do so, passing to his controller intelligence on CIA-planned operations for Albania and details of the three groups of six agents who were to be parachuted into the Ukraine, where the largest group of anti-Soviet partisans was situated. So accurate was this information that he was able to supply the exact co-ordinates of the landing zone.

He wrote later that he did not know what happened to those who were parachuted in, but added with his usual cynicism that he could make a pretty accurate guess as to their fate.[44]

Before departing for Washington, Philby was briefed on an American project, codenamed VENONA (see Chapter 7), to crack the Soviet intelligence and diplomatic cipher, made possible by the careless wartime slip of an overworked cipher clerk in Moscow. Despite the suspicion with which some of the ring were now regarded, it was VENONA that proved to be the final undoing of The Cambridge Five.

* * * * *

In the spring of 1944 Maclean was posted to the British embassy in Washington. Both he and Melinda were delighted, for it improved Maclean's career chances and Melinda was pleased to be on home soil and away from the bombing and deprivations of wartime London. 'It was soon borne in on me that Donald Maclean was regarded as a coming man,' Robert Cecil wrote when he, too, was posted to the Washington embassy in April 1945; 'he had acquired an air of authority, tempered by just sufficient consideration for others to pass as a good fellow'.[45]

Soon after arriving, Maclean was promoted first secretary and thanks to his friendship with a senior British diplomat, who thought highly of him, he became involved in a high-level committee relating to the Anglo-American participation in the development of the atomic bomb. Then, in February 1947, he was appointed joint secretary of the Combined Policy Committee, which co-ordinated the research and development of nuclear weapons and nuclear power in the United States, United Kingdom and Canada. This gave him access to material infinitely more important to Moscow than anything that might have crossed his desk in London.

More important posts followed as on 1 September 1948 Maclean was appointed head of Chancery at the British embassy in Cairo. Aged just 35, this made him the youngest counsellor in the Diplomatic Service. Like Philby, he seemed destined to reach the top of his profession. But during his time in Washington he had had a narrow escape from detection, and the virulently anti-Communist Senator Joseph McCarthy was on the rise, making a right-wing United States, unilaterally armed with the atom bomb – the first successful Soviet atomic test was not until August 1949 – a real and present danger to everything Maclean held dear. So it was not surprising his nerves began to fray, and towards the end of their time in Washington Melinda had complained of his moodiness and drinking bouts. When he arrived in Cairo his problems were compounded by the stupidity of his new NKVD handler, and The Centre gave him little guidance. Despite this, the intelligence he passed to The Centre during his time in Cairo was substantial. For instance, when Ernest Bevin, the British foreign secretary, addressed the British cabinet in September 1948 on the Berlin Crisis, the cabinet minutes, thanks to Maclean, were available to Stalin early the following month. So too was material relating to Anglo-American disagreements on the crisis – intelligence that could have persuaded Stalin to wait out the winter to see if the Allied airlift of food and fuel into the beleaguered city would fail.

However, eventually, the strain overwhelmed Maclean and in December 1949 he added a note to some classified documents he passed to his handler requesting that The Centre release him from his espionage role. His handler ignored the plea, and so did Moscow, and though in April 1950 he repeated the request, this also seems to have been ignored, though it could have been simply refused. Whichever it was, his drinking bouts became so overwhelming that it affected his memory. On one occasion, finding a dinner invitation on his desk for the previous evening, he rang his hostess and apologised profusely for not attending, citing the pressure of work as the reason. There was a pause at the other end of the line before the woman said: 'But Mr Maclean you *were* there.'

Inevitably, it all came to a head in one disastrous incident when he wrecked an apartment belonging to two girls from the US embassy. He was sent home for psychiatric treatment but by the autumn he was back at the Foreign Office in London as head of its American Desk. This was a prime posting which he would never have been given if the British ambassador in Cairo had submitted, as he should have done, a report on Maclean's behaviour – yet another case of the old boy network protecting its own.

* * * * *

At around the same time as Maclean was sent back to London, Cairncross was transferred to MI6's political branch (section 1) covering Germany and the countries on its eastern borders. This enabled him to pass an MI6 report on the plans Himmler was making to form a Nazi underground resistance, and a survey by MI6 on the Soviet Union between the years 1939–44. As a token of their gratitude The Centre sent him £250 in October 1944, though he himself admitted, in thanking The Centre for the money, that the previous eighteen months had been a lean period for him, but that he intended expressing his gratitude by redoubling his efforts in the future. This he did by reporting in February 1945 that within the next fortnight the Germans would launch a counter-offensive against the Red Army in two places, one of them Pomerania; that the British were intercepting Soviet radio-telephone messages in certain areas; and passing the details of British agents in South America, the Iberian Peninsula and some of the Scandinavian countries. This last especially pleased The Centre, which graded it very important and instructed the *rezidentura* that Cairncross be thanked and given a present.

At the beginning of 1945 the Treasury had asked MI6 for Cairncross to be returned and this request was granted in June. The move was approved by The Centre, as it knew Philby was covering the work of MI6 for them more than adequately. Cairncross was initially posted to the Treasury Department that handled War Office estimates. It is not known what documents he passed, but a snippet of information he gained from an MI6 colleague, that the Poles had broken the Red Air Force cipher, must have been received with special appreciation. Though Yuri Modin says otherwise in his book, in October 1945 the *rezidentura* broke contact with Cairncross, probably as a security measure following the defection in Ottawa of Igor Gouzenko. This hiatus lasted until February 1948 when the newly arrived Modin established contact with Cairncross. Initially the Scot's vagueness and unpunctuality infuriated Modin, but the two men soon reached a rapport, and in July 1948 Cairncross began passing documents relating to War Office personnel.

Then, in January 1950, Cairncross arrived at their meeting with a large quantity of files and a note for Modin to pass to Moscow. The note said he had been appointed Treasury representative to the Western European Union – an early self-defence pact involving several European countries – which meant that all the Union's military documents would be available to him, as well as that of Britain's Defence Committee. The *rezidentura* was delighted and reported to The Centre that it was possible to judge from what Cairncross had passed at a meeting in February, 'that documents of the highest secrecy pass through his hands. KAREL's [another cover name for Cairncross] new appointment opens to us great possibilities for acquiring interesting material. Among the papers passed by KAREL are a few files related to the atomic problem.'[46]

Modin would have known from his time at The Centre that Cairncross had been the first to alert Moscow of his country's involvement in developing a nuclear weapon. So when the Scot mentioned at one of their meetings that he shared a room with a colleague who dealt with atomic energy, Modin asked him to get a copy of the key to his colleague's safe so its contents could be photographed. It was a risky business to remove them from the building, so Modin provided Cairncross with a camera.

But the results were either out of focus or underexposed, or the papers were only partly photographed. Modin put this down to Cairncross's mechanical incompetence, but it could equally have been that the spy was scared out of his wits.

When the Korean War broke out in July 1950, Cairncross was passed documents relating to the conflict.[47] But his relationship with his immediate superior was bad and in September he was transferred into a section that proved a cul-de-sac. However, by May 1951 he had managed to have himself transferred from the Treasury to the Ministry of Supply and the following month he was able to bring to a meeting a large packet of documents. But by then Burgess and Maclean had fled the country, and the rumours about their treachery spread rapidly through the corridors of Whitehall. It was not long before MI5 was knocking on Cairncross's door.

* * * * *

In the summer of 1950, Burgess sent Philby a letter saying that he had been posted to Washington and asking if he could stay with them until he had found an apartment. Philby later wrote in his memoirs[48] that normally it would be quite out of the question for two agents to live under the same roof, but added that the circumstances were not normal: their friendship stretched back to their Cambridge days when he had given Burgess a donation for the casualties of the Austrian *Schutzbund* rising in February 1934. Later, he had recommended Burgess to the Soviet secret service, and Burgess had repaid the compliment by helping Philby join MI6. Burgess had also been Philby's courier in Spain and they had later worked together in MI6. Their association was therefore public knowledge, so having his friend to stay on a temporary basis would have been regarded as perfectly acceptable. Besides, he wanted to keep an eye on Burgess, whose drunken shenanigans too often threatened to end in a scandal. But barely had Philby told Burgess he could stay than the embassy security officer showed him a letter from London warning him of Burgess's arrival. The letter gave a list of Burgess's shortcomings, and warned there might be worse to come. 'What does he mean "worse"?' the worried security officer asked Philby. 'Goats?'[49]

Although on at least one occasion Burgess did act outrageously, he proved a useful courier between his host and Philby's new handler, Valeri Makayev (codenamed HARRY), in New York. As Philby had access to the code-breaking VENONA programme (see Chapter 7), it did not take him long to realise that the cover name HOMER in the VENONA decrypts referred to Maclean and that the FBI would eventually be able to deduce this. Philby knew that Maclean would almost certainly crack under interrogation. He informed The Centre via Makayev of the imminent danger Maclean posed to the whole ring, and received the reply that Maclean should stay put for as long as possible while a plan to exfiltrate him was drawn up which would be put into operation before the FBI closed in.

During the winter of 1950–51 it did begin to close in: by December 1950 the list of suspects had narrowed to thirty-five, and by April it had been reduced to nine. Then a few days later a newly decrypted cable indicated that in June 1944 HOMER's wife had been expecting a baby and was living with her mother in New York. The description fitted Maclean and no one else. The game was up for the diplomat, but Philby knew there would be time to arrange Maclean's defection, as it would take those investigating the case a while to find sufficient evidence to convict him (they were never able to); the evidence VENONA provided, apart from being far too secret to reveal, would never have stood up in a court of law. But Philby also knew he was in great danger, and demanded Maclean be exfiltrated to the USSR immediately so that he, Philby, would not be compromised.

The question was: how could Philby warn Maclean in London, especially as Maclean would already be under discreet surveillance? It was Burgess who had the answer. He arranged to be sacked and sent back to London after deliberately causing a series of anti-American incidents. Before he left he promised Philby he would not go with Maclean to Moscow; if he did, Philby knew he was bound to be exposed.

On his arrival in London on 7 May 1951, Burgess went to see Blunt and asked him to deliver a message to Modin that Maclean was about to be arrested, and that Maclean was in such a nervous state that he was sure he would break down immediately he was interrogated. Within 48 hours The Centre had agreed that Maclean should defect and for him to make the necessary arrangements, but Maclean was in such turmoil that he initially refused to go. Modin insisted, and insisted, too, that Burgess must escort Maclean to Moscow. Burgess, remembering his promise to Philby, refused, but eventually gave way when Modin implied that he did not have to go all the way to Moscow, and that in any case he would be free to return. This proved to be untrue.

By now the British foreign secretary had approved the interrogation of Maclean and, though it was later denied, it was probably due to take place on Monday 28 May. However, on the previous Friday the London *rezidentura* arranged for the two absconders to leave Maclean's home on the Surrey–Kent border, and drive to Southampton to catch a weekend pleasure steamer that stopped at various French ports. There were two reasons for choosing this means of escape: the surveillance of Maclean stopped at 8 p.m. every day and at weekends; and no passports were required for passengers on the ship they were using.

The next morning the two spies left the boat at St Malo and made their way to Moscow. In Britain no one knew for certain what had happened. A Europe-wide hunt for them proved fruitless. Soon it was generally known that they had defected, but no official Soviet confirmation was forthcoming until Khruschev gleefully announced it during his visit to the Britain in 1956.

After the defection of Burgess and Maclean, Philby was recalled to London, as the head of the CIA had announced he was no longer acceptable as a liaison officer. He was grilled by MI5 officers but protested his innocence, and he still retained a core of supporters within MI6. Apparently, no one present at an MI5 inquiry thought him innocent, but there was insufficient evidence for a prosecution to succeed. Although he was granted a modest pension, he now had no job and no prospects, and spent the next few years freelancing as a journalist and ghostwriter, until in 1956, with the help of friends in MI6, he was sent to Beirut as a freelance for *The Economist* and *The Observer*. Aileen had died in 1957 and in Beirut he started an affair with his future third wife, whom he married in 1959.

MI5 never gave up attempting to find sufficient evidence to secure a confession from Philby, and in January 1963, armed with new information about the spy's prewar recruiting activities,[50] his friend Nicholas Elliott extracted a partial one in exchange for immunity from prosecution. Double-dealing to the last, Philby told his KGB handler that more interrogations would follow, making his position precarious, but did not tell him he had already confessed.

The Centre reacted quickly and before the end of the month Philby was aboard a Soviet freighter heading for the Soviet Union. There he wrote his memoirs, was decorated with the Order of the Red Banner and the Order of Lenin, had a four-year affair with Melinda Maclean, and in 1971 married a Moscow resident after his third wife died. He died in 1988 and was buried with great ceremonial pomp. Safely out of the way, he is now highly regarded in Russia as the KGB's most successful operator, but many remained suspicious of him to the end. Indeed, Nicholas Elliott wrote that after the collapse of the Soviet Union, one KGB officer said he was not at all sure 'that Philby had not been fooling them all along and that they had had a dread that he might one day turn up at the British embassy in order to be permanently repratriated'.[51]

* * * * *

Immediately Blunt knew Burgess and Maclean had defected, he rushed round to the former's flat and tried to clear it of any incriminating evidence. However, in his haste he overlooked some of Cairncross's handwritten notes about a confidential prewar Whitehall discussion, and MI5 found them. Unfortunately for Cairncross, John Colville, who had been assistant private secretary to the Prime Minister, Neville Chamberlain, at the time of the discussions, had recorded the presence of Cairncross in his diaries, and was able to identify him as the writer of the notes. After putting Cairncross under surveillance, during which time the Scot was almost caught meeting his controller, Yuri Modin, MI5 started interrogating him. He was forced to leave the Treasury, but, as with the others, there was not enough evidence to prosecute him, and in 1952 he left the country with his wife, whom he had recently married, after Modin had given him a large sum of money. He eventually confessed in 1964 and was publicly exposed in 1990 when *KGB: The Inside Story*[52] was published. Of all The Five, he probably did the most long-term damage to western interests but, ironically, was the only one to live out the remainder of his life in some degree of contentment.

When Modin told Blunt that The Centre also wanted him to defect, Blunt refused. 'I know perfectly well how you people live,' he told Modin, 'and I can assure you it would be very hard, almost unbearable, for me to do likewise'[53] – a comment that Modin said left him speechless. Soviet intelligence then seems to have severed all connections with Blunt, though in 1954 Modin did get him to agree, reluctantly, to pass £5,000 to Philby, who was in financial straits. After several attempts by MI5, he confessed in 1964. In return he received immunity from prosecution and was allowed to continue as Surveyor of the Queen's Pictures. The Queen knew about him, of course, and Blunt was told he must never come face to face with her. His treachery became an open secret in Buckingham Palace, and on one occasion, when a visitor was being shown round, Blunt was passed in a corridor. 'That's our Russian spy,' the visitor was informed with a chuckle.

Blunt was eventually publicly exposed in 1979 in Parliament by the then Prime Minister, Margaret Thatcher, and he was stripped of his knighthood. Goronwy Rees, who had always disliked Blunt and thought him a fraud, was dying in hospital at the time, and he watched the drama unfold on television. 'Got you, you swine,' he said, before falling into a coma.[54] However, when an attempt was made to strip Blunt of his emeritus professorship, it was voted down. At least the world of art scholarship still appreciated his talent. He died of a heart attack in 1983, never having shown even a hint of remorse.

* * * * *

Nicholas Elliott wrote that he had heard from an impeccable private source that The Five had all come under suspicion during Stalin's era when the First Chief Directorate acquired a new and very experienced broom, Mrs Zoya Nikolayevna Ryskina. On reading their files she concluded they were all under MI6 control and recommended they be assassinated. Their case officers protested against such extreme action, and her recommendation was not accepted. But as Elliott commented: 'What a lot of trouble would have been saved if Mrs Ryskina had had her way.'[55]

NOTES

1. For a perceptive analysis of the books published in this era, see Knight, A., 'The Selling of the KGB', *The Wilson Quarterly*, Vol. 24, 2000 (www.wilsonquarterly.com/archive).

2. Damaskin, I. with Elliott, G., *Kitty Harris: The Spy with Seventeen Names* (London, 2001). Kitty died in 1966.

3. Kerr, S., *International Journal of Intelligence and Counter-Intelligence* (vol. 14, no. 1, 2001).

4. Damaskin and Elliott, *op. cit.*, p. 153.

5. Borovik, G., *The Philby Files* (Little, Brown, 1994). The details of what happened to some of Philby's handlers is on p. x.

6. Connolly, C., *The Missing Diplomats* (London, 1952) p. 15.

7. Elliott, N., *Never Judge a Man by His Umbrella* (London, 1991) p. 183.

8. Cecil, R., *A Divided Life: A Personal Portrait of the Spy Donald Maclean* (London, 1989) p. 5.

9. Borovik, *op. cit.*, p. 29. Deutsch's immediate superior in London was Aleksandr Orlov, codenamed SCHWED (Swede). Orlov's story is related in *Deadly Illusions* (London, 1993), and its authors, John Costello and Oleg Tsarev, claimed that he was the mastermind behind the recruitment of The Cambridge Five. However, as Christopher Andrew and Vasili Mitrokhin point out in their book *The Mitrokhin Archive* (London, 2000) p. 78, senior Soviet bureaucrats commonly claimed, and were credited for, the achievements of those under them. They also pointed out that the KGB's successor, the Russian Foreign Intelligence Service (SVR), which sponsored *Deadly Illusions*, would be keen to inflate Orlov's importance as someone who had made western intelligence agencies look foolish by working under their noses for more than thirty years without being detected.

10. Printed as part of *The Private Life of Kim Philby: The Moscow Years* (London, 2000) by Rufina Philby, with Hayden Peake and Mikhail Lyubimov.

11. Damaskin and Elliott, *op. cit.*, p. 148. Courtesy Damaskin.

12. Instead, Burgess was awarded what was known as an aegrotat, awarded to those who could not take their exams because of illness.

13. Carter, M., *Anthony Blunt: His Lives* (London, 2001) p. 161.

14. Rees, J., *Looking for Mr Nobody: The Secret Life of Goronwy Rees* (Phoenix Paperbacks, London, 1994) p. 82.

15. Carter, *op. cit.*, p. 163.

16. *Ibid.*, p. 118.

17. West, N. & Tsarev, O., *The Crown Jewels* (London, 1998) p. 133.

18. *Ibid.*, pp. 205–06.

19. Cairncross was an expert on the works of this seventeenth-century French playwright, and later wrote several books on him. The Centre seemed unaware that, when allotting codenames to their agents, their choice could help reveal the real name of those they were trying to protect.

20. Borovik, *op. cit.*, p. x. Maly was posthumously rehabilitated in 1956.

21. When Germany invaded the USSR in June 1941, the NKVD re-employed Deutsch, and in 1942 sent him to South America as an illegal. His ship was sunk by the Germans on its way to New York and he drowned.

22. Sentenced to five years in a labour camp by his Moscow masters, Grafpen was, nevertheless, luckier than many others. He survived the Gulag, and after being rehabilitated in 1956 was awarded the Order of the Red Banner. He died aged 96 in 1987.

23. West and Tsarev, *op. cit.*, p. 213.

24. Modin, Y., *My Five Cambridge Friends* (New York, 1994) p. 100.

25. Tom Bower, *The Independent*, 10 October 1995.

26. West and Tsarev, *op. cit.*, p. 214.

27. Andrew, C., and Mitrokhin, V., *The Mitrokhin Archive* (London, 2000) p. 150.

28. West and Tsarev, *op. cit.*, p. 234.

29. Philby, K., *My Silent War* (London, 1968). The book was published in ten other countries before it appeared in a Russian edition in 1980.

30. Andrew, C., *The Defence of the Realm: The Authorised History of MI5* (London, 2009) p. 270.

31. West and Tsarev, *op. cit.*, p. 173.

32. Andrew, *op. cit.*, p. 269.

33. *Ibid.*, p. 261.

34. *Ibid.*, pp. 289 and 292.

35. West and Tsarev, *op. cit.*, p. 148.

36. *Ibid.*, pp. 170–71.

37. *Ibid.*, p. 147.

38. West, N., review of Christopher Andrew's *Authorfd History of MI5* (op. cit.) in *International Journal of Intelligence and Counter-Intelligence* (vol. 23, no. 4, 2010). Volkov's full statement is in West, N., *Historical Dictionary of Cold War Counter-Intelligence* (Lanham, MD, 2007) pp. 359–61.

39. Modin, *op. cit.*, p. 150.

40. Andrew and Mitrokhin, *op. cit.*, p. 202.

41. Jeffery, K., *MI6: The History of the Secret Intelligence Service, 1909–1949* (London, 2010) p. 490.

42. *Ibid.*, p. 709.

43. Borovik, *op. cit.*, p. 252.

44. Philby, *op. cit.*, p. 159.

45. Cecil, *op. cit.*, p. 73.

46. West and Tsarev, *op. cit.*, p. 223.

47. Maclean also passed intelligence on the Korean War which Robert Cecil, his deputy at the American desk, assessed 'of inestimable value in advising the Chinese and the North Koreans on strategy and negotiating positions'. Quoted in Andrew and Mitrokhin, *op. cit.*, p. 203.

48. Philby, *op. cit.*, p. 165.

49. *Ibid.*, p. 166.

50. In 1962, the MI5 officer, Victor Rothschild, happened to meet Flora Solomon in Israel. Solomon, a former mistress of Kerensky, the leader of the Menshivist party in 1918, was so disgusted by Philby's pro-Arab newspaper articles that she told Rothschild that Philby had attempted to recruit her to the Communist cause before the war, and Rothschild got her to repeat her accusation to MI5. Related in Rose, K., *Elusive Rothschild* (London, 2003) p. 230.

51. Elliott, N., *With My Little Eye* (London, 1993) p. 96.

52. By Christopher Andrew and Oleg Gordievsky. Gordievsky, a KGB officer, was an MI6 mole from 1974 until he defected in 1985.

53. Modin, *op. cit.*, p. 222.

54. Carter, *op. cit.*, p. 473.

55. Elliott, *op. cit.*, p. 96.

4

The Singing Valet

Espionage is not always committed by dedicated idealists, or by patriots. Some are motivated by self-interest and greed, and a few who operated during the Second World War saw an opportunity to make money after it by writing about their adventures in colourful terms.

At that time the general public knew far less about spying than they do now. In Britain the official records were still closed; the word 'secret' meant just that, with the government of the day not even acknowledging that MI6 existed. This was fertile ground for the spy with an exaggerated story to tell and a publisher willing to peddle it. More importantly, it could be embellished without contradiction, for those who knew the truth were obliged to keep their mouths shut. The story could be officially denied, but as the truth could not be told the general public believed what it wanted to believe. So the authors of these books, which often sold in many thousands, were heavily promoted as individuals of exceptional daring who had a thrilling tale to tell.

Such a person was Elyesa Bazna, codenamed CICERO by the Germans. As one blurb writer remarked: 'if Bazna had never existed it would have been necessary for Graham Greene to invent him, for he was a character with delusions of grandeur equipped with a do-it-yourself spy kit'. This is certainly true, but the irony is that Bazna nevertheless perpetrated one of the most successful acts of espionage against the British during the Second World War. He published his side of the story in 1962, but prior to this Ludwig Moyzisch, CICERO's case officer; Walter Schellenberg, Moyzisch's immediate superior; and Franz Von Papen, the German ambassador to neutral Turkey, wrote in their memoirs[1] their versions of what became known as 'Operation Cicero'.

THE GERMAN PERSPECTIVE

The English edition of Moyzisch's book was published in 1950, the same year as it first appeared in Germany. The book had a strapline across the front of the dust jacket: 'The Espionage Sensation of the War', though the publisher's preface admitted the story was incomplete. The book caused something of a furore in Britain and questions were asked in Parliament, but it took many decades for the relevant documents to surface, and for the whole story to be told.

From the first Moyzisch emphasises the tangled rivalries in the higher echelons of the Nazi leadership and the intelligence agencies they controlled. He plays down – in fact fails to mention – that he belonged to the Foreign Intelligence Service (Amt VI), a department of the *Sicherheitsdienst* (SD), the SS's security service headed by Walter Schellenberg. The SD was part of the *Reichssicherheitshauptamt* (RSHA or Reich Security Main Office), which also ran the Gestapo. By October 1943, when CICERO became active, the RSHA was run by the notorious Ernst Kaltenbrunner, who was later hanged for war crimes.

Moyzisch's wartime cover was as the assistant commercial attaché in the Ankara embassy, and in his book he disingenuously uses this appointment to hide his Nazi secret service affiliations, something his ambassador, Franz Von Papen, was quick to point out in a postscript he wrote for the book. At the same time Von Papen also made it clear that all political matters were handled by himself and his legitimate diplomatic staff, and that the author would therefore not have known how – or if – the intelligence received from CICERO was exploited or not. This is a point worth remembering, as Moyzisch always maintained the Germans did nothing with the intelligence they received, disinformation that helped the British downplay the affair after the war.

Von Papen was not an out-and-out Nazi though, as a former German Chancellor, he had facilitated Hitler's rise to power, which doubtless gave him some protection from the cut-throat element in the Nazi Party. He was a wily, old-style diplomat who had the experience and the guile to counter the Allies' efforts during the latter half of 1943 to bring Turkey into the war on their side. He reported to the *Auswartige Amt* (German Foreign Office) headed by Von Ribbentrop whose dislike and jealousy of Kaltenbrunner was well known. If Moyzisch had not had the misfortune to be landed with the CICERO case it was unlikely that he would have become enmeshed in the power struggle between these two Nazi warlords. On the other hand, CICERO possibly saved him from being posted to the horrors of the Eastern Front, a fate he said his superiors threatened him with in September 1943 if he did not start delivering some high-grade intelligence.

In his book Moyzisch relates that on the night of 26 October 1943 he went to bed early but was woken by a call from the wife of the *chargé d'affaires*, Frau Jenke, saying he was urgently needed at their apartment. Being the sister of Von Ribbentrop, she was not to be argued with and the sleepy official did as he was bid. When he arrived Frau Jenke pointed to the sitting room and told Moyzisch that there was a 'strange sort of character' in there who wanted to sell something to the Germans. Would he please deal with it; and when he had finished would he turn off the lights and close the front door as she had sent the servants to bed.

Moyzisch entered the sitting room.

> I guessed that he was in his early fifties. He had thick black hair, brushed straight back from his forehead, which was fairly high. His dark eyes kept darting nervously from me to the door and back again. His chin was firm, his nose small and shapeless. Not an attractive face on the whole … the face of a man accustomed to disguising his true feelings.[2]

In halting French the man explained that he had access to highly secret papers from the British embassy, that he wanted £20,000 sterling for the two rolls of film he had taken of the documents, and £15,000 for each subsequent roll. Perhaps remembering the threat of being posted to the Eastern Front, Moyzisch resisted the urge to throw the man out, but listened to his proposition, and after some hesitation agreed to contact Berlin. He would then give Berlin's response when the man, who would call himself 'Pierre', telephoned him the following week. If Berlin agreed to the deal, they would meet that same evening to make the exchange. If Berlin did not agree, well – and the man gestured in the direction of the Soviet embassy nearby – there were others who would be interested. As Moyzisch let him out of the front door the man turned and said: 'You'd like to know who I am? I'm the British Ambassador's valet.'

Moyzisch and Von Papen both agreed that, however sceptical they were of the valet's offer, the German foreign minister must be informed, and a telegram was dispatched telling Von Ribbentrop the facts and asking if the offer was to be accepted. If it was, the money should be sent by special courier and arrive not later than 30 October. 'Alleged valet was employed several years ago by First Secretary, otherwise nothing much known here.'[3]

When Von Ribbentrop received the signal he consulted Schellenberg as it was a matter for the SD. Schellenberg later wrote in his memoirs[4] that his first reaction to the incident was astonishment and disbelief. However, during his career in secret intelligence he had often had to take risks, and had acquired an intuition as to whether one was worth taking. In this instance, the fact that any payment would be on delivery of the material gave some security, particularly if the film could be inspected before payment was made. Also, he was pretty sure the matter would be handled by Moyzisch who he knew to be both experienced and clever. They decided it was worth the risk, and a signal was sent, saying the valet's offer was to be accepted, provided every precaution was taken. A special courier would deliver the money and a report was to be sent immediately the documents had been delivered.

As Schellenberg surmised, Moyzisch did handle 'Pierre' judiciously. When the valet rang at the appointed time the German alerted the embassy photographer that he would be needed later that evening. He met 'Pierre' as arranged and took him to his office. He then removed a bundle of notes from his safe and counted them out in front of the man whose eyes, he could see, were swimming with greed. 'Pierre' handed over the two rolls of films, but when he reached for the money Moyzisch put his hand on the pile, saying the films had to be developed before he would pay him. Moyzisch describes this as a tense moment, but when 'Pierre' immediately agreed, the attaché felt, for the first time, the man was probably genuine. He soon knew the rolls of film were genuine, too, for once developed they showed crystal clear prints of fifty-two recently dated documents, mostly correspondence between the British ambassador, Sir Hughe Knatchbull-Hugesson, and the Foreign Office in London.

Moyzisch worked through the night, following the photographer's instructions on how to enlarge the prints, and then took them back to his office and locked the door. As he studied them more closely, his fears of a posting to the Eastern Front must have receded as his astonishment grew. The documents were obviously genuine; obtaining photographs of them was a coup any secret agent would dream about. 'Even at a glance I could see that the valet's service to the Third Reich was unbelievably important. His price had not been exorbitant.'[5]

The experienced Von Papen also had no doubts about their authenticity and noted that details of the Lend-Lease *materiel* the Americans had sent the Soviet Union during the course of the previous two years was particularly important. He informed Moyzisch that the valet should have a codename and suggested CICERO, the name of the famous Roman orator, saying it seemed a felicitous one.[6]

When Schellenberg saw the photographs in Berlin he, too, realised their importance, and ordered they be immediately made available to Hitler through Himmler; requested the head of the Army's deciphering department to come to his office to receive the material to help work on deciphering the British Diplomatic Code; ordered the relevant experts to compile a list of questions which, when answered by Ankara, would confirm to Hitler the reliability of the source; and informed the under-secretary of state of the situation and asked him from which budget the money should be taken.

Berlin, particularly Von Ribbentrop, was more sceptical and insisted the source's *bona fides* had to be established before his intelligence could be accepted, and in the following weeks the astute Moyzisch began slowly extracting the necessary information, discovering that the valet's motive for spying derived from his hatred of the British because an Englishman had killed his father in a hunting accident; and that he did know at least some English, though he continued to deny this. He also insisted that he worked alone, though one of the photographs showed a document being held by him, identified by a signet ring he wore on his forefinger.

These inconsistencies reinforced the opinion of the sceptics in Berlin that the valet was a British plant. But, as Schellenberg pointed out, though CICERO might be untruthful it didn't mean his material was fake, and he revealed in his memoirs that German cryptologists found it of great use in deciphering some of the diplomatic code employed by the British. He also wrote that the documents contained the codename for the planned Allied invasion of France, though in fact the word OVERLORD was not to appear in Bazna's filmed documents for some weeks.

At their second meeting Moyzisch had to admit that he did not have any more English currency when CICERO handed over two more rolls of film, but the spy simply shrugged and said he could pay him later, but that he required a new camera and plenty of film for it. This Moyzisch agreed to, as he did CICERO's request that in future he should be picked up by car at a prearranged rendezvous in an old part of the town where the streets were dark and narrow.

The two films were developed, and by early the following morning forty prints were spread out on Moyzisch's desk. To his astonishment they included the initial minutes of the Moscow Conference being attended by the foreign ministers of the three major powers, and their military advisers, as a preliminary for the Teheran Conference the following month.

On 4 November a courier arrived from Berlin carrying a suit-case filled with English banknotes that totalled £200,000, all of it designated for CICERO. As if aware of the money's arrival the valet rang the very next day to make a new appointment, and that evening, when Moyzisch approached the agreed rendezvous, a torch was flashed in his direction. It could only be CICERO, the German knew, and thought it a melodramatic and quite unneces-sary gesture, but reminded himself how unpredictable the spy was proving to be. He slowed near the shadowy figure, and leant back and opened the rear door. In a flash CICERO was in the back seat, and instructed Moyzisch to drive to the new part of Ankara. Had Moyzisch got his £30,000? Moyzisch nodded, and put the bundle on the front seat beside him. CICERO leant forward, took the money, and replaced it with another roll of film that Moyzisch quickly pocketed.

When Moyzsich showed the developed prints of this latest film to Von Papen, the ambassador gave him a signal from Von Ribbentrop, which summoned Moyzisch to Berlin for a meeting. He was to take all the material, and a seat had been reserved for him on a plane leaving Istanbul in two days' time. However, when the plane refuelled at Sofia, Moyzisch says he was transferred to another one. This had been sent by Kaltenbrunner who, he was told, would see him immediately he arrived.

In Berlin Moyzisch was interrogated at length by Kaltenbrunner and his staff while the films and photographs were examined by experts. They agreed the documents were authentic but doubted that CICERO took the photographs unaided, which pointed to the possibility of the valet being a plant. Kaltenbrunner, too, expressed his doubts, but was more interested in telling Moyzisch that he, Kaltenbrunner, was in charge of the CICERO operation, not Von Ribbentrop. They then discussed CICERO's personality and motives – an adventurer, vain, and ambitious, was Moyzisch's verdict, but in his opinion genuine. When Kaltenbrunner heard that CICERO's father had been killed by an Englishman, he demanded to know why he hadn't been told this, as it could be 'the key' to CICERO's actions. When Moyzisch replied that he had already reported this to Von Ribbentrop, Kaltenbrunner snarled that the foreign minister must have deliberately kept this information from him.

The parlous state of relations between Kaltenbrunner and Von Ribbentrop was further underlined for Moyzisch when he went to see the foreign minister. As two of Kaltenbrunner's officials were escorting him, Von Ribbentrop declined to see him, and two Foreign Office officials examined the documents instead. They also thought them genuine, but warned Moyzisch that Von Ribbentrop was convinced CICERO was a British plant, a position the foreign minister confirmed when he saw Moyzisch a few days later. At the end of the meeting he ordered Moyzisch to remain in Berlin, pending further investigations and discussions. Moyzisch protested, saying he needed to return to receive more CICERO intelligence, but Von Ribbentrop was adamant.

'I now found myself being kept on ice, as the saying was,' Moyzisch wrote. 'It happened frequently in Berlin. Any official who for any reason had fallen out of grace was left to twiddle his thumbs until the sun of superior benevolence should shine on him once again. In such circumstances it was best not to ask why. In my case it just happened that two powerful men were quarrelling, and I had the bad luck to be caught between them.'[7]

Moyzisch was not left on ice for long as it soon become clear he was being kept in Berlin to promote the Foreign Ministry's coup in discovering CICERO. He was wined and dined and partied, and introduced to a whole succession of influential individuals who were delighted to meet him and seemed to know more about his activities in Ankara than Moyzisch would ever have been prepared to admit; and he was relieved, when on 22 November, he was ordered back to Turkey. On his arrival at his office his secretary said that a certain 'Pierre' had called him several times and would call again that afternoon. When they met Moyzisch paid CICERO for the last roll of films, but refused to pay for a roll the spy said he had been forced to expose as Moyzisch had not been there to receive it. Schellenberg had already instructed Moyzisch that he was to keep Von Papen informed about his activities, as he, Schellenberg, considered it essential they trusted one another. However, Moyzisch now received a written order from Kaltenbrunner that he was to send all future CICERO intelligence to him direct; on no account was he to show any to Von Papen or to discuss the operation with him. Moyzisch ignored this directive as often as he dared, a brave, even reckless, decision which Von Papen acknowledged in his postscript to Moyzisch's book.[8]

Another problem now arose for the hard-pressed German intelligence officer. For some time CICERO had wanted to be paid in American dollars for one of his rolls of film and Moyzisch eventually arranged this by taking some of the English pounds Berlin had sent him to the German embassy's bank in Ankara. The manager was only too happy to oblige, particularly as one of his business customers had just brought in a large amount of American dollars and wanted to exchange them for English pounds. However, some time later the manager contacted Moyzisch and said that an Englishman had bought the pound notes from his customer and had taken them to London where, unfortunately, they had been found to be counterfeit.

When Moyzisch informed Berlin about the counterfeit currency he was told to keep quiet about it and to refund the bank from embassy funds. However, it left the German wondering if the rumours of an operation he had heard about in Berlin – to print counterfeit pounds to undermine the British currency – were more than just rumours. He therefore sent some of the money he had received to be independently tested, but these were found to be genuine. Relieved, Moyzisch put this curious incident out of his mind and it was not until after the war, when the German operation to print counterfeit pound notes was made public, that Moyzisch deduced that the money he had paid CICERO had been largely fake.

* * * * *

By December, Moyzisch noted the improvement in the spy's appearance, and his fingernails, previously bitten to the quick, were now elegantly manicured. He talked incessantly about his rosy future and how he was going to spend his fortune.

However, there was soon a dramatic incident that rattled the spy badly. During a routine meeting Moyzisch realised a long, dark limousine was following his car. Try as he might he could not shake off his pursuer. In and out of the narrow streets Moyzisch drove as fast as he could, his tyres screaming on the bends, while CICERO, plainly terrified, crouched on the back seat. Eventually, by doubling back and then driving at breakneck speed down the city's main central boulevard, Moyzisch shook off his pursuer, and after taking more evasive action, dropped CICERO near the British embassy. He had no idea who had been following them, but reasoned it was connected with CICERO. That was the evening, Moyzisch decided later, when the whole operation began to turn sour.

CICERO's most productive month was December when every courier flight to Berlin took with it top-secret documents, so important in Moyzisch's estimation, that even the quarrel between Kaltenbrunner and Von Ribbentrop took second place to their contents. One roll of film held the minutes of the first part of the Cairo Conference and of the Teheran Conference[9] at which some of the war's major decisions were taken. These included an agreement that Turkey should be persuaded to join the Allies before the end of the year and that Stalin, if he agreed to co-operate in other areas, should be handed part of Poland and be allowed to form a puppet communist government in Warsaw.

At around this time the spy gave Moyzisch a small packet that contained the wax imprints of the keys to the ambassador's safe for Berlin to copy. He was in such fine form, and so full of himself, he also insisted on singing Moyzisch arias from *I Pagliacci* to show what a splendid voice he had. Then, just before Christmas, he delivered a roll of film of top-secret documents on Anglo-Turkish relations. According to Moyzisch, these revealed that the Allies were winning the argument to draw Turkey into the war. Firstly, Ankara was prepared to allow Britain to infiltrate more technicians into the country to prepare Turkish air bases for a proposed Allied invasion of the Balkans. Secondly, it would allow the British to construct radar stations in Turkish Thrace to guide Allied bombers attacking the Romanian oil wells.

Moyzisch realised such intelligence was far too important to keep from the German ambassador, whose work to keep Turkey neutral Moyzisch whole-heartedly endorsed, as he did Von Papen's

desire for a negotiated peace to end the war. Deciding it was essential to make a strong protest about the radar stations to the Turkish
foreign minister, Numan Menemencioglu, Von Papen pretended
that he had heard about them through loose talk by the British
air attaché, and warned that German reprisals, such as bombing
Istanbul, were inevitable if they were built. In his memoirs Von
Papen wrote that the foreign minister seemed astonished at what
Von Papen knew. He immediately related their conversation to the
British ambassador and the very next day the latest batch of photographed documents from the valet that Von Papen studied on his
desk contained a telegram from Hugesson to the British Foreign
Office saying that the German ambassador knew more than was
good for him …

Moyzisch could not avoid forwarding the prints of these documents to Berlin, though he rightly feared the consequences. Sure
enough, he soon received a letter from Kaltenbrunner. accusing
him of a gross breach of discipline for ignoring his orders. Only
sheer luck prevented him from being sent to the Eastern Front
immediately: one of the items on the Teheran Conference agenda
stated that the Allies would soon start an all-out bombing campaign against the capitals of those Balkan countries allied to Hitler.
The first target was to be Sofia, the capital of Bulgaria, which up
to that time had suffered only sporadic air attacks. The date for the
raid was 14 January 1944.

When Berlin received this information Moyzisch was told that if
such a raid took place it would definitely prove CICERO's documents were genuine. To prevent any Allied suspicions of leaked
intelligence, Sofia's air defences would not be reinforced; instead it
would be left to its fate.[10] On the morning of 15 January, Moyzisch
called the German consulate in Sofia with a heavy heart, and was
told that the whole town was on fire and there had been heavy
civilian casualties.

From then on only Von Ribbentrop still refused to believe
CICERO's intelligence was genuine, and having read the minutes
of the Allied meetings Moyzisch believed he knew why. For he saw
with 'brutal clarity' that what he was reading was a clear and coher-
ent plan of his country's total destruction, a vision Von Ribbentrop
would never admit to himself, much less to Hitler.

It was this total blindness to reality, Moyzisch believed, that
caused CICERO's material to be ignored by Berlin, and in his

memoirs Von Papen confirms that he never received any instructions from either Hitler or Von Ribbentrop on the general policy
he should pursue with Turkey, and that he was left entirely to his
own devices. However, he totally rejected Moyzisch's assertion
that almost no use was made of the intelligence the valet provided.
On the contrary, he regarded it as priceless as it allowed him to
combat the decision at the Moscow Conference to force Turkey
into the war before the end of 1943, that CICERO kept him fully
informed of the talks at the Cairo Conference between Churchill
and Roosevelt and the Turkish President, and how the Turkish
Government were able to resist the intensifying Allied pressure to
join the war.

* * * * *

In early January 1944 Moyzisch acquired a second secretary,
whom he called Elisabet, to help him with his extra workload.
The daughter of a German diplomat based in Sofia, she had spent
her formative years in the United States. Elisabet, by all accounts,
was highly strung. The early raids on Sofia had upset her and her
father was anxious for her to move to a neutral country. Moyzisch
had heard about her through Von Papen's press attaché, a friend of
his called Seiller, at whose apartment Moyzisch sometimes used to
meet CICERO. On paper she seemed ideal – a linguist with sec-
retarial experience whose father was a respected German diplomat
– and Moyzisch urged Berlin and Von Papen that he be allowed
to employ her. This was eventually agreed, but Elisabet, though
attractive, was excessively temperamental and nervous. Only time
would tell why this was so.

At around the same time as Elisabet arrived in Ankara CICERO
told Moyzisch that several men had arrived from England and
were prowling around the building, and that the ambassador's safe
had been fitted with an alarm system. The valet did not, of course,
know why this had happened, and Moyzisch did not tell him. But
he turned down CICERO's attempts to extract more money, and
refused to pay when CICERO produced details of the embassy's
petty cash expenditure. However, Berlin thought differently and
Moyzisch was forced to pay, but he informed CICERO that he
was well aware of the game the valet was playing. CICERO then
relented and said he would photograph only documents marked
'secret' or 'most secret'. From that time they often conversed in

English, which Moyzisch remarked later, was a considerable improvement on his horrible French.

Because CICERO could not now find suitable material to photograph, Moyzisch wrote that he saw less of him in February, but at the beginning of March some of the documents on the film he did deliver included the codename OVERLORD. Its meaning remained obscure but the context in which it was mentioned indicated it was of a military, not diplomatic, nature; and from other documents already photographed Moyzisch claims to have deduced that it was the codeword for the second front which Churchill had promised Stalin would come in 1944. He sent a signal to Berlin suggesting this, but received a cool reply: Possible but hardly probable.

Moyzisch claims this was the last roll of film he received from CICERO. He did see him once more to make a final payment – the total he had passed to the valet was an astonishing £300,000 – and again a few days after 'that ghastly April 6th, a day which, I imagine, decided his fate as it did mine.'[11] This was the day that Elisabet disappeared.

Elisabet had always proved difficult, and seemed offended whenever Moyzisch failed to take her into his confidence. Towards the end of March, while Moyzisch was away, she opened a letter addressed to him. She was correct to do so as Berlin had forgotten to mark it for his personal attention, and it appeared to be just routine correspondence. In fact it was anything but that, and as soon as Moyzisch returned to the office, she asked him, apparently quite innocently: 'Who is CICERO?' Moyzisch brushed her question aside, but was alarmed to see, when he read the letter, that its contents made it obvious that CICERO referred to an operation in the British embassy.

A few days later Moyzisch agreed to go shopping with Elisabet to act as her interpreter, and while she was choosing what to buy CICERO entered the store. The two men ignored one another, but when Elisabet still could not find what she wanted, and Moyzisch's Turkish proved unequal to the task of helping her, the valet offered to help. He had no idea who she was – a girlfriend perhaps? – but he helped her get what she wanted. CICERO then bowed to her, gave Moyzisch a knowing wink, and left the shop.

Shortly afterwards, Elisabet asked if she could spend Easter weekend with her parents in Budapest where her father had now been posted. Von Papen and Moyzisch had already decided the girl was far too temperamental and difficult, and had agreed that her father should be asked to take her home on account of her hysterical behaviour. So her request seemed the perfect solution: once she had left for Budapest her father would be asked to keep her there, and her belongings would be forwarded.

Moyzisch agreed to see her off, but she never turned up at the station. He rushed to her apartment, but the girl she shared it with said she had left earlier that afternoon, taking all her belongings with her. Moyzisch now thought the unthinkable. Recently a senior Abwehr (German Military Intelligence) officer in Turkey had deserted to the Allies. Rats leaving the sinking ship. Could Elisabet be another, Moyzisch wondered? The Turkish minister of the interior, when Moyzisch sought his help in finding her, thought that that was exactly what had happened, though he hoped for the Moyzisch's sake he was wrong. Moyzisch did, too. Employing a traitor meant the Eastern Front would be insufficient punishment for him. More likely, he would end up in a concentration camp; Kaltenbrunner might even have him tried and shot.

As Moyzisch feared, once Kaltenbrunner heard of Elisabet's disappearance, he ordered Moyzisch back to Berlin. That same day Moyzisch received a note from a friend in the Foreign Ministry in Berlin warning him he was suspected of abetting the defection of his secretary, and that he should therefore ignore the order. That night he received a succession of anonymous telephone calls, urging him to defect. He refused them all and eventually, in desperation, cut the telephone cord. Nevertheless, he decided not to catch the plane, and feigned illness for not doing so.

Shortly afterwards CICERO asked to meet him and told him that Elisabet had defected to the British, but was still in Ankara. He asked Moyzisch how much Elisabet knew about him, and whether she had taken any of the photographs with her. Moyzisch told him she had not taken any – he had already checked his safe – but that she knew the valet's codename … 'and perhaps more'. He noticed how CICERO looked a beaten man, quite sick with fright. They shook hands and Moyzisch never saw him again.

As for Elisabet, Moyzisch wrote at the end of his book that he had heard when she had left Turkey her usual slovenly appearance had been transformed. Her long, bedraggled fair hair, had been replaced by a short, black coiffure, and she was dressed in smart

New York clothes with heavy make-up, but he gives no further explanation of her behaviour.

Meanwhile, Turkey's continuing prevarication about joining the Allies had produced a stand-off with them. This, the Turkish Government knew, it could not afford, so on 20 April the Turkish foreign minister informed Von Papen that Turkey was going to break off diplomatic relations with Germany on 1 May. From that date Turkey would no longer supply Germany with vital war materials including chromium, an essential component of high-grade armour plate. This was a setback for Germany and Von Papen was recalled to Berlin immediately. But though Von Ribbentrop issued a communiqué that the ambassador would not be returning to his post in the immediate future, this order was immediately overturned by Hitler at a meeting he held with Von Papen and Von Ribbentrop.

Von Papen's description of this encounter clearly conveys the reactions of the Nazi leadership to the intelligence being sent to them from Turkey. When Von Papen raised the matter of the decisions reached at the Teheran Conference that CICERO's documents had provided, Hitler retorted that the intention of the Allies to bring about the complete destruction of Germany had been made clear by Roosevelt's demand for Germany to surrender unconditionally, which he had announced after the Casablanca Conference the previous January. Everything else, Hitler was convinced, was just propaganda designed to soften the German nation and to make such surrender acceptable. But the Atlantic Wall would stop the British and Americans in their tracks, and once they were repulsed the Russians would soon be brought to a halt. Von Papen saw Von Ribbentrop nod his agreement and recognised there was no point in continuing the conversation.

CICERO'S TALE

Bazna's book was published in 1962, written in collaboration with a German journalist. In it Bazna states he was born in 1904 in Pristina, now the capital of the independent state of Kosovo, but then part of the Ottoman Empire. Later his family moved to Istanbul and in the aftermath of the defeat of the Empire during the First World War he was employed by a French transport unit, France being one of the occupying powers. Having left school without any practical skills or academic qualifications, but with an inflated idea of his own worth, he soon found himself in trouble.

He spent three years in a French penal camp where he acquired a grounding in the French language.

Released early, when the occupying powers signed a treaty with the new Turkish government, Bazna joined a commercial vehicle company in Marseille, where he incidentally learnt the skills of a locksmith. He returned to Istanbul and was employed in several capacities, ending up as the servant-driver of the Yugoslav ambassador in Ankara. One day his employer heard him singing while he washed the ambassador's car. He told him he had a fine voice and suggested it should be properly trained, and he also encouraged his servant's interest in photography, at which he obviously had a talent.

CICERO began attending the local conservatoire, and music, in his words, became his consolation for living the life of a servant to a foreigner, a *kavass* as the Turks contemptuously called them. He became consumed by the desire to be a great singer, worked hard at improving his voice, and after seven years decided he was ready to launch his career. He handed in his notice, but his first concert flopped and he was soon back at work, this time as the driver for the American Military attaché. Then, in 1942, he began working for the first secretary at the German embassy, Albert Jenke, using the name of Diello. To show off to his wife – who lived in the city with their four children – he began photographing some of Jenke's correspondence and took a picture of himself lying on the drawing room sofa. Some of the letters he found were from Frau Jenke's brother, Von Ribbentrop, Hitler's foreign minister.

Unhappily for CICERO, Jenke must have got wind of his prying and sacked him, but the experience of working for important people on opposing sides in the war gave him the idea of acquiring the confidential documents of one power and selling them to another – in other words to become a spy. This, he reasoned, would be an exciting way to earn a living and was about the only method by which he could ever hope to accumulate sufficient money to live in the manner he believed his due. And what better place was there to pursue such a career than in Ankara, the capital of a neutral power and one of the war's principal centres of espionage?

To further this aim CICERO successfully applied for the post of chauffeur and general handyman to the first secretary at the British embassy, and it was not long before he had the opportunity to read memoranda about British intentions in Turkey that his employer had carelessly left in an unlocked drawer. It was a promising start, made more promising by the love affair he soon began with Mara, the family nurse. However, he eventually realised that if he was to make the kind of money he wanted he would have to find a more important source of intelligence; and by devious means he manoeuvred himself into being employed as the valet of the 57-year-old British ambassador, Sir Hughe Knatchbull-Hugesson, an old-style diplomat of proven ability but eccentric habits, who was also a talented artist and pianist.

One of the peccadillos CICERO discovered about his master was that he preferred to work at home, not in the embassy located next to his residence. So CICERO started his spying career by carefully inspecting the layout of the house. To his satisfaction the ambassador's study, located on the first floor above the kitchen, was thickly carpeted so no one would hear him moving around in it when Hugesson was out. He then timed how long it took to move between various rooms, and noted where he could hide documents in an emergency. He may have been an ill-educated servant, but he had sufficient savvy to follow that old military adage that time spent in reconnaissance is rarely wasted.

CICERO noted that all the ambassador's papers were stored in red boxes and were brought each day from the embassy to his residence. At the end of the working day documents that still needed attention were returned to their red boxes, and were locked by the secretary in her safe before giving the key to Sir Hughe. More importantly, CICERO discovered that the documents needing the ambassador's urgent attention were transferred to a black box, which Sir Hughe took to his bedroom to study at night where he often worked into the early hours of the morning. No wonder, CICERO thought, that the ambassador needed the sleeping pills that lay on his bedside table.

To test the ambassador's alertness, CICERO took from his bedroom dressing table a sketch Sir Hughe had been working on and secreted it behind a painting of King George V on the ground floor. When he returned it three days later, it was clear that Sir Hughe had not missed the drawing as he did not comment on its disappearance. That, and the fact the ambassador wrote poetry, settled CICERO's nerves completely, and from then on he felt boundlessly superior to him.

Sir Hughe's vagueness, combined with a daily routine by which CICERO could set his watch, made the ambassador the

ideal victim. Confident now that his espionage plans would succeed CICERO constructed a method of photographing the
documents in his servants' quarters. He bought a more powerful
bulb for his lamp, and purchased four metal rods and a metal
ring. He used the rods to support the ring and hold it firmly in
place as a kind of tripod. He then fixed his old Leica camera to
the ring, with the lens pointing downwards through the ring's
centre. When rigged, he was able to take photographs of any
document by placing it directly under the lens of the camera
and illuminating it with the lamp. When not in use he disguised
this contraption by making two of the rods into a tie rack and
another two into hanging rails for his washing, and he concealed
the ring by disguising it as part of his ashtray.

He then found a method of accessing the ambassador's papers. He
bought some wax, which became malleable when he warmed it in
his hand, and bided his time. Inevitably, one morning the ambassador
carelessly left the keys to the safe, and to the red and black boxes, on
his bedside table while he had a bath, and it took CICERO only a
moment to take impressions of them with the wax. Later he had
duplicates made by a locksmith who had, at one time, worked for
him in the Istanbul municipal transport department.

With the help of Mara, he had already photographed documents
in the possession of Hugesson's first secretary – one of them, so
CICERO claimed, was a list the names of all the British agents
in Turkey – and by 26 October he had two rolls of film totalling
fifty-two photographs. He now decided the time had come to
act and in a state of high excitement, he approached his former
employer, Herr Jenke, who had recently been made *chargé d'affaires*
to the German ambassador, Franz Von Papen. Jenke listened to his
former servant and was no doubt impressed by his knowledge of
photography, if not by what else he had to say. CICERO told him
that he was able to use his Leica camera at the British embassy
and take photographs, not with a long-distance lens but an ordinary 1.2 or 1.5 lens. He was therefore in a position to photograph
documents, and all those he had so far taken were marked 'secret'
or 'most secret'. He then demanded £20,000 sterling for the two
rolls of film he had already taken, and added that any future roll
would cost £15,000. This had Jenke reaching for the telephone
to summon the embassy's security officer, Ludwig Moyzisch, an
SS Lieutentant-Colonel (*Obersturmbannführer*).

CICERO repeated his demand to Moyzisch. He also wanted a new camera, and for every roll he gave Moyzisch he was to receive another in return, as he did not want to risk being seen buying film. He would ring Moyzisch at his office at 3 pm on 30 October and give the name 'Pierre'. They would agree where to meet, and when Moyzisch produced the cash CICERO would hand over the film. CICERO told him he was willing to wait while the films were being examined and Moyzisch need not hand him the money until he was satisfied that the rolls were worth the price he was demanding. Surely, nothing could be fairer than that?

Moyzisch agreed that nothing could, and a few days later CICERO rang at the appointed time and met Moyzisch that evening, and they walked to the Nazi security officer's house. Once in his study Moyzisch unlocked the safe and showed CICERO the money wrapped in a newspaper. He then demanded the rolls of film and after having them developed gave the £20,000 to CICERO, and also presented him with a brand-new Leica camera and some film. They drank amicably to the deal with whisky, but the valet brushed aside a receipt Moyzisch wanted him to sign. He then said he would have another roll of film ready the next day, and that when they met Moyzisch should provide him with a revolver. It was difficult to know which piece of information upset the German more – the revolver or the proximity of their next meeting as he protested he would not be able to get more money at such short notice. He needn't worry, CICERO replied loftily. Moyzisch could pay him later. He would allow him credit.

Their next meeting was brief. CICERO handed over the roll of film – the photographed documents concerned the recently held Moscow Conference – and Moyzisch handed him a revolver.[12]

It seems that the valet, though he had to ask Moyzisch to have one of the ambassador's keys re-cut, was now able to examine the contents of the boxes almost at will, while his master was out on official business, playing the piano which he did most afternoons, or when he was heavily asleep at night, having taken a sleeping pill. CICERO photographed those items he judged important, like the ones containing the names of famous people he had heard of: Stalin, Churchill, Roosevelt, Eden. Some he could see had details of the Allied efforts to entice Turkey to join the war. To emphasise his own, important role in preventing this – and probably to persuade the reader that patriotism as well as money motivated him

– CICERO wrote that Von Papen, because of what he knew, was able to intervene successfully with the Turkish Government, and prevent the country from being involved in a bloody war. So the answer the Turkish foreign minister, Numan Menemencioglu, gave to the British ambassador was no. He CICERO knew this because he had photographed it.

As the weeks passed CICERO's pile of money grew and grew. He set Mara up in a love nest, spent lavishly on them both, and spread the remainder of the notes under the carpet in his bedroom in the embassy. Every so often he would roll back the carpet and savour the riches beneath it. As the weeks passed, and the horde of notes became larger and larger, CICERO dreamt of building himself a hotel in a Turkish resort. Later, when he had fears of his espionage being uncovered he removed the money to the house he had rented for Mara.

Every time they met, Moyzisch questioned CICERO about his motives. Although CICERO knew exactly what these were – money and the buzz of earning it dangerously – he continued to justify his espionage to himself as a means of keeping Turkey neutral. As Moyzisch would have found this unconvincing, instead CICERO spun his yarn about his father being killed by an Englishman in a hunting accident.

CICERO liked to show off. He would boast to Moyzisch that he was using the ambassador's telephone to call him, and described how he would enter the ambassador's bedroom in the middle of the night, unlock the black box, take out the documents in it, and return to his bedroom on the ground floor to photograph them. Once, when returning them, he knocked over the glass of water with which the ambassador had taken his sleeping pills. The glass broke; Hugesson stirred but did not open his eyes; and CICERO retreated, leaving the broken glass where it lay, rightly guessing his master would think he had broken it himself in his sleep.

One day the haul from the black box included a telegram Hugesson had drafted for dispatch to the Foreign Office in London. The sentence in it about Von Papen knowing more than was good for him immediately caught CICERO's eye and sparked fear inside him. The spy's nerves were already on edge as the previous evening Moyzisch's car had been followed as the two men were making their usual swap of cash for the latest roll of film. Unable to shake off the mystery driver CICERO had jumped from the car. He watched their pursuer speed by and just caught a glimpse of his smooth young face. Now real fear of discovery flooded his mind: if Von Papen knew something he shouldn't have concerning British interests, it could only have come from the copies of the telegrams he was supplying to Moyzisch. And the mysterious driver who had pursued them so tenaciously knew it too…

CICERO's fears multiplied when that evening Mara said she knew he was working for the Germans. She had overheard the first secretary telling his wife that the Germans had an excellent source of information that might have come from inside the embassy itself, and soon deduced this could only be him. CICERO froze. Was she blackmailing him with the unspoken threat of unmasking him in order to keep her good life going? It seemed quite likely, and when he went to work the next morning his fears were amplified when he noticed a man standing across the road from the embassy gates. As CICERO drew nearer the man cupped his hands to light a cigarette, and the match illuminated the man's smooth, young face.

* * * * *

One afternoon while the ambassador was playing the piano he asked his *kavass* to bring him a glass of orange juice, and after fetching it for him CICERO remained for a moment to listen. When Hugesson paused to drink the juice the spy remarked how well he played. Then, perhaps spurred on by the music that had he had just heard, the valet suddenly began singing an aria from Wagner's opera, *The Flying Dutchman*. The ambassador, being the civilised man he was, was impressed and said so. He played the first notes of a German *lieder*, and looked up questioningly at his servant. CICERO knew it well and began to sing, and Hugesson accompanied him.

When they had finished CICERO knew he had nothing to fear from Hugesson who had already said how pleased he was with him, and was now full of praise for his voice. However, the valet knew he had a lot to fear from the men to whom he served tea in the ambassador's office shortly afterwards. They had been flown from England to improve the embassy's security system, and CICERO recognised this could only mean the British suspected a leak of confidential information, and that it came from their Ankara embassy.

At around this time the spy mentions a niece called Esra. Requested by her father to find the attractive 17-year-old some work in Ankara, CICERO obtained the agreement of Lady Knatchbull-Hugesson for the girl to stay in the embassy until she had found herself a permanent position. The ambassador's safe now had an alarm system but this did not deter CICERO. He arranged for Esra to remove the fuse that controlled the system when he wanted access to it, and carried on his espionage as before. Esra proved a useful and resourceful accomplice. She soon replaced Mara in CICERO's affections, and when Mara went to England with the first secretary and his family, the valet promptly installed Esra in his rented house.

As 1943 drew to a close CICERO began seeing the word OVERLORD in the confidential telegrams he was photographing; and when one said that if Turkey came in on the side of the Allies it would free up the escort vessels so urgently needed for OVERLORD he realised this could be the codename for the Second Front which had been discussed at the Teheran Conference. He wrote that he had already begun speculating on the meaning of Operation OVERLORD and that the strange expression recurred more and more often in the telegrams and documents that he was photographing. Rather grandiosely he remarked in his memoir that he was the first person on the Axis side to come across the codename and that he later discovered he was the first to alert the Germans to it.

One day, when calling Moyzisch to make a new appointment, CICERO spoke to his case officer's new secretary. To CICERO, the inveterate womaniser, she sounded attractive. However, when he gave his codename 'Pierre', and she asked him coyly what his real name was, CICERO brushed her curiosity aside. Then, by chance, without knowing who she was, he met her in an Ankara store accompanied by Moyzisch. They exchanged a few words, but she only told him she was German. Later, he saw her again, in the Ankara Palace Hotel, this time escorted by the man with the smooth, young face, who had last been seen watching him outside the British embassy ...

Shortly after 6 April CICERO heard from the ambassador's chef that a secretary called Cornelia Kapp had disappeared from the German embassy, and had probably defected. Such events were common knowledge amongst the Turkish domestic staff of

1. Pit (right) and Pan in front of one of the station wagons just before the start of Operation SALAM. (Eppler, *Operation Condor*)

'The English Patient' Laszlo [A]masy in the uniform of a captain [of] the Hungarian Air Force Reserve. [L]ubassek, *A Szahara Buvoleteben*)

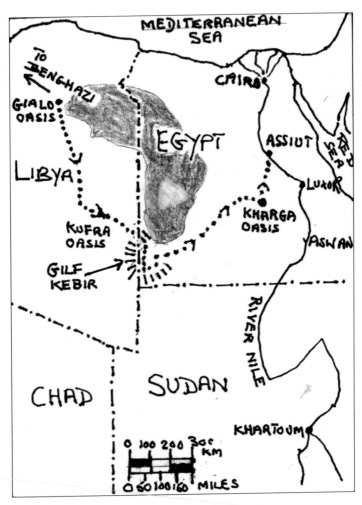

3. Map of Almasy's epic journey across the desert. (Author)

4. The pro-German Cairo belly-dancer Hekmat Fahmi (Mosley, *The Cat and the Mice*)

Major A.W. Sansom, the British Field Security officer who tracked down the spies in Cairo. (Eppler, *Operation Condor*)

DR. RICHARD SORGE

1M DDR

1895-1944

DR. RICHARD SORGE

HELD
DER SOWJETUNION

6. Soviet Stamp issued in 1964. One of the ways the USSR belatedly honoured its most important Second World War spy. (Wikimedia Commons)

7. Miyake Hanako, Sorge's last mistress at his house in Tokyo. (Whymant, *Stalin's Spy*)

Guy Burgess, the brilliant but unstable
KVD double agent who died a broken man
Moscow. (KGB archives)

9. The art historian and traitor, Anthony
Blunt. He died unrepentent in 1983.
(KGB archives)

. The high-flying diplomat, Donald
aclean, was exposed by VENONA
crypts, and defected in 1951. (KGB
chives)

11. John Cairncross, the last of The
Cambridge Five to be unmasked.
He probably did more damage to his
country than any of the other members
of The Cambridge Five. (KGB archives)

12. 'Kim' Philby, arguably the most committed and astute double agent of them all, has been called 'the spy of the century'. He had blood on his hands and even those in the Soviet Union, to where he defected in 1963, did not trust him. (Borovik, *The Philby Files*)

13. A photograph of a disguised Kitty Harris from the KGB archives. Her lovers included American Communist, Earl Browder, and Donald Maclean. (KGB archives)

14. The Austrian-born Arnold Deutsch recruited The Cambridge Five in the 1930s. (Damaskin, *Kitty Harris: The Spy with Seventeen Names*)

15. Grigory Grafpen who replaced Deutsch and Maly in April 1938. He soon became a victim of Stalin's purges. Miraculously he survived, and after Stalin died was rehabilitated and decorated, and lived until he was 96. (Damaskin, *Kitty Harris: The Spy with Seventeen Names*)

16. Bazna, dressed here for a concert, failed to make his mark as a singer. He was much more successful as a spy. (Bazna, *I Was Cicero*)

17. The book that first revealed to the British public the extent of espionage in the British embassy in Ankara in 1943. (Author)

18. Arch enemies at Hitler's headquarters, 1942: Franz Von Papen, the wartime German ambassador to Turkey (left) and the Nazi Foreign Minister, Joachim Von Ribbentrop. (Franz Von Papen's Memoirs)

19. Ludwig Moyzisch, Bazna's controller in Ankara. (Bazna, *I Was Cicero*)

20. The British Embassy in Ankara, the site of one of the most successful acts of espionage against the British during the Second World War. (Bazna, *I Was Cicero*)

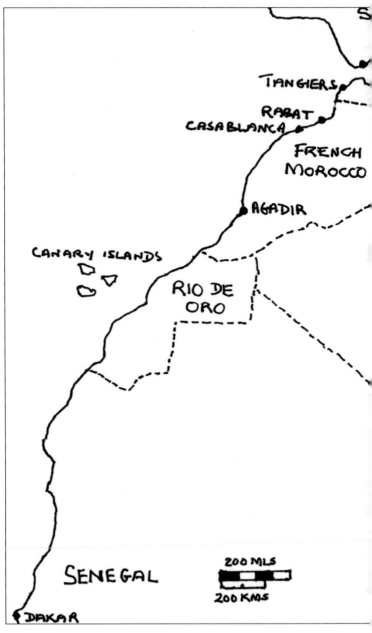

21. Map of North Africa. (Author)

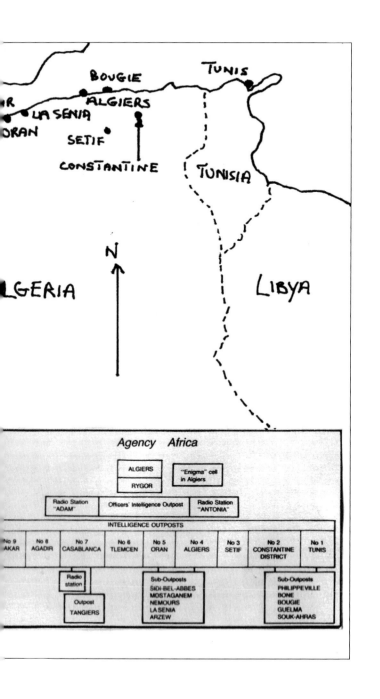

BOUGIE

TUNIS

ALGIERS

?R

LA SENIA

ORAN

SETIF

CONSTANTINE

TUNISIA

N

LGERIA

LIBYA

Agency Africa

ALGIERS	"Enigma" cell in Algiers
RYGOR	

Radio Station "ADAM"	Officers' Intelligence Outpost	Radio Station "ANTONIA"

INTELLIGENCE OUTPOSTS

No 9 AKAR	No 8 AGADIR	No 7 CASABLANCA	No 6 TLEMCEN	No 5 ORAN	No 4 ALGIERS	No 3 SETIF	No 2 CONSTANTINE DISTRICT	No 1 TUNIS

		Radio station		Sub-Outposts SIDI-BEL-ABBES MOSTAGANEM NEMOURS LA SENIA ARZEW			Sub-Outposts PHILIPPEVILLE BONE BOUGIE GUELMA SOUK-AHRAS	
		Outpost TANGIERS						

22. After the fighting: Daphne Tuyl, the only female British agent in North Africa, with one of Roosevelt's 'twelve apostles' Colonel John Knox (left), whom she later married. In the centre is Marshal Juin who commanded the French armies opposing the Allied landings in North Africa, November 1942. (Slowikowski, *In the Secret Service*)

23. The American General Devers, who commanded the Allied forces which landed in the South of France, August 1944, decorating Rygor with the American Legion of Merit. (Slowikowski, *In the Secret Servic*

24. Colonel 'Tar' Robertson, the highly successful head of MI5's Double-Cross section. (Popov, *Spy/Counterspy*)

5. Dusko Popov (right) a Dubrovnik café efore the war with is elder brother Ivo. vo was also a double gent who pretended o be a collaborator German-occupied ugoslavia. (Miller, *Codename Tricycle*)

26. The German parachutist, Karl Richter (centre), at the spot where he landed in Hertfordshire in May 1941. He is indicating to the commandant of Camp 020, Colonel 'Tin Eye' Stephens (left, smoking), where he had buried his equipment. He was executed in December 1941. (IWM HU66766)

27. The only German spy known to evade capture was Wilhelm Ter Braak (real name Engelbertus Fukken). He landed near Cambridge in November 1940 and – despite being reported as suspicious by a local landlady – eluded capture until April 1941 when he shot himself in a partly built Cambridge air-raid shelter. (TNA, KV 2/114)

28. Sir John Masterman, who ran The Double Cross System. (Popov, *Spy, Counter-Spy*)

29. The parachutist, Wulf Schmidt, with the transmitter with which he sent false messages to his Abwehr controllers. Given the codename TATE – after Harry Tate, a well-known music hall comedian of the time – he was one of the most successful agents in The Double Cross System. After the war he settled in England under the name of Harry Williamson. (TNA, KV 2/62)

30. Elizabeth Bentley, the 'Red Spy Queen', giving evidence to the Committee on Un-American Affairs in 1948 against the OSS officer, Duncan Lee, who is sitting behind her. (AP/Wide World)

. Jacob Golos (real name Jacob Rasin) was Elizabeth entley's Soviet controller in the United States – and er lover (KGB archives)

32. The Russian-born William Weisband was an expert in signals intelligence. He worked for the American Armed Forces Security Agency (later the National Security Agency) and was almost certainly the first to reveal the VENONA programme to Soviet intelligence. (Nigel West)

33. The British scientist J.B.S. Haldane, codenamed INTELLIGENSIA by the Soviets, who worked on highly secret projects for the British Admiralty during the war. VENONA decrypts indicated he was head of X Group that passed intelligence to the Soviet GRU. (Nigel West)

34. The brilliant cryptographer, Meredith Gardner (left), and his team working on VENONA decrypts at Arlington Hall in 1946. It was before the age of computers. (Nigel West)

35. Arlington Hall, Virginia, where, for several decades, VENONA decrypts were laboriously unravelle It was the American equivalent of Britain's Bletchley Park Code & Cipher School. (Nigel West)

embassies, CICERO later wrote, and that contact between them was not confined to gossip as alcohol was often exchanged, so that staff in the German embassy were well supplied with whiskey and the British with Moselle or hock.

CICERO also linked the girl's disappearance with the fag-end of a conversation he had overheard between the ambassador and his first secretary, that someone had been flown to Cairo where she was being thoroughly interrogated. This half-heard remark enveloped him in a sense of doom. In his mind the defector was connected to Moyzisch, that she had been the one who had asked CICERO for his real name, and was the one he had met with Moyzisch in the Ankara shop. What's more, she was the one he had seen accompanying the man with the smooth, young face at the Ankara Palace Hotel …

Shortly afterwards, CICERO saw the same, smooth-faced young man again, standing near the British embassy's trade entrance, and on impulse decided to follow him. He trailed him to a block of modern flats where many foreigners lived, and the man let himself into the building with a key. From then on, as often as he could, CICERO kept watch on the building. One day his patience was rewarded, and he saw the man approaching the block of flats. With him was a British WRNS with short black hair. She looked nothing like Cornelia Kapp, yet there was something familiar about her gait, the way she held herself, but it wasn't until the couple had disappeared inside the building that the valet realised it had indeed been her.

That decided him, and as soon as he could he arranged a meeting with Moyzisch and told him he was not going to work for him anymore. He also demanded to know what Kapp knew about him. Moyzisch assured him she knew nothing, but CICERO did not believe him. He decided the time had come to cut and run. He gave in his notice on 20 April, put all his money in a bank deposit box – it now amounted to the enormous sum of £300,000 sterling – packed Esra off to a hotel, disposed of his rented house, and dumped his Leica camera and equipment.

Once he had worked out his notice CICERO began his new life. He rented a smart apartment, began trading in second-hand cars, took as his mistress a Greek singer who had a first-class figure but a third-class voice, and divorced his wife (he later remarried). Even his ambition to build a luxury hotel began to take shape when he joined a consortium that was given financial backing by the Turkish government. Most importantly, as time passed, he knew the authorities would not trouble him. The British might know he was a spy, but they had no evidence and probably had no wish to publicise what had happened.

Then it all went pear-shaped. After he had paid one of the companies working on the hotel in the pound notes from his horde, it was discovered they were forgeries. His company's assets were frozen, and the courts, though they eventually accepted he had not circulated the forged money deliberately, ruled that he still had to pay the contractor. From being rich and free he became poor and debt-ridden, earning what he could by giving singing lessons and selling second-hand cars. Once when he arranged a concert to earn some extra money his creditors moved in and took it all. When he heard that the film *Five Fingers*,[13] based on Moyzisch's book, was being shot in Turkey, he contacted the producers and suggested he play the main character himself, or he would be willing to act as a consultant. His offer was declined. He even attempted to sue the German Federal Government for a pension as he believed he had been cheated of proper payment for his wartime work. His book was a last desperate attempt to earn good money from his wartime activities, but by one account he ended his days working as a night-watchman in Munich before dying in 1970.[14]

WHAT REALLY HAPPENED (MORE OR LESS)

The CICERO affair was not the first time security at the Ankara embassy had been brought to the attention of the Foreign Office. On 19 October 1941 Guy Liddell, Director of MI5's Counter-Intelligence, recorded in his diary that ISOS (decrypts of the Abwehr's hand ciphers) indicated the Abwehr had two spies in the British embassy; and on 3 November he noted that the Germans had had access to a diplomatic bag containing re-ciphering tables which, luckily, were able to be withdrawn from use before they became operational.[15]

At around the same time the Soviet authorities informed the Foreign Office, via the British ambassador in Moscow, that someone in Hugesson's residence had been opening his safe every night and making its contents known to the Turks. When questioned, the ambassador made such an astonishing reply that one can only assume his sense of humour – which was apparently well developed – had got the better of him. He said he thought the Foreign Office 'had greatly exaggerated' how often his safe had been opened and that 'he did not think it was being opened more than once a week at the maximum.'[16]

This revelation sent Sir John Dashwood, MI6's deputy security officer, flying to Ankara at the earliest available opportunity to investigate the embassy's security. Not surprisingly, he found it poor with several other infringements coming to light, and Hugesson quite oblivious of his obligations to follow Foreign Office security procedures. He noted that the ambassador even argued that as his safe was being opened it was better – contrary to Foreign Office rules – to carry any confidential documents he wanted to read to his bedroom in a box. This he proceeded to do even after the safe in his residence was moved in January 1943 to the Chancery (embassy building) 60 yards away.

The problem with Hugesson was that, though a first-rate diplomat, he belonged to a previous era. Probably a strong supporter of the ethics of Henry L. Stimson, a US secretary of state during the 1920s, who pronounced that 'gentlemen did not read each other's mail', his disdain for espionage and all those connected with it knew no bounds. He was, for instance, hardly on speaking terms with the embassy's MI6 security officer and apparently disliked the SOE (Special Operations Executive) in Turkey even more. This must have made Dashwood's task a difficult one, and despite a thorough investigation he was unable to find the two Abwehr plants in the embassy, or who was rifling the ambassador's safe in his residence.

Another example of Hugesson's insouciance came in January 1943 when it was discovered that his butler rang the German embassy to report the ambassador's departure for Adana to meet Churchill. Not unreasonably, the Foreign Office asked Hugesson if he was satisfied there was no further chance of the butler contacting the enemy. Hugesson replied that he wasn't, but he couldn't possibly dismiss the butler before he had found a suitable replacement! The Foreign Office put its foot down and the butler eventually left on 15 May 1943, and was replaced by a footman.

Hugesson's cavalier attitude to the dangers of espionage is also recounted by Sholto Douglas, the RAF's C-in-C Middle East, who stayed at the Ankara embassy early in 1943 while negotiating British defences for Turkish airfields. On his arrival, Hugesson asked him if his briefcase contained any secret papers. If it did 'you'd better let me have it to lock away in my safe for the night. Too many of our servants seem to be spies.' When Sholto Douglas asked why they weren't dismissed, Hugesson replied airily that they were good servants 'and in any case any others we might get would also probably be spies.'[17] He was certainly proved right about that.

As these incidents occurred a matter of months before Bazna was employed in July 1943, it is not inconceivable that the future valet knew about the embassy's lax security, and deliberately targeted it.

Guy Liddell, who strongly believed the division between the two secret services should be functional and not geographical, was a fierce critic of MI6's handling of Ankara's poor security. He believed MI5's expertise in counter-espionage was much greater than that of MI6, and that the former should have been called in to help. However, the Foreign Office baulked at any outside assistance, and, quite wrongly, did not even inform MI5 about events in Ankara. As Liddell pointed out, MI5 had a general interest in knowing about any cases of espionage in British embassies abroad as MI5 could be looking for a spy in Britain when in fact he was in a British embassy abroad. He felt so strongly about this that in January 1943 he even mentioned to Anthony Blunt that, because of the several leakages that had occurred, he thought it important to get an MI5 operative into the Ankara embassy, though there is no evidence this happened. Then, on 20 January 1944, he recorded in his diary that Dashwood was again being sent to Ankara to investigate a leakage there, but that he was unlikely to clear the matter up as he had 'no experience whatsoever of investigation'.[18]

This time Dashwood planted fake documents in boxes left in the Chancery and the ambassador's residence, one of which was a forged War Cabinet paper, artfully constructed by Victor Cavendish-Bentinck, the chairman of the Joint Intelligence Committee. This produced no results as CICERO had by now ceased his espionage. He and the other servants were thoroughly vetted by Dashwood who reported that the butler spoke a little English, but that none of the others was known to be able to read it and 'all the indications are against them being able to do so', which shows how thoroughly CICERO duped him. That the valet was clever, as one expert on the history of intelligence[19] has stated, cannot be in doubt. He also duped Nicholas Elliott, an MI6 officer based in Istanbul. 'That an illiterate and unprepossessing person such as Cicero could have had the technical expertise to photograph these documents seemed surprising,' Elliott later wrote. 'I remember him quite vividly from the times I had stayed with the Hugessons and he had laid out my clothes. So far as I could make out he did not speak more than a few words of English.'[20]

Dashwood also noted that the valet and two other servants regularly entered the ambassador's study and had access to his bedroom suite, and that Hugesson kept his working papers in a black box in his bedroom overnight. He carried its key with him, along with a key to a red circulation box in which papers were taken to and from the Chancery. It was all strong circumstantial evidence, in Dashwood's opinion, that the documents had been taken from one of the boxes while in the ambassador's residence, though Hugesson stoutly maintained that it was more likely to have happened on the train to or from Cairo.[21]

When Sir Alexander Cadogan, the permanent under-secretary at the Foreign Office, read Dashwood's report he wrote to Hugesson pointing out that documents in his possession were still being incorrectly handled so as to make it possible for an enemy agent to get hold of them. As one commentator has pointed out, such flouting of Foreign Office regulations should have drawn a tart rebuke from Cadogan, 'an official known for his acid tongue'.[22] Instead, the permanent under-secretary wrote mildly that he must ask Hugesson in future to do all his work in the Chancery, and not to take any papers to his residence. Hugesson complied, but by then the damage had been done.

It wasn't until the war had ended and more of the facts were known that Cadogan realised that the ambassador's behaviour had seriously endangered the country's security as well as the reputation of the Foreign Office. He confided in his diary that Snatch (Hugesson's nickname) should really be court-martialled; instead, on 28 August 1945, he sent Hugesson a severely worded, formal reprimand. This was never made public, and Hugesson remained at his post as ambassador to Belgium – where he had been appointed in September 1944 – until he retired on a full pension in 1947. For the remainder of his life – he died in 1971 – he blithely continued to deny he had done anything wrong, a stand in which he was no doubt encouraged by the low-key approach the Foreign Office had taken to his behaviour.

* * * * *

It was Allen Dulles, the Swiss Director of OSS, who provided
the first 'hard information'[23] that identified the Ankara leak-
age as coming from a source in the British embassy codenamed
CICERO. This intelligence originated from a German Foreign
Office official, Fritz Kolbe, who from August 1943 occasionally fed
Dulles German Foreign Office documents he had microfilmed.[24]
Kolbe, an anti-Nazi out to promote a compromise peace with the
Allies, sometimes visited Bern as a courier, and the documents he
delivered to Dulles over the Christmas holidays in 1943 included
the first three telegrams from Von Papen that summarised the early
photographed documents Moyzisch had shown him. On 1 January
1944 Dulles notified his colleagues in Washington that Von Papen
had obtained documents on which 'he clearly placed great value
and which, seemingly, were taken from the Zulu [British] Embassy
through a source he designated as Cicero', and that he had passed
this information to his MI6 counterpart in Bern, Count 'Fanny'
Vanden Heuval, for onward transmission to London.

However, on 10 January 1944 Dulles had to tell Washington and
London that Kolbe had been unable to identify who CICERO
was. Then, on 15 January 1944, President Roosevelt cabled
Churchill that the OSS had reported through their intelligence
sources that Von Papen had learnt that (1) a Turkish air base 'would
be ready by 15 February for receiving twenty United Nations air
squadrons and that in the event of these squadrons going there,
two programs called ACCOLADE and ANVIL[25] would be put
into effect and Allied submarines would be permitted to enter the
Black Sea', and (2) that a 'German agent secured British report
on Turkish-British relations'. This information, he told the Prime
Minister, 'comes from a good but not sure source. I am merely
passing it on to you for what it is worth.'

In a telegram drafted for him by the head of MI6, Churchill assured
the President that 'our respective Intelligence Services are closely collaborating on this subject' and that the leak would be thoroughly
investigated, but attempts to unravel what really happened had to
wait until the war ended and the principal players rounded up and
interrogated. Moyzisch was arrested when he arrived at Liverpool on
26 May 1945 en route for Germany aboard the SS *Drottningholm*.
He was dispatched to MI5's Camp 020, at Latchmere House, near

Richmond, and held there for several months for questioning, as was Schellenberg. Maria Molkenteller, the AmtVI translator of CICERO's documents, was also flown from Germany and questioned; and SIME's (Security Intelligence Middle East) Cairo interrogation of Moyzisch's secretary, Cornelia Kapp, which had taken place the previous year, was made available to Moyzisch's MI5 interrogators.

The reason for Kapp's defection is at least partly explained in a 'Footnote to Cicero' by Dorothy J. Heatts which was released onto the CIA website in 1994, though probably written many years earlier.[26] Its source is the American who helped Kapp escape to Cairo, and makes clear that she was not an Allied spy planted on Moyzisch, but simply someone desperate to return to the United States. To achieve this, her Ankara dentist agreed to put her in touch with a US Foreign Service officer who was another patient of his. When they met, Kapp told him she would feed information to the Americans in exchange for a guarantee that they would return her to the United States.

Though no such promise was forthcoming, she nevertheless began passing whatever intelligence she could find. But she was no spy and when, within a matter of weeks, Moyzisch arranged for her to visit her parents, all expenses paid, she feared she had been discovered and was in fact being returned to Germany for trial and possible execution. She panicked and demanded her contact get her out of the country immediately, and he agreed to help. Suitably disguised she hid for a week with two US embassy secretaries while arrangements were made to exfiltrate her to Cairo. However, when she arrived there 'it was rather a shock to her', as one of the summaries of her interrogations recorded, 'not to be received with open arms, but to be segregated and interrogated. She was in a very hysterical condition, and drugged herself lavishly with luminol. Finally she calmed down and gave some useful information about the organization and personalities of the SD in Ankara.'

The summaries of Kapp's interrogations reveal that when she defected she brought with her a number of telegrams between Ankara and Berlin that she had copied during her last two weeks at work, 'of which the most important refer to the CHURCHILL-ROOSEVELT-STALIN meeting, to Rumanian attempts to secure a separate peace, and to negotiations for Arab union.' She also had verbal information about Turkish neutrality pacts with Germany and Bulgaria, but overall her SIME interrogators assessed her information as being 'either too brief or too vague to be of major importance'. She also knew about 'the mysterious S.D. agent' called CICERO, and gave details of his telephone calls to Moyzisch and the code employed by them for their regular meetings, but her information on him was classed as 'tantalizingly meagre'. Once the Americans had extracted from her all that she knew, she was returned to the United States, where she was interned, and she later married, had children and settled in California.

Kapp's Cairo interrogations did not add much to MI5's knowledge of 'Operation Cicero', but what she had told SIME intelligence officers about Moyzisch's contact with the spy did force Moyzisch's hand. Up to that point he had categorically denied having any knowledge of espionage in the British embassy, and that all he wanted was to be reunited with his family as quickly as possible. But by August he was 'piping up well', according to one interrogation report after he was confronted with Kapp's evidence and he 'confessed to the Cicero affair which he states, convincingly, was more important from the point of view of results than the rest of his work in Turkey put together and which he evidently considers is as good as a rope round his neck.'[27]

He must therefore have been immensely relieved when he was returned to Germany – and his family – in October 1945, having told his interrogators what he knew: after first meeting CICERO at the embassy apartment where Jenke lived with his wife, he stated that he went to Jenke's bedroom to report. Jenke had told him that the man had previously worked as a servant of his, that his name was Ilja, and that his visit and offer to spy had been unsolicited. He had told Moyzisch to keep in touch with Ilja and to report immediately to the German ambassador. This Moyzisch did and was told by Von Papen that the necessary money would be available if the information proved worthwhile. A few days later Ilja had phoned Moyzisch and had arranged to visit him that evening, using the embassy's back door. When they met, Ilja had produced two undeveloped Leica films and stated his terms: 5,000 Turkish pounds per film and a salary of 15,000 Turkish pounds a month irrespective of whether he delivered any films. At that time £1 sterling equalled 4.8 Turkish pounds.[28]

The films were developed and shown to Von Papen who had cabled summaries of them on 3, 4, and 5 November to Von Ribbentrop, and had probably also authorised the initial payment in Turkish pounds. On 6 November Moyzisch flew to Berlin with all the material so it could be examined to see if it was genuine. The first two rolls of film, as listed in one MI5 report dated 8 August 1945, comprised a) a questionnaire in two parts drafted by Hugesson, headed respectively 'What I want to Know' and 'what the S. of S. [secretary of state, ie Anthony Eden] will want to know', with an annex headed 'Memorandum on the state of British preparations for war (dumps, communications, etc.) in Turkey on 21 October 1943'; b) a document dated 7 October and headed 'the Immediate Aims of British Policy towards Turkey – Brief for the Secretary of State'; and c) a document of the same date and headed 'Long Term British Policy towards Turkey – Brief for Secretary of State'.[29]

In Berlin Moyzisch had met Kaltenbrunner who had expressed his doubts that CICERO was genuine, but who had then berated Moyzisch for not ensuring Amt VI would take all the credit for the coup. He had not met Von Ribbentrop, who was out of Berlin, and the official he had met had insisted on keeping the films so they could be thoroughly examined, which caused a clash between the Foreign Ministry and the SD. Consequently, Moyzisch had been forbidden to show any further material to Von Papen, though it had been decided that Ilja's cover name, CICERO, should be retained. Moyzisch, he assured his interrogators, had never known Ilja's real name, which by August 1945 the Foreign Office had identified as being 'pretty certainly' Ilyas Bazna.

Back in Ankara, Moyzisch had faced the displeasure of both Jenke and Von Papen over the arrangements he had been forced to agree to in Berlin. He had resolved this by promising to show any future material to Von Papen provided Berlin was not told. His meetings with CICERO had been resumed after he had been instructed to accept CICERO's terms of payment. These had been increased after three weeks to 10,000 Turkish pounds per film, and the valet had also asked for a Leica camera. The two men had met frequently until March 1944 and Moyzisch had calculated that during this time he had been given between forty and fifty rolls of film, though sometimes one might just contain three or five photographs of a single document. The photographs, so CICERO had told him, had been taken in the morning, when the ambassador had been in his bathroom, and in the early afternoon when he had gone into town to play the piano.[30]

Because thumbs and fingers that appeared on several of the developed photographs, Moyzisch had thought CICERO probably did have an assistant in the embassy, and that Schellenberg had agreed with him on this point. CICERO had never seen the developed films, so had been unaware that any suspicions had been aroused by some of them. In December 1943 he had given Moyzisch the impressions of two keys which Moyzisch had sent to Berlin. The locksmith who had cut them had commented that 'in his experience of impressions of keys taken by criminals, he had never seen a neater job'. For obtaining the impressions, CICERO had been paid 50,000 Turkish pounds.

When asked by his interrogators if there had been any other penetrations of the British embassy, Moyzisch replied that in 1941 Dr Viktor Friede (the Abwehr's head of intelligence in Ankara at that time) had shown him a book of photographs and particulars of all the British embassy staff and that one of his contacts 'had obtained, through a man, a number of cinematograph films from the British embassy, which were of great interest to the Propaganda Ministry; these were transported from the British Embassy to the German embassy in a sack.' When asked why CICERO had stopped spying, 'Moyzisch states that this was fear of discovery. Throughout, Ilja was very nervous and scared he might be caught, but towards the end he was even more so than before, trembling violently whenever they met.'

* * * * *

To the great discomfort of the Foreign Office, well aware of the damage 'Operation Cicero' might have on its reputation, US Army intelligence officers in Germany were the first to interrogate Maria Molkenteller after an informer had told them she had worked for the SD. The Foreign Office asked 'what this woman knew' and urged that CICERO's activities should not be given any more publicity than was necessary. An MI6 officer even suggested the Americans be asked not to mention the matter in their report as it was purely a domestic matter. If they were, they ignored the request, and after their interrogation of Molkenteller they sent their report to MI5, and then released her into British custody.

Molkenteller seems to have had a retentive memory and was able to list the translated CICERO documents in some detail as well as corroborate the statements of other participants. According to her, CICERO had photographed the documents while Hugesson had been 'in the next room playing the piano' and that the ambassador 'liked to have him around' as CICERO was supposed to have had a fine voice. CICERO, she said, had photographed about 130-150 tel-egrams between the ambassador and Eden and Churchill, as well as such minutiae as a list of Christmas boxes, a salaries list, two personal letters from King George VI, and a report on the bad behaviour of a staff member who was going to have an illegitimate child.

Another report states that 'Molkenteller also disposed of the myth of CICERO's mastery of photographic technique – the photostats [*sic*], she says, showed many duplicates, and some of the manuscript notes were largely indecipherable.' An Amt VI colleague of Molkenteller, who ran the English desk, remarked that many of the documents were very dated and only of historical interest, though the ones concerning Anglo-Turkish relations were considered to be extremely valuable from the point of view of foreign policy.

Molkenteller's statement also confirmed that Bazna's book was not entirely fictitious when she told her interrogators 'that CICERO was in the habit of waiting in the dark in one or other of the less frequented side streets of Ankara where he was picked up by a German car driven by one of the Consuls. The car did not usually draw up for CICERO who had the knack of getting in it at walking pace. He would hand over what he had inside the car and would get out, again at walking pace, in some other unfrequented side street. They always changed the streets.'

There also seems to have been a basis of truth in the story that Moyzisch and Bazna were followed one night by a car, for Molkenteller said that she was told that in January 1944 there had been a near-collision between the German car and an English one, with the latter deliberately trying to drive into the former. It had been decided that the British were probably watching CICERO and he was told to lie low for several days.

* * * * *

Although Hugesson published his memoirs, *Diplomat in Peace and War*, in 1949 he made no mention of 'Operation Cicero'. It was an omission one commentator later noted by writing: '"A period of some difficulty followed" was how he described what his colleagues thought was the greatest breach of FO security prior to the Burgess and Maclean affair.',[31] and it was not until 15 January 1950 that the British public was made aware of what had happened, when The *Sunday Express* headlined a full-page article 'A War Spy in the British Embassy'. This revealed that a Belgian newspaper was publishing 'an astonishing story' based on Moyzisch's book which 'tells how in 1943 the Germans obtained vitally important Allied war secrets by paying £300,000 in sterling to the valet of the British ambassador in Turkey, Sir Hughe Knatchbull-Hugesson. In this way, it is said, they learned of the Moscow and Casablanca conference decisions, details of the bomber offensives, and plans for the final invasion of Europe. They also obtained the key to the British diplomatic code.'

The article included an interview with Hugesson who accepted that a leakage had occurred, but that the story had been exaggerated. He played down the whole incident, giving the impression that it was of no importance and of little consequence, which is no doubt how he perceived it. However, he was less sanguine about any adverse impression his own behaviour socially might have caused, and emphatically denied that he had accompanied his valet on the piano while CICERO sang, remarking this was 'absolute poppycock'.

The *Sunday Express* article prompted a question in the House of Commons and on 18 October 1950 Hansard records that the secretary of state for Foreign Affairs, Aneurin Bevin, was asked: 'in view of the fact that top secrets, including Operation OVERLORD, were stolen from our Embassy in Turkey and transmitted to the Germans, whether an enquiry has taken place; what has been the result; and what instructions had been issued to prevent a repetition.' Bevin replied that:

> … no such documents were actually stolen from His Majesty's Embassy during the war. But an inquiry into the occurrences to which the hon. member refers reveals that the Ambassador's valet succeeded in photographing a number of highly secret documents in the Embassy and selling the films to the Germans. He would not have been able to do this if the Ambassador had conformed to the regulations governing the custody of secret documents. New instructions have since been given to all concerned and other measures have been taken to prevent such leakages occurring again.

This did not satisfy the questioner:

> Is it not a fact that the statement published in the book [by Moyzisch] in which this question arose caused a good deal of public anxiety; and if it was the case that the Overlord plans were in fact not stolen, why did not the Foreign Office issue a denial of the statement?'

Mr Bevin:

> The actual document was not stolen. I admitted that photographs were taken, which is the same thing.

It might seem surprising that Bevin failed to deny categorically that CICERO ever had access to the Casablanca conference decisions or details of the bomber offensives, much less to the OVERLORD invasion plans, but it was not known at the time – nor is it now – exactly what CICERO photographed, as the prints sent to Berlin were apparently never recovered. Perhaps it was a case of the less said the better, though the Foreign Office would have known that Hugesson never received any detailed information about OVERLORD as the operation was one of the most closely guarded secrets of the war.

Luckily, for the Foreign Office and Hugesson no one asked what action had been taken against the ambassador in question. However, the film *Five Fingers*, which repeated the myth that OVERLORD secrets had been betrayed, did spur Hugesson to try and make sure he would die with his reputation intact, the laws of libel, and a Foreign Office keen to protect its own, no doubt giving him the necessary protection while he was alive.

However, some myths refuse to die and Hugesson's obituary in The *Daily Telegraph* of 23 March 1971 stated that CICERO had made microfilms of the Normandy invasion plans which he had extracted from his employer's safe, while *The Times* obituary of the same date was sufficiently unclear to make it necessary for a Foreign Office official to write a supplementary obituary. Then, during the 1970s and 1980s, writers on espionage – beguiled perhaps by new revelations of the brilliant successes of British wartime strategic deception – started promoting the view that there was more to 'Operation Cicero' than met the eye, and that the valet had in fact been under British control all along. This was officially denied, but it nevertheless muddied the waters enough to cast doubt on the unpalatable truth that the British had been caught with their pants down. Perhaps this is why the authorities kept the relevant files under lock and key for such an inordinate amount of time.

ENVOI

A summary of 'Operation Cicero', prepared in 1979 for the fourth volume of F.H. Hinsley's official history, *British Intelligence in the Second World War*, pulled no punches on what happened: 'The possible damage to the Allied cause by the CICERO leakage must be considered under two heads: military and diplomatic, and it cannot be emphasised too strongly that the potential damage in both fields was enormous'.

This, in rather cooler language, the official history acknowledged when it was published in 1990, but concluded that it was unlikely that the leakage did any great damage to Allied interests. However, no mention was made of the summary's remark that Moyzisch insinuated that 'the Germans became aware that there was no genuine threat of an Allied move into the Balkans. If this particular statement is true – and it rests on an entry in Jodl's diary [Jodl was head of the OKW's Operation Staff] – then perhaps CICERO earned all the money the Germans paid him.'

The summary did not expand on this statement, nor did the official history mention Jodl's diaries, and it was left for others to comment. One historian pointed out that in February 1944 Jodl 'had remarked in his diary under the heading "Results from Cicero": Overlord = Major invasion from Britain'; and added that the controversial historian David Irving had found intelligence summaries from CICERO in the German archives, and that some mentioned the codeword OVERLORD.[32] Another wrote that in the same month, February 1944, Jodl also noted in his diary that intelligence from CICERO indicated that a British offensive in the eastern Mediterranean was no longer imminent. The British were merely posturing while really preparing for an invasion of northern France the following spring, and that Jodl's analysis implied that troops in the area could be moved and used on other fronts.[33]

In fact, on 13 February, the German High Command (OKW) had indicated that it wanted to move two divisions in the Balkans either to France, to help repel the upcoming invasion wherever it might land, or to Italy where the Germans were still stubbornly defending the northern part of the country. Two weeks later the German intelligence evaluation service, *Fremde Heere West*, made clear that Turkey's refusal to enter the war meant that neither the Mediterranean nor the Balkans were currently threatened. This assessment was soon reinforced by the C-in-C of Army Group F in the Balkans, Field Marshal Maximilian Von Weiches, who agreed that any Allied action in Thrace or Turkey was most unlikely.

Hitler knew all about CICERO, and was apparently kept regularly informed on the intelligence the valet provided. Though the Führer was highly sceptical about all intelligence reports, this did not prevent him, and Von Ribbentrop, from using them to reassure the leaders of Hungary and Bulgaria that they were safe from any Allied offensive, with Von Ribbentrop pointing out that Ankara's resistance to British pressures to join the Allies lessened still further the likelihood of any attack. Also, on one occasion at least, Hitler used CICERO's intelligence to brief his generals, telling his Army chief of staff on 27 December 1943 that the British wanted to force Turkey into the war by 15 February.

The information CICERO provided on the Teheran Conference was also used for German propaganda as another extremely successful spy, Rygor Slowikowski, related in his book[34]: 'Do you know the terms of the agreement reached between Roosevelt, Churchill and Stalin at the Teheran Conference?' he asked the head of OSS, General Donovan, in 1944, adding that 'It is well known that the Germans, via Radio Wanda, have been broadcasting to our troops at Monte Cassino [in Italy] telling them not to fight for the Allies who sold Poland to Stalin at Teheran!'

This is surely evidence that CICERO's intelligence did influence those controlling German strategy. Equally clear is its influence on Von Papen who made good use of it to warn off the Turks from entering the war. By doing so he probably delayed their country from severing relations with Germany, and thus maintained for a few extra precious weeks vital Turkish exports for the German war machine.

Great damage to Allied interests CICERO may not have inflicted; damage he certainly did, not only to the Allied war effort but to the mutual trust that governed post-war Anglo-American intelligence co-operation.

NOTES

1. Bazna, E., *I was Cicero* (London, 1962); Moyzisch, L., *Operation Cicero* (London, 1950); Schellenberg, W., *The Schellenberg Memoirs* (London, 1956); Von Papen, F., *Memoirs* (London, 1952).
2. Moyzisch, *op. cit.* p. 31.
3. Moyzisch *op. cit.* p. 40.
4. Schellenberg op. cit. p. 388.
5. Moyzisch *op. cit.* p. 54.
6. Moyzisch later wrote that Von Papen decided to use the Roman orator as

Bazna's codename because 'his documents are so very, very eloquent', but Von Papen does not mention this in his memoirs.

7. Moyzisch *op. cit*, p.100.

8. Moyzisch *op. cit*, p.207.

9. The Cairo Conference was held in two parts, from 23 to 26 November and from 3 to 7 December 1943. The Teheran Conference, at which Stalin, Roosevelt and Churchill met for the first time, took place from 28 November to 1 December.

10. Schellenberg says the city did receive a warning but there was not much the defences could do to stop the raid. See Schellenberg *op. cit.* p.396.

11. Moyzisch *op. cit*, p.167.

12. Moyzisch does not mention supplying Bazna with a revolver, and in his memoir the spy never mentions it again. It was probably introduced into the narrative to spice it up.

13. The film rights to Moyzisch's book were bought by Darryl F. Zanuck for Twentieth Century Fox. Directed by Joseph Mankiewicz and starring James Mason, *Five Fingers* appeared in 1952. It proved very popular, but spread the myth that CICERO had passed the plans of OVERLORD to the Germans. Mankiewicz thought Bazna 'the most obvious-looking villain I have ever met', though this comment appears to have been made solely for the purposes of publicising the film.

14. Wires, R., *The Cicero Spy Affair* (London, 2009) p.188.

15. West, N. (ed.), *The Guy Liddell Diaries, Vol 1* (Taylor & Francis, 2005) pp.184 & 187. The editor notes that Bazna was involved in these early incidents, but there is no evidence of this.

16. FO 370/2930.

17. Douglas, W. & Wright, R., *Combat and Command: The Story of an Airman in two World Wars* (London, 1966) pp.543–44, quoted in Wires *op. cit.* p.52.

18. West, N. (ed.), *The Guy Liddell Diaries, Vol II* (Taylor & Francis, 2005) pp.256, 38 & 163.

19. Doerries, R., *Hitler's Last Chief of Foreign Intelligence: Allied Interrogations of Walter Schellenberg* (Portland, OR, 2003) p.369, n. 126.

20. Elliott, N., *Never Judge a Man by his Umbrella* (Salisbury, 1991) pp.136–37. Quite why Elliott thought being unprepossessing had any connection with technical ability is hard to understand. It is equally hard to avoid concluding that his comments, along with Dashwood's, that the valet was 'too stupid to make a good spy', reflect the innate superiority of so many upper-class Englishmen at that time. Hugesson was a typical example, and it could have caused a catastrophe.

21. Leakages were obviously common in Turkey. In December 1943 the US State Department informed the Foreign Office of one about the Cairo Conference, which it reported as coming from the Hungarian Legation in Stockholm. Though the British embassy in Ankara suggested this was because of a breach in Turkish ciphers, ULTRA intelligence indicated that the Turkish foreign minister was keeping the representatives of several other countries – including China, Yugoslavia, and Greece – fully in the picture on the progress of his country's negotiations with the British.

22. Baxter, C., 'Forgeries and Spies: The Foreign Office and the Cicero Case' in *Journal of Intelligence and National Security* (Vol 23, December 2008) p.815. The author is indebted to this article for its succinct summary of the various minutes and memoranda concerning security at the Ankara embassy.

23. The phrase used in a detailed summary in TNA KV6/8 of 'Operation Cicero' written in 1979 for the fourth volume of F.H. Hinsley's official history, *British Intelligence in the Second World War* (London, 1990). What follows, unless otherwise annotated, comes from the same source, which was released into The National Archives in 2005.

24. Kolbe approached the British in Bern first, but was turned down. Dulles gave him the codename 'George Wood' and he became one of the war's top agents for the OSS, delivering a large number of important German Foreign Office documents. See Wires, R., *The Cicero Spy Affair* (London, 2009) p.128, and Delattre, L., *A Spy at the Heart of the Third Reich* (London, 2003) p.134.

25. ACCOLADE was the codename for an Allied amphibious assault on Rhodes and other islands that never took place. ANVIL was an early codename for the Allied landings in the south of France. It was launched in August 1944 under the codename DRAGOON.

26. 'Footnote to Cicero' released onto the CIA website, 18 September 1995. See www.cia.gov/library/center-for-the-study-of-intelligence and search for Cicero.

27. KV2/169.

28. Schellenberg's interrogation in Camp 020 confirms that Moyzisch obtained the Turkish currency for CICERO with forged British notes the SD supplied. These were part of a RSHA operation codenamed BERNHARD. The original plan to wreck the British economy by disseminating this false currency was cancelled and the notes were used instead for various purposes including support for intelligence operations abroad.

29. Later documents included details of the meeting at the first part of the Cairo Conference in November 1943 between Anthony Eden and the Turkish foreign minister, and Operation SATURN, a plan to prepare Turkish airfields for Allied fighter squadrons. Churchill discussed SATURN with a Turkish delegation headed by President Inonu at the second part of the Cairo Conference in December 1943 before drafting the plan for the British chiefs of staff on 6 December. A copy of it was given the same day to Inonu and Hugesson. The substance of this document was cabled to Berlin by Von Papen on 14 December 1943.

30. Moyzisch's statement is confirmed by an anecdotal but first-hand source, Nicholas Elliott. However, Elliott, a wartime MI6 officer, may well have had access to summaries of Moyzisch's interrogation before writing his chapter on CICERO for his book, *Never Judge a Man by his Umbrella* (London, 1991) p.139. Hugesson's draft diaries, held in the Churchill Archives, Churchill College, Cambridge (KNAT 1/14), make frequent reference to his love of music and his piano playing, but do not mention keeping a room in Ankara to practise.

31. Denniston, R., *Churchill's Secret War* (London, 1997) p.129. In fact, Hugesson's draft diaries make it clear that he was referring to the very difficult negotiations to persuade Turkey to enter the war.

32. West, N., *Unreliable Witness* (London, 1984) p.140. If this is so, the summaries have been lost.

33. Wires *op. cit.* p.161. By March Soviet advances deemed it necessary to keep the two divisions in place, anyway.

34. Slowikowski, R., *In The Secret Service: The Lighting of the Torch* (London, 1988) pp.242–43.

5

The Spy who Made Porridge

The contribution of Polish intelligence to the Allied war effort during the Second World War is not as widely known, or appreciated, as it should be. Yet the Poles were the first to break the German Enigma machine cipher that gave the Allies such a vital edge over the Axis; the first to report the holocaust; and the first to give details of the V-1 flying bomb and the V-2 rocket that could have brought Britain to its knees in 1944. Around 1,500 Poles also played an important part in the French Resistance that included, as this chapter describes, the spy ring known as Agency Africa. One of the war's most successful espionage operations, it made a vital contribution to the success of the Anglo-American landings in North Africa (codenamed TORCH) on 8 November 1942.

'The *scale* of Agency Africa should be emphasised,' one commentator has noted. 'On the eve of Torch, its network, organised into intelligence officers, outpost commanders, agents, associates and informants, constituted a vast and complex human pyramid, two radio stations, and its own counter-intelligence outpost.'[1]

Albeit without the knowledge of the spy ring's Polish leader – a highly regarded 45-year-old professional intelligence officer, Major Mieczyslaw Slowikowski – the information the agency sent to the Polish High Command's II Bureau in London was automatically passed to MI6, which directed the agency's activities via the bureau. But it is typical of the scant attention the agency received after the war that it is not mentioned in either the relevant British official history on intelligence[2] or the authorised history of MI6;[3] and though President Roosevelt's personal representative in North Africa, Robert D. Murphy, expressed his gratitude at the time to Slowikowski and his network for their contribution to the planning of TORCH, he does not mention this in his book, *Diplomat Among Warriors* (New York, 1964), which describes his wartime role in French North Africa.

While Slowikowski's personal contribution to TORCH was recognised – by the Americans with the Legion of Merit, by the British with the OBE (Order of the British Empire), and by the Poles with the Gold Cross Merit with Swords – after the war he was obliged to continue working until he was 70, as a metal polisher in a British factory. This does not reflect well on those who could have ensured that such a courageous individual was better treated by a country that owed him so much. Regrettably, he was not alone. Despite their contribution in deciphering German Enigma traffic, both of the Poles who ran the Enigma interception outposts in France and Algiers died in obscurity in Britain after the war, one of them while living on national assistance. It is therefore ironic that on visiting London in early 1943 Slowikowski was told by Commander Wilfred Dunderdale, MI6's liaison officer with Polish intelligence, that when peace came, if he'd been British, he would never have had to work for the rest of his life, such was his contribution to the war effort. A further irony is that, while running Agency Africa, Slowikowski notionally became quite a rich man with the investments he made of the funds the French government-in-exile gave him to run the agency.

That Slowikowski remained in the shadows after the war was no doubt partly due to the veil of secrecy behind which he ran his network during it. He used a variety of aliases and his true identity was known only to a handful of his closest associates. His cover was above reproach, and the extreme caution with which he worked reflected his disciplined, methodical approach. Little wonder that he chose 'Rygor' – it means 'rigour' in Polish – as his *nom de guerre*. But like all good agents he knew when to break the rules and make them work to his advantage, as he did by having his wife and young son living with him. Whoever heard of a spy travelling with his family? Even so, as he openly admitted, he was lucky, very lucky indeed.

Lack of documentation was another reason the spy ring and its leader remained almost unknown for decades. Practically all the archive of the Polish General Staff's II Bureau was destroyed at the end of the war to avoid it falling into the hands of the Stalin-backed Polish government. Some of it was handed over to the British authorities 'on trust',[4] but subsequently disappeared, and only one or two of Rygor's original signals survive from the period before the TORCH landings. However, he retained the registers in which he listed the numbered signals sent to, and received from, London, and briefly noted their contents. It was these registers that became the factual backbone of his history of the network, *In the Secret Service: The Lighting of the Torch*, which was published in Polish in 1977. An English edition was delayed eleven years, ostensibly because of the secrecy that surrounded the breaking of the German Enigma machine cipher with which Slowikowski had been indirectly connected, but more probably because of the reluctance of the authorities to make public how shabbily he had been treated.

Though few traces remain in British archives of the original intelligence Slowikowski supplied, John Herman, in his afterword[5] for Slowikowski's book, writes that some of Agency Africa's information can be traced in the Foreign Office, War Office and cabinet papers in The National Archives at Kew: 'They contain numerous examples of intelligence sent from North Africa where the precise source is not given, but attributed to "reliable" or other sources, which appears to tie up with Agency Africa's messages.' But, as he points out, some historians take the view that 'if there is no document, it never happened', making it doubly difficult for the agency's achievements to be given the recognition they deserved, even if this had been genuinely desired by anyone, which apparently it wasn't.

To add insult to injury, for many years America's OSS (Office of Strategic Services, the wartime equivalent of the CIA) continued to take much of the kudos for the intelligence Slowikowski's network had provided. Rather late in the day this misconception was corrected when the official history of the OSS was published in 1976. This states that the 'pre-Torch and Torch activities in North Africa received special attention in this volume because they were the main reason the OSS survived. Without this evidence to the JCS [Joint Chiefs of Staff] of its value, it would most probably have been dismembered.'[6]

* * * * *

Following the defeat of Poland in October 1939, and then its division and occupation by the USSR and Nazi Germany, about 45,000 Polish troops escaped to France, and a Polish government-in-exile was formed in Paris. By June 1940 the numbers had increased to around 80,000 men. They were commanded by General Sikorski, and included elements of the Polish Air Force. However, they had still not been properly equipped when the Germans invaded France in May 1940, and suffered heavy losses during the fighting that followed. When, on 16 June, Marshal Pétain, the new leader of France, called for an armistice, Sikorski refused to accept it and announced that his forces would continue to fight with their British allies. Between 20,000 and 35,000 Polish troops, along with the Polish government-in-exile, escaped to Britain from Dunkirk and other French ports. Others crossed into neutral Switzerland where they were interned, and some, especially those who had close ties with France, joined the Resistance.

Under the terms of the armistice, signed on 22 June 1940, Pétain was allowed a small lightly equipped standing army on mainland France, but the air force was demobilised. The French Navy, the fourth largest in the world, remained intact but was confined to various ports where it was to be decommissioned. The Germans occupied northern and western France down to neutral Spain, roughly totalling two-thirds of the country, and the Atlantic coastline was declared a military zone. The rest, known as the free zone, was divided from the occupied zone by the demarcation line that ran laterally across the country from just east of Tours.

Pétain and his government were based in the town of Vichy, which gave the collaborationist regime its name. On paper it governed both zones as well as the three French North African colonies, Tunisia, Algeria and French Morocco. Under the terms of the armistice Pétain had complete executive power in the free zone, but the occupied zone was subject to the German authorities based in Paris. This was the theory; in practice, Pétain became no more than a puppet dictator where the Germans increasingly pulled the strings, though initially his government strove to keep a degree of independence. For instance, it maintained diplomatic relations with the United States, and other neutral nations, and in espionage matters it executed or incarcerated German and Allied agents with equal impartiality.

After the fall of France, a small group of Polish army officers, headed by Slowikowski, started an escape network to Britain for stranded Polish personnel. By September 1940 the organisation had acquired a radio and codes to communicate with the Polish General Staff's II Bureau in London. On 16 September it reported that this new clandestine organisation was based at Marseille, where special units were producing exit visas (in the prefectures) and visas (in the foreign consulates) for those wishing to escape. It wanted to start intelligence operations in France, and preparatory steps had already been taken in this direction, but it needed instructions as well as money and technical assistance. The II Bureau replied positively and nominated Rygor's deputy, Major Wincenty Zarembski, alias 'Tudor', as chief of intelligence in France while Rygor was appointed head of evacuation.

Right from the start, one of the organisation's biggest problems was to prevent it being infiltrated by German agents. On one occasion a suspected German informer, posing as a Polish artillery officer who had escaped from a German POW camp, was requesting quick evacuation. However, a friend of the artillery officer knew he had died in the camp, and told Rygor that the man could not be genuine. The two were brought together, but neither recognised the other. Furthermore, though the man spoke fluent Polish, he did so with a slight foreign accent; and when it was found that his identity card had been tampered with – the card was genuine, but the stamp on the photograph was forged – it was established beyond doubt that the man was an imposter.

Luckily the organisation was not without friends in the local French administration. One of them, Marcel Dubois, the anti-Nazi deputy *commissaire* for public security in Marseille, was particularly helpful, and did not hesitate to offer his co-operation when needed. At an arranged time he sent a 'taxi' to take the man – and two of Rygor's intelligence officers who pretended they were also being evacuated – to the demobilisation camp, through which all evacuees passed. The road to the camp was heavily wooded and close to a rocky coastline with high cliffs. The 'taxi' stopped, the man was shot and his body thrown over a nearby cliff, Rygor knowing that if it was ever found Dubois himself would officially investigate the circumstances of the man's death. Such swift executions, and they were not infrequent, were known as 'wet jobs'.

Not long afterwards, Rygor heard through his Polish secret service contacts in occupied France that Dubois had been blacklisted as an anti-collaborationist. He warned the *commissaire*, who obtained a transfer to a similar post in Rabat before the authorities could move against him, and in due course was able to show his gratitude for Rygor's prompt intervention.

Rygor soon found that the Germans, acting through their Armistice Commission with its paraphernalia of Gestapo agents and informers, were making it all but impossible for Polish troops to escape to England or neutral Spain by sea. Apart from finding their way across the Pyrenees into Spain, which many did, the only escape route left was to France's North African colonies. Despite the disruption of war, passengers and freight continued to flow between French Mediterranean ports and French North Africa, and Rygor decided to try and smuggle escapees aboard the ships plying these routes. He therefore employed one of his men, Lieutenant Kiersnowski, to fraternise with seamen in Marseille, and he found them perfectly amenable to taking stowaways, and a price of 100–300 francs – around £25–75 in today's money – per person was agreed.

Rygor wrote later of the hazards involved, describing how, in the dead of night, Kiersnowski collected the escapees from an assembly point and took them to where small boats were waiting to take them to the ship. To avoid detection by the port police, this was approached from the seaward side with the escapees boarding by rope ladders. They were then taken to their hideouts, where they had to remain while the boat was at sea and in the port. The number of escapees varied but there were often around forty.

> The entire operation had to be effected quickly, in complete silence and under cover of darkness. The hideouts were very uncomfortable, usually in those parts seldom visited by the ship's officers, e.g. coal bunkers, boiler rooms, etc. Great physical stamina was required to remain constantly in the same place in a foul atmosphere and tremendous heat … The effort in boarding such a large group can be imagined.[7]

To handle the escapees, a series of outposts in North African ports had to be formed to organise them and send them to safe houses. They were then taken to Casablanca in Morocco, as it was thought to be the safest port from which to smuggle the evacuees to Gibraltar. Due to the distances involved this was no easy task. Nor was it a simple matter to transport the stowaways between Tunisia and Algeria to Morocco, as the borders between the three countries were guarded and it was necessary to have a special travel permit.

Despite these difficulties Rygor managed to dispatch members of his escape organisation to Tunis, Algiers, Oran and Casablanca, and they reported back that the local authorities in these ports were more amenable than on mainland France and that it should be possible to shelter stowaways and eventually evacuate them. By February 1941 several hundred soldiers had taken this route before the escape line was discovered and closed down. However, between June 1940 and May 1941 the organisation helped nearly 3,000 men escape to England to join the Polish forces there, a considerable achievement.

* * * * *

With Rygor's escape organisation in place in North Africa by early 1941, Zarembski ('Tudor') suggested to him, after being asked by London for information about the area, that he should form an intelligence network there. Rygor agreed, and on 1 May 1941 London nominated him its chief and ordered him to move to Algiers as soon as possible. It indicated that the network would be mostly employed obtaining military intelligence, identifying Vichy French units, military garrisons and personnel of major importance, though once started the agency supplied political and economic intelligence as well.

Covering so vast a land mass was a huge task, as it stretched from Dakar on the west coast of Africa to the western borders of Libya. But Rygor had an exceptional talent for making the right contacts in the right places and using them to his advantage, and he and his secret service colleagues already had, or soon acquired, influential connections amongst the Polish communities that had sprung up in French North Africa. This social network apart, Rygor was also helped by anti-collaborationists working for the Vichy authorities; by the various embryonic resistance movements that slowly began to emerge; and by American diplomatic and intelligence organisations before and after the United States entered the war in December 1941.

The agency's work was made easier by the fact that bribery in North Africa was commonplace – 'for a bit of money you can buy anyone in Morocco,' the head of the Gestapo there remarked[8] – so it was often possible to buy your way out of trouble. Initially, Rygor was provided with 500,000 francs, but later money became a constant cause for concern. As he pointed out, too many espionage rings were compromised by 'dubious financial transactions. The disposal of money in the Secret Service must, therefore, be effected very carefully and with great skill. This is a cardinal point.'[9]

To operate properly in French North Africa, and to move between the three countries, it was essential for Rygor to arrive there legally. He managed to acquire a forged French passport in the name of Stawikowski, an alias under which he was working in France, but he also needed the necessary entry visa, which proved difficult to come by. The Polish intelligence officers who were to accompany him fared better and had the necessary social connections. One had no trouble getting to Algeria, as General Weygand – who was shortly to become the Vichy government's delegate general in North Africa – was an old family friend. The contacts of another, who was to work in Casablanca, provided him with a genuine French passport; and a third was married to a Breton countess who had relatives in Algiers.

Eventually, Rygor's wife, Sophie, solved his visa problem by suggesting she write to the wife of *Commissaire* Dubois, expressing their wish to escape the harsh living conditions in Marseille and to join them in Rabat. This discreet hint received a prompt and positive reply, and before long Rygor had his visa, signed by Dubois. With the *commissaire*'s name now behind him, Rygor also managed to obtain the necessary paperwork for his family who were to follow later. On 19 July 1941 he sailed for Algiers with one of his secret service colleagues, a journalist called Count Henry Lubienski (*nom de guerre* 'Banuls'), who had obtained a visa in order to research a book, and had with him some useful letters of introduction.

* * * * *

Algiers at that time was a hotbed of intrigue and espionage. The spies of the German and Italian Armistice Commissions, backed by their consulates, were everywhere. Nevertheless, Weygand, who was no friend of the Germans or the Italians – or the English for that matter – was determined to maintain a greater degree of independence for the North African colonies than was possible for mainland France, though Rygor doubted if Weygand could for long resist German pressure, or the demands of Pétain, to introduce collaborationist policies.

After the Royal Navy's bombardment of the French fleet at Mersel-Kébir (Oran) in July 1940 – to prevent it falling into German hands – and the abortive attack by British and Gaullist forces on Dakar in September 1940, the British were universally loathed in French North Africa and had no diplomatic representation there.

The Americans, on the other hand, were well liked. As well as maintaining diplomatic relations with the Vichy government, they were strongly represented diplomatically in French North Africa, where their policy was to support the colonies to maintain their independence from the Germans. They had a Consulate General at Algiers and Casablanca, and consulates in Oran and Tunis, and their representation was further strengthened in mid-1941 when a dozen diplomatically accredited vice-consuls were posted to the US consulates in Algeria, Morocco and Tunisia.

These new diplomats were responsible to President Roosevelt's personal envoy to North Africa, Robert Murphy, who in February 1941 had signed a commercial agreement with Weygand. Under this accord the role of the twelve vice-consuls was to ensure that US aid shipments to French North Africa were not diverted to the Axis, but their true purpose was to gather military intelligence for the Office of Co-ordinator of Information (COI), which became the OSS in June 1941. The vice-consuls were known as Roosevelt's 'Twelve Apostles';[10] and it is an interesting fact that the American president had already identified North Africa as the most likely initial landing place for Allied forces to reconquer Europe and defeat Germany, and was making early preparations for such an operation even though the United States was still neutral.

The Poles, too, were well liked for fighting so tenaciously alongside the French, and were at first given a degree of freedom by the French North African authorities. But the political and military situation was constantly in flux, and Rygor knew that caution and prudence were the watchwords by which he must work. He decided the more important centres such as Algiers and Oran would be targeted first by his intelligence teams, with Tunisia, Constantine, Morocco and Dakar being covered later. Finding the right French commanders for these espionage outposts was crucial if all the military bases were to be properly monitored. Once this was achieved, 'then the network would spread its antennae into the main railway centres, mining districts, industry and agriculture until it covered all the military and economic life of French North Africa'.[11]

How all the intelligence gathered was to be transmitted to London could have posed a problem for Rygor. But before leaving for North Africa he had learnt that a clandestine Franco-Polish wireless cell near Nîmes in southern France, codenamed 'Cadix',[12] had opened an outpost in Algiers, codenamed 'Kouba' after the villa in which it was based. 'Cadix' deciphered German Enigma radio traffic, transmitting the results to London, and Rygor was ordered to use 'Kouba' to forward his intelligence to 'Cadix' for onward transmission to London.

To facilitate this process, Rygor moved into the same hotel as Major Maksymilian Ciezki,[13] alias 'Mathew', who ran 'Kouba', and they soon established a secure routine for exchanging radio messages. The first one from London required Rygor to report on the anti-aircraft defences in French North Africa; what war materials were being shipped to Germany; and the condition of the railway system in Algeria. He was also asked whether an outpost had been formed in Dakar and if a two-way radio set (called a 'hurdy-gurdy' by the Poles) could be established there.

Rygor thought some of these requests unreasonable, and his exasperation increased when the following morning he decoded another signal requesting him to report on the condition of the French battleship *Richelieu*, anchored in Dakar harbour and crippled by a recent British carrier air attack. He was to send London the thickness of armour on her gun turrets, the calibre of her guns, the position and armoury of the local coastal defences, and what armoured vehicles, if any, were in the immediate area! Not knowing that Polish intelligence in London was receiving its orders from MI6, Rygor was baffled by this request. He assumed that at least some of the queries must be of British origin – in fact, the September 1940 Anglo-French attack on Dakar was being planned – but he was astonished that II Bureau had so little inkling of the difficulties facing him. 'I had only been here for five days, hadn't been able to begin work, and was not even certain whether it would be possible at all. Dakar was over three thousand kilometres away, accessible only by air, and to those holding special French permits.'[14]

Even if the agency had somehow acquired this information in time, it is doubtful if the *Richelieu*'s powerful guns, which helped repulse the Anglo-French forces, could have been neutralised. However, by the autumn of 1942 Rygor had found a suitable agent for Dakar, an elderly Frenchman codenamed 'Albert', a First World War veteran with extensive military knowledge. He was able to supply much of the intelligence MI6 was continuing to request, including the disposition of the port's defences, the morale of the French sailors, and the ammunition supplies and equipment of the ships in the harbour. He also gave a detailed description of the *Richelieu* – a continuing concern for the British Admiralty – and told the interesting story that by the time the Anglo-French expedition had been withdrawn in September 1940 the battleship had had only enough 15-inch ammunition for one more salvo, after which she would have been the proverbial sitting duck …

* * * * *

On 31 July 1941, his tenth day in Algiers, Rygor set Agency Africa on a proper footing. He had already appointed two intelligence officers, putting Lubienski ('Banuls') in charge of Oran and giving Lieutenant Gordon, alias 'René', who had previously run Rygor's evacuation post in Oran, the responsibility for Algiers. Now the three of them sat down in Rygor's hotel room with a bottle of wine to thrash out how the spy ring was to work. Both 'Banuls' and 'René' were novices at espionage, so Rygor started by telling them the first cardinal rule: no written notes, especially no names and addresses, as this could expose the whole network; they had to learn to memorise such details, and they had to hammer this point into all the agents they employed. Secondly, no female agents, not because he thought them in any way inferior to men as spies, nor was he against women – 'on the contrary … But when men and women work together, sooner or later a physical attraction may develop between two agents. This could produce jealousy amongst the others which in turn, could cause unnecessary conflict and friction in work which should otherwise run smoothly.'[15] Thirdly, real names were never to be used and agents were to avoid contact with one another, reports and other documents being passed by a third person who would act as a 'post box'. This person would know nothing about the spy ring, but would merely receive material from an unknown person identified by a password, who would then hand it to another unknown person identified by a second password.

Rygor also emphasised that, as it was a Polish network, only Polish methods of work would be employed; only Poles were be appointed intelligence officers, who would be directly responsible to Rygor; and only they would know his identity. Whenever an agent was accepted, after a probationary period he would be given an agency number that would be known only to London and Rygor, never to the agent. It was to be made clear to agents, who came from all walks of life, that they were working for France

against Nazi Germany, and they had to be ideologically motivated – only later were some put on the payroll. They would all
be French citizens living legally in the colonies, though later some
non-French individuals were employed. However, known Gaullist
supporters were not to be recruited, as this might alert the French
authorities who were extremely hostile towards de Gaulle, and
their hostility might endanger the whole network. Also, agents
were not to admit any connection with the British, 'as they are
hated here'.

The exact details of what agents were expected to discover about
the French armed services were also agreed before Rygor ended
the conference by giving his two officers their orders: 'René' was
to locate and reconnoitre all military garrisons in Algeria, while
'Banuls' was to find a suitable 'post box' and start recruiting agents
for the Oran department – from where he soon provided interesting details of a military hydroplane base, and the coastal defences
around Oran and Mers-el-Kébir. All intelligence was to be passed
to London in summary form by radio, the full reports being taken
by courier to Zarembski ('Tudor') on the mainland, who would
forward them to London via Madrid.

On 8 August the agency's naval expert, Lieutenant Jekiel
('Doctor'), arrived from Marseille, en route for Casablanca, though
tragically he never got there. His first assignment was to keep a
watch on the port of Algiers, and the shipping movements in and
out of it, before reporting to Rygor each evening at 8 p.m. By the
end of August, when Rygor's records showed that sixty messages
had been transmitted to London and sixteen had been received,
the spy ring was fully operational in Algiers and Oran, and had
begun answering some of London's more reasonable queries. For
example, when a puzzled British Admiralty wanted to know the
origins of merchant ships whose names began with 'Saint', it was
soon discovered that 'Saint' identified them as Allied vessels requi-
sitioned by the Vichy government. The Admiralty would also have
been grateful for the agency's information about the French fleet's
flagship, the cruiser *Dunkerque*. This modern warship had survived
the British attack at Mers-el-Kébir. So three days later she was
attacked again, this time by British torpedo aircraft, and sank in
shallow water.

The letters of introduction 'Banuls' had brought with him proved
invaluable. One of them introduced him to a local anti-Vichy

government official who agreed to co-operate with the agency, and supply the names of reliable recruits in Algiers and Oran. Another helped Rygor obtain a meeting with the head of the local Polish community,[16] an elderly businessman-lawyer who had good connections with the local administration and the police. By a stroke of luck that seemed to happen so often to Rygor, the businessman was seeking a partner to provide capital to establish a porridge factory, and at the end of July a meeting between them was arranged. The businessman told him the firm was to be called Floc-Av (an acronym for flakes of oats, though the porridge was actually made from barley) and that the necessary machinery and raw materials were available. It would be, the businessman enthused, the first of its kind in French North Africa, would be sold through local chemists, and, most importantly, had received the blessing of the authorities. The capital he needed from Rygor was 100,000 francs.

The idea attracted the Pole. With luck, he reasoned, it would give him the cover he required to remain in Algiers, and would establish him locally as a businessman of substance as well as giving him the freedom of movement he needed. Nevertheless, he deliberately hesitated, saying that his stay in Algiers was only temporary, and not having a permanent residence permit made it difficult for him to come to a decision. The businessman rose to the bait and immediately replied that his connections in Algiers would ensure that this small matter could be satisfactorily resolved. This vital point agreed, Rygor shook hands on the deal, knowing the money involved was a small price to pay for such suitable cover. Later, rather more reluctantly, he also agreed to invest in a pig farm, as the animals could be fed on the waste from the production of the porridge that would otherwise have cost money to dispose of. As the farm was sited close to Maison Blanche airfield, where all incoming aircraft for North Africa had to land, Rygor even found this a useful acquisition, as he could stand high up on one of the pig bunkers with his binoculars and identify what Axis military aircraft were arriving and departing.

Other agency members also found Floc-Av useful cover, as Robert Ragache, alias 'Paul', a Merchant Marine captain who became the outpost commander at Oran, and Paul Schmitt, alias 'Lucullus', the outpost commander at Constantine, were hired as company salesmen. Rygor reasoned they could do the job as well as the next man, and it gave them greater freedom of movement, for as porridge salesmen they would have easy access to military and naval bases, and airfields, and perhaps even to warships and cargo boats. It amused him greatly that in talking to them in his capacity as commercial director, neither knew he was also directing their secret service activities.

However, a stumbling block to the plan soon arose as the Floc-Av chairman, despite his assurances, had been unable to arrange a permit for Rygor, but in September Marcel Dubois resolved the matter when he turned up unexpectedly in Algiers. He suggested Rygor and his family visit him in Morocco a few days before their visas expired. He would then issue them with new Moroccan visas and ones for a three-month stay in Algeria, and this arrangement could be repeated as often as necessary. This proved the ideal solution for Rygor, as it meant he could travel between the two countries as frequently as he liked, and he went there twice more in 1942 on agency business. On his second visit a friend of Dubois sold him a fish factory in Agadir, Morocco's most southerly port, as cover for his trips within the country, and Rygor then recruited the previous owner to run the port's intelligence outpost.

* * * * *

Rygor's order never to make written notes was later ignored by one of his officers with serious consequences. However, it was impossible to run the agency without paperwork: ledgers, files and account books were all needed, as was a safe place to keep them On returning from buying stationery and a typewriter, Rygor encountered the hotel's proprietor and explained he was opening a business in Algiers and that his family was about to join him. The proprietor was delighted, and offered to rent him an apartment within the hotel, and in one of its rooms he found a secure hiding place to conceal all the agency's documentation.

Rygor's agreement to become Floc-Av's commercial director added a three-hour stint to his daily routine, now divided as follows: between 0900 and 1200 he dealt with the agency's administration and with coding and decoding radio messages; between 1200 and 1400 he went down to the port and observed the movement of shipping, had lunch, and conducted any necessary business in the town. Then he either relaxed for an hour if he could, or did more administration before spending the next three hours in the Floc-Av offices. Dinner was between 1800 and 1900, and he would then spend the rest of the evening receiving and reading his intelligence officers' written and oral reports, which he edited and encoded before passing to 'Mathew' for transmission to 'Cadix'. It was a heavy schedule, but once his wife, Sophie, had arrived with their young son, Rygor's burden was eased. She became the go-between with 'Mathew', and within a short time had learnt how to help Rygor code and decode messages. She also began delivering and picking up material from the local 'post box'.

By September 1941 the Vichy government had begun to tighten its grip on its colonies: pro-German propaganda was everywhere, and food rationing and wine restrictions were tightened, as more and more was exported to mainland France for German consumption, a situation which enabled a black market to flourish. The police and their numerous informers rigorously enforced new regulations forbidding anyone to listen to the BBC, and the press began an anti-Semitic campaign. This harsh new environment encouraged small anti-Vichy resistance groups to spring up, principally in Oran and Algiers. These were to prove useful to the Allies when they landed, but initially they lacked cohesion and a unified leadership.

None of this prevented Rygor from pressing ahead with the enlargement of the spy ring. On 1 October, Maxime de Roquemaure, alias 'Morel', was appointed to the new intelligence outpost in Tunis and on 12 October Rygor's complement of intelligence officers was completed by the arrival of Lieutenant Rombeyko (*nom de guerre* 'Mustafa') from Marseille.

* * * * *

All seemed to be going well when, out of the blue, Rygor was arrested on returning from his first trip to Morocco. He was taken to the Office of Public Security where he was questioned by a Vichy inspector of police from Marseille. The inspector was keen to know his connection with Lt Jekiel, the ring's naval expert, whose work in Marseille of issuing false passports had now unfortunately resulted in his arrest in Algiers. It was a nasty moment that could have ended in calamity for the agency. Luckily for Rygor, the chief of the Secret Police in Algiers was the anti-Vichy *commissaire*, André Achiary, for whom Rygor had been given a password in Marseille with which to identify himself if the need arose. He asked to be shown into the *commissaire's* office and when the two men were alone, Rygor mentioned the password and asked Achiary if he recognised the phrase. Achiary, astonished, admitted that he did and Rygor then revealed who he was and said he was in trouble. Achiary soon settled the matter. He concocted a report about his 'interrogation' of Rygor, and then arranged to have the Pole's hotel apartment 'searched' before he was released because of what Achiary tactfully called 'insufficient evidence'. It was the start of an important collaboration between the two men. However, Achiary could not help Jekiel, who remained in the local military prison until he was sent to mainland France to face trial.

Though Rygor remained unscathed from his first brush with the Vichy authorities, it brought home to him what a precarious existence he was leading. He therefore took the precaution of removing his 'office' to a large house owned by a strongly anti-German family called Aboukaya, who, being Jewish, had been deprived of the right to work, and were only too eager to help. As a further precaution 'René', who had now become known to the police because of his connection with Lieutenant Jekiel, was spirited away to the British consulate in neutral Tangiers, and in due course reached London via Lisbon.

Having lost two valuable intelligence officers, Rygor decided it would be insecure to replace them: he, 'Banuls' and 'Mustafa' must now run Agency Africa by themselves. 'Banuls' became the contact for the intelligence outposts in Oran, Tunis and Constantine – where the agency's third intelligence outpost was opened in December 1941 – while 'Mustafa' became the contact for Maurice Escoute, alias 'Curly', the new intelligence outpost commander for Algiers. 'Curly' was a French tax collector and a committed socialist whose job allowed him to travel throughout Algeria without difficulty. 'Mustafa' also took over watching the port of Algiers, which had been Lieutenant Jekiel's temporary responsibility. Despite the extra work this involved, the vetting and recruitment of local agents continued to grow, though it was not until March 1942 that the head of the Casablanca intelligence outpost, Lieutenant Edward Przesmycki, alias 'Vincent', was appointed to replace the imprisoned Lieutenant Jekiel.

Rygor also found a solution to London's seemingly impossible request for the agency to involve itself in counter-intelligence as well as intelligence gathering. He suggested to Achiary, who willingly agreed, that the agency should finance him to supply intelligence on the activities of the German and Italian consulates, the two armistice commissions, and the various spies and informers they employed. This added to the strain on Rygor's financial resources, and increased demands from London for more intelligence obliged him to ask for more funds which, despite repeated requests, were not forthcoming.

November 1941 was a bad month for Polish intelligence in France: an important Polish agent based in Paris was betrayed by his mistress, who was codenamed 'La Chatte'.[17] This brought about the destruction of his network and forced 'Tudor' into hiding in Marseille (he was later picked up by an aircraft and evacuated to England). It also proved a bad month for Algeria, as Weygand was ordered back to Vichy. His civilian duties became the responsibility of a strongly collaborationist civil servant, who introduced stringent Vichy policies and strengthened collaborationist organisations such as the youth movement, *Chantiers de la Jeunesse*. The Gestapo, already present in Algiers as 'advisers', now virtually took control of security.

Despite the increased dangers, intelligence continued to flow to London with eighty-four signals being dispatched in December. Some were routine, but others not only answered queries but contained intelligence of help to the Allies fighting in the Mediterranean and Middle East theatres. One expert on signals intelligence in these theatres later wrote that probably the most useful information the agency supplied – not available from any other source – were its signals identifying which French bases were being used to facilitate the transit of German aircraft to Libya, and the 'extent to which supplies for the Afrika Korps travelled the same route'.[18]

However, the most startling intelligence London received that month was in a letter from Rygor to MI6's Liaison Officer, Commander Dunderdale, dated 11 December 1941:

> I have received the following telegram from our Chief Agent 'AFR' sent and received on 10th instant. 'I have been for some time in direct contact with [the divisional commander] General Charbonneau and officers of the II Bureau of the divisional staff at Oran. There is a strong military organisation at Oran which wishes to revolt on a day signalled from London.

Total about 16,000 men as well as 150 aircraft from the air base at Lasenia. The coastal defence will be neutralised on the whole Oran coast. The navy does not present any difficulties …'

'They are asking for extensive help and material,' Rygor added, and wrote that he had told them to stay their hand until an answer had been received from London. He concluded: 'A similar business is being prepared in Algiers.'

London's response was immediate. A high-level meeting took place at the War Office, and on 12 December a signal was sent to Rygor. 'Great interest aroused,' it began, but more details were requested which Rygor did his best to provide. On 23 December he specified that the help required was 'aircraft and armoured equipment', and on 27 December he further qualified the necessary conditions for any revolt: 'The entire action is dependent upon the outcome of the Libyan campaign and adequate material assistance', which sounds as if those planning the action had got cold feet. Anyway, by now London was expressing doubts, and on 6 January it asked if the 'whole action in Algiers and Oran is really serious' and what Rygor meant by 'the help should have an American character' – perhaps the first time the question had arisen of the Americans taking the lead in any action in North Africa.[19]

Nothing came of the rumblings of discontent among the French armed forces against its Vichy masters, but the incident must have reassured planners that, if they played their cards right, the planned landings (TORCH) could take place unopposed. London was also much more positive about a closely related action of Rygor's which he described in a signal sent on 23 December. In this he informed London that a conference had just taken place unifying the anti-Vichy resistance movements in Algiers and Oran. He had suggested this to Achiary, citing the Polish resistance movement as an example to follow. Achiary had agreed, and the meeting took place in his apartment with representatives from both areas. Rygor chaired the meeting but made it clear that, while he was prepared to offer help and guidance – and money, though he had little left to give – he could not be actively involved in fighting to replace the Vichy government, as this was a purely French affair.

It was agreed the two resistance organisations should be unified under the overall command of General de Gaulle, and one of the first actions agreed upon was to counter Vichy propaganda by painting slogans everywhere in red paint. Judging by the reaction he received, Rygor wrote later, his message 326 had created a stir, as London wanted full details on the new movement's character, strength and composition, and 'whether help was required and a representative from London was considered necessary'.[20]

Having an organised and disciplined resistance movement in the two major ports certainly helped those landing there when TORCH was launched.

* * * * *

Shortly after Christmas Day 1941, Rygor met the two US vice-consuls in Algiers, John Knox and John Boyd, a contact initiated by 'Banuls'. Before he had been forced into hiding, 'Banuls' had started taking English lessons from an Englishwoman, Daphne Tuyl. He soon learnt that she knew John Knox (whom she later married), and after his first lesson 'Banuls' casually told her that he thought that some kind of Polish spy ring was working in Algiers, guessing Daphne would pass this on to Knox. She did, and Knox turned up at the next lesson, and another meeting was then arranged at the consulate when it was agreed that in future the consulate would forward the agency's pouch to London via the British consulate in neutral Tangiers.[21] This was a great relief to Rygor, as 'Tudor' was in hiding and Rygor had no means of sending to London the bulkier items of intelligence material he had been accumulating. It also meant that most intelligence could be sent by pouch and that only the most urgent information needed to be radioed to London – a great saving in time.

Rygor agreed to return to the consulate on 2 January 1942 with his first pouch. On 8 January he signalled Colonel Gano, the head of the II Bureau in London, that he had talked to the two vice-consuls 'as an Ally who had an intelligence network already in place, and in the course of the conversation I became convinced that the consulate had no intelligence information from Northern Africa nor any of its ports'.[22] When the vice-consuls asked how they could help, Rygor replied that he would like to send all his more bulky documents by diplomatic pouch. The Americans willingly agreed and it was settled that every week Rygor would personally go to the consulate to hand over the pouch. Though, as he pointed out to Gano, US Department of State regulations did not permit it to be sealed, it was 'the safest and the quickest way' to get the pouch to London. He could not have known that it was anything but that.

Immediately that Rygor knew the pouches could not be sealed, he of course realised the Americans would read what was in them before they were delivered to the British consulate in Tangiers. He had no objection to this, only asking that Washington be notified that the source of the intelligence was the Polish Army's Intelligence Service Agency Africa in North Africa. He repeated this request when he met Robert Murphy, who replied, with what Rygor later described as an enigmatic smile: 'Naturally it is understood that this is part of our gentlemen's agreement!'[23] What never occurred to Rygor was that Murphy and the vice-consuls were now busily forming their own intelligence network for the OSS, and that this would take the credit for the agency's work!

As it happened, Daphne Tuyl was already in touch with the British consulate in Tangiers, as she belonged to a resistance cell formed by Escoute ('Curly') before Rygor had even arrived in Algiers, and was probably the only British agent on French North African soil. Her speciality was helping British service personnel, and others, to escape arrest. This she did with remarkable efficiency. For instance, on one occasion, right under the noses of the port authorities, she organised a sailing boat to take four escapers to Gibraltar. When 'Curly' became the head of the agency's Algiers intelligence post, it was accepted that she would continue to send, separately from the agency, the cell's intelligence to London via Tangiers. She was not to know, of course, that both cells were passing identical information to MI6!

In her memoirs, Daphne Tuyl recounts how she and 'Curly' came to be assured that Achiary was working with them. One rainy night the car of the Italian general working for the Italian Armistice Commission was ambushed in an Algiers street. The general and his escorts were beaten up, and one man was killed, but by the time the police arrived the attackers had disappeared. The next day Achiary visited the general in hospital, expressed his sincere regrets, and suggested he provide one of his detectives as a bodyguard – an offer the general gladly accepted. Actually, the assailants were Achiary's own men acting on his orders. 'Perhaps they went at it a little too wholeheartedly,' Tuyl wrote:

> ... but they were Corsicans, and the Italians, their hereditary enemies, occupied Corsica. From then on, until the landings in November 1942, Achiary's man, acting as a bodyguard, reported

all the movements of the Italian Armistice Commission, set up
a microphone in their conference room and acted as our peri-
scope or 'seeing eye' on all their plans.[24]

Sometimes Tuyl's method of communication with Tangiers went
awry.

It was not long before I began to get messages from Tangiers
through the [US diplomatic] pouch and work began in earnest.
My orders and questions were typed on a square of paper about
half the size of an ordinary envelope in minute letters. The paper
was very light and thin, made of rice wafer so that in case of
emergency I could swallow it and it would dissolve, leaving no
trace in the stomach. On one occasion I made the mistake of
folding it and putting it in a breast pocket. It stuck together and
melted into a sticky mass with the heat of my body. Fortunately
I had read it and committed most of it to memory.[25]

* * * * *

In February 1942, Rygor heard that 'Morel', the commander of the
intelligence cell in Tunis, and two of his agents had been arrested,
and that the Tunisian police, now alerted to the existence of the
agency, suspected it was centred on Algiers. 'Banuls' then came to
him and said that two men had been questioning the porter of his
hotel about a man whose description he fitted. Rygor told him
to leave the hotel at once, after informing the hotel proprietor he
was leaving Algiers immediately, and, with his wife, take refuge in
Rygor's office at the Aboukayas' house. This prompt action saved
'Banuls', for very early the next morning the two men returned
to his hotel to arrest him. A complete disaster had been narrowly
averted, but damage had been done as the 'post box' in Algiers was
arrested when the man's name was discovered amongst the documents belonging to 'Morel'.

Rygor's messages for more funding had been ignored by London
for some time now, and the network had only been kept afloat
because of his high standing among the local business community.
This allowed him to borrow from local banks against his alleged
'fortune' in Switzerland, which had been his cover for financing
Floc-Av. But by February 1942 the agency's financial situation was
dire. It had a debt of 170,000 francs and only 3,858 francs in cash.

Only Rygor's monthly salary of 8,000 francs just kept it solvent. Eventually, money did arrive, via the US consulate in Lisbon, but it was in Portuguese escudos, the one currency that could not be exchanged on the black market! In despair Rygor tendered his resignation – it was refused – and the escudos were returned to Lisbon, and eventually yielded 517,500 francs. Then London arranged for another 600,000 francs to be transferred from Shell in London to its office in Algiers. The local Shell manager, a Frenchman, proved most helpful, for when Rygor went to collect the money he gave him all the information he needed about the North African reserves of motor fuel that London had requested earlier.

When 'Mathew' had to return to mainland France, Rygor asked London for his own 'hurdy gurdy'. In due course, this arrived via the US consulate, but Rygor could not at first find anyone to work it. However, in April 1942 – the month Rygor and his family, for better security, moved to a rented apartment – one of the agency's agents, Joseph Briatte, volunteered. As he was also a radio technician, Rygor bought a shop as a cover for him in the Arab quarter that sold and repaired radio equipment; and after the war, as a reward for his outstanding work, the Polish authorities gave Briatte the premises, and he was also awarded a high Polish decoration.

Briatte's cover proved very suitable, especially as it was allowed by the authorities to have an aerial for carrying out transmission tests for the ships' radios that Briatte repaired. The 'hurdy gurdy' was secreted in an empty radio casing and placed on a shelf with other equipment. When it was time to transmit, the aerial was simply plugged in. However, Rygor always made sure the shop had armed men in and around it. If it came to a shoot-out with those searching for the transmitter – the German and French counter-intelligence authorities knew it existed, but had been unable to locate it – Rygor was sure he would have the advantage of surprise, and that escape would be simple as it was virtually impossible to find anyone in the Arab quarter. As an extra security, and to relieve the pressure on the transmitter, a second one was installed with an operator in an Algiers villa specially purchased for the purpose.

The arrest of 'Morel' and his wife, and the narrow escape of 'Banuls', inevitably attracted the attention of the mainland Vichy police, and in March, Achiary told Rygor that a specialist in counter-espionage, *Commissaire* Begue, would shortly arrive in Algiers with the specific task of tracking down those running Agency

Africa and breaking up its network. He would be bringing his own agents with him, but even so, Achiary assured Rygor, Begue was a stranger to Algiers and would be forced to co-operate with him. One of Begue's agents was his very attractive 'wife'. According to Tuyl, she was a pickpocket who had been plucked from gaol and told that 'if she did a good job [of helping Begue] she would be freed and paid well into the bargain'.[26]

By March 1942, the ports, administrative offices and military bases of the coastal cities were being watched all the time, though the network still needed to be extended to inland towns. By now Rygor controlled about a hundred principal agents, who had their sub-agents, who in turn had their informers, and so on practically *ad infinitum*. 'One never really knew how many there were,' Rygor wrote later, 'since only the most important ones had agency numbers. I felt like an enormous spider enveloping ever-larger spans of territory in its web'.[27]

The vigilance of the agency's spies watching the ports produced dividends when, the following month, Rygor received a report that a 200-ton ship had loaded diesel oil and food in Algiers port, and had sailed that night. It returned the following morning without its cargo and there were strong rumours at the port that it was refuelling and re-provisioning German U-boats at sea. Similar incidents with other ships followed and Rygor's description of them was dispatched to London. They were, he said, Spanish ships flying a German flag, which had been built and purchased in Belgium. From their size, build and camouflage, it was easy to guess from the gossip of the crew in port that they were taking aboard far more diesel than they needed. 'It was difficult to pinpoint the supply zone – at sea east of Algiers and probably different in each case; the diesel being pumped into the submarine at sea.'[28] No doubt the Royal Navy made good use of this intelligence.

Counter-intelligence work continued to be required by London, especially on German spies in North Africa, and there was a constant exchange of information on this subject. With *Commissaire* Begue and his 'wife' still searching for 'Banuls' and other members of the ring, Rygor felt obliged to ask Achiary for further assistance. However, Achiary was himself now under suspicion as a Gaullist supporter. Instead, he suggested that Inspector Lofredo, one of his most trusted officers and a fervent anti-collaborationist, would help, especially as his job anyway was to investigate all those suspected of being foreign agents. Rygor knew Lofredo and trusted him. He asked the Frenchman to head the agency's counter-intelligence outpost for both Algeria and Tunisia, and Lofredo agreed enthusiastically. Shortly afterwards, the Vichy authorities dismissed Achiary and posted him to Setif in north-eastern Algeria as commissioner for the town and district. This was a severe blow for Rygor, but luckily – and Rygor remained remarkably lucky – Lofredo was appointed to Achiary's old post. Achiary's experience and dedication was not totally lost to the agency, as he agreed to command intelligence outpost number 6, giving special attention to the ports of Bougie and Djidjelli.

In June and July 1942, twenty new agents were taken on, most of them to cover the interior. London also arranged that Rygor should receive extra help in the form of three Polish intelligence officers. They were flown to Gibraltar, but there were delays, and they were not landed, on a beach near Oran, until September. The operation was scrupulously planned, and was disguised as an overnight camping trip with a tent being erected on the beach. Once the trio had landed, five French agents were taken aboard, the agency having hidden them after they had escaped from mainland France following the betrayal of the Polish agent's Paris network by 'La Chatte'.

Ragache ('Paul'), the commander of the agency's intelligence outpost at Oran, met the Poles. He had brought blank identity cards with him, and he only needed to add the 'mugshots' the agents had with them, and to endorse these with the police station's rubber stamp provided by one of its anti-Vichy *commissaires*. One of the Poles, a naval officer, was attached to the Oran outpost to keep an eye on Mers-el-Kébir; another went to Constantine; and the third was sent to Algiers where he took over from 'Banuls' who had been forced to take refuge in an Oran safe house to avoid the continuing attentions of Begue and his pickpocket 'wife'.

* * * * *

In June, Rygor met Roosevelt's special envoy, Colonel Solborg, who had arrived from London on a fact-finding mission. They talked in Polish – Solborg's mother came from Poland – and both agreed that North Africa was the best base from which to invade Europe and that Italy should be the initial mainland target once Sicily had been taken. The French armed forces in North Africa,

Rygor assured Solborg, were largely anti-German in sentiment; the Arabs had no political role; and the French colonial population were no supporters of Pétain and Vichy. It was therefore likely that any invading force would meet only token resistance – provided the operation was American and not British. Soon after his meeting with Solborg, Rygor began regular discussions with Murphy who, in July, introduced him to Colonel William Eddy, the senior OSS officer in North Africa. Eddy wanted the agency to take on sabotage work, but Rygor refused, saying that this meant building up a network completely separate from the agency, and he was not prepared to do this.

By September 1942 there were rumours of an American landing; of the Germans countering this threat by invading themselves; and of an armed insurrection by French forces if the Americans did land. Rygor signalled London that the resident minister in Morocco had informed the Vichy government that the Americans were looking for landing sites there, and that the lighthouses near Oran had therefore been extinguished. In Algeria the Vichy authorities were equally jittery and the Armistice Commission ordered the army to take up defensive positions around major ports with others being closed. It also ordered additional coastal patrols and improved defences for Maison Blanche airfield.

The TORCH planners had been well aware for some time that, if the landings were to succeed, the British had to be kept in the background and that the Americans would take the lead in any negotiations. General Eisenhower was to command the landings overall, and on the night of 21 October 1942 his deputy, General Mark Clark, was landed from a British submarine – disguised as a US Navy one – on a beach near Algiers with a small party of American officers. They were met by Murphy and two of the 'Twelve Apostles' and taken to a nearby farmhouse where the negotiations were held. The Americans' main task was to negotiate with the disaffected officers of the local French IX Corps, but those taking part, and they included representatives of local French Resistance groups, also had to agree a new French commander-in-chief and a new political structure after the Vichy authorities had been deposed. It was a tall order and much confusion ensued as the French were under the impression the landings were still in the planning stage, while the Americans were intent on concealing the invasion date, but eager to discover the attitude and intentions, politically and militarily, of the disaffected French. They impressed those present by saying the invasion force would amount to 500,000 Allied troops, supported by 2,000 aircraft and a major battle fleet. (In fact only 112,000 landed during the first few days.)

The Americans then suckered the French into giving them the intelligence they needed, including their dispositions to defend the beaches. As one American writer has commented, 'the deceit and bravado' of the meeting caused a series of political and military disasters in French North Africa, but he added that though 'some called the American (Murphy's) duplicity "a virtual double cross by the Americans", London and Washington truly feared that the French would betray Torch if they had known the D-Day time and date, forces size, and landing sites'.[29]

But when the landings took place on 8 November 1942 the Germans were taken by surprise. British deception plans had led them to believe the task force convoy crossing the Atlantic was heading for Dakar, while the two from Britain were destined for Malta and an invasion of Sicily. French forces defending the North African beaches had also been deceived, and when they realised this they fought back in some places. There were no preliminary bombardments by the naval task forces, as it was hoped the French would not oppose the landings. In some places they did so, particularly the French naval forces loyal to Admiral Darlan, the commander-in-chief of the French armed forces, who had just arrived in Algiers. But by the end of D-Day the town and port of Algiers were in the hands of the Eastern Task Force, which comprised both British and American troops, many of the former allegedly dressed in American uniforms. The only significant fighting in the port took place when the Vichy authorities attempted to quell a coup by 400 local French resisters. The Central Task Force took Oran two days later. The same day the Western Task Force captured Casablanca, where the fiercest fighting took place. Once the landings were consolidated, the Allied forces moved eastwards to take Tunisia.[30]

In mid-December 1942, Rygor was summoned to London where officers of the Polish High Command were quite open about their lack of interest in him or his spy ring, and made him realise that only the British and Americans had some appreciation of his achievements. It was a bitter pill to swallow. However, it was agreed the agency should continue, though reduced in size and with a different role, and in February 1943 Rygor returned to Algiers and his family.

In 1944 the agency merged with the intelligence department of the Polish II Corps fighting in the Italian campaign, but on his return to London in September that year Rygor found there was no place for him in the Polish command structure there. Instead, he was posted to Crieff in Scotland as chief of staff of the Infantry Training Centre, where he began writing his book about Agency Africa. This does not disguise his bitterness at the way the agency was treated, or the way Poland had been betrayed when Britain and the USA allowed Stalin to take over his country. Polish servicemen, he pointed out, did not even participate in the Allied victory parade – presumably so as not to offend 'Uncle Joe', as the British people had called Stalin during the war, with badly misplaced affection.

However, there must have been one consolation for Rygor. Agency Africa had shown him to be not only one of the outstanding intelligence figures of the Second World War, but an astute and canny businessman; for in the short time the porridge factory existed – it closed the day the landings took place – it made a profit of 36,000 francs that covered at least some of the costs of running the agency. What's more, Rygor even recouped the French government's capital, which he had invested in Floc-Av, when he sold his shares to the chairman.

NOTES

1. Herman, J., 'Agency Africa: Rygor's Franco-Polish Network and Operation Torch' in *Journal of Contemporary History* (vol. 22, no. 4, 1987) p. 683. Perhaps this article was a corrective to an earlier one in the same journal that described Agency Africa in a footnote as a 'small-scale Polish espionage network' working for MI6!

2. Hinsley, F.H. *et al.*, *British Intelligence in the Second World War*, 4 Vols (London, 1978–90).

3. Jeffery, K., *MI6: The History of the Secret Intelligence Service, 1909–1949* (London, 2010).

4. The phrase Dr Paul Latawski used during his discussion on the 'Historiography, Issues and Controversies of the Polish Intelligence Contribution in the Second World War', which took place at a conference at Lady Margaret Hall, Oxford, on 6 May 2006.

5. Slowikowski, R., *In the Secret Service: The Lighting of the Torch* (London, 1988) pp. 263 and 250.

6. Kermit Roosevelt's introduction to *The Secret War Report of the OSS* (New York, 1976) p. x.

7. Slowikowski, *op. cit.*, p. 25.

8. Kitson, S., *The Hunt for Nazi Spies: Fighting Espionage in Vichy France* (Chicago, IL, 2008) p. 35.

9. Slowikowski, *op. cit.*, p. 151.

10. Their story is told in *FDR's 12 Apostles* by Hal Vaughan (Lyons Press, Guilford, CT, 2006).

11. Slowikowski, *op. cit.*, p. 56.

12. In his book Slowikowski describes 'Cadix' by the cryptonym 'Whirlwind'. However, this appears to have been the *nom de guerre* of Lieutenant-Colonel Gwido Langer, chief of the Polish General Staff's intelligence station '300' in Avignon, to which 'Cadix' was connected. Like Ciezki (see n. 13 below), Langer played a vital role in deciphering German Enigma cipher machine signals.

13. Ciezki (1898–1951) was a key figure in breaking the code of the German Enigma cipher machine. In March 1943 he was, with his chief, Colonel Langer, arrested while trying to escape into Spain. They were both interned in an SS concentration camp, but survived the war.

14. Slowikowski, *op. cit.*, p. 62.

15. *Ibid.*, pp. 66–67. An English female agent (Daphne Tuyl) did work for Rygor indirectly, though he probably did not know it.

16. Stirling, T. *et al.* (eds), *Intelligence Co-operation between Poland and Great Britain during the Second World War: Vol. 1: The Report of the Anglo-Polish Historical Committee* (Vallentine Mitchell, 2005). In his paper, 'North Africa', Andrzej Peplonski says (p. 249) that the II Bureau forbade Slowikowski to request 'assistance from the Polish consulate General in Algiers, the Honorary Consulate [*sic*] in Casablanca, or contacting the Polish community.' This statement appears on p. 15 of the Polish edition of Slowikowski's book, but there is no mention of these restrictions in the English edition.

17. This was Mathilde Carré, a French nurse whose nickname derived from her habit of always beginning her radio messages: 'The cat reports ...'. She was recruited as a double agent by the Germans, and when she came to England an attempt by the British to make her a triple agent failed and she was imprisoned. After the war she was deported to France and sentenced to death, but was reprieved. She was released in 1954, and published her memoirs, *I was the Cat* (London, 1960).

18. From a review of Slowikowski's book by Dr Ralph Bennett in *Journal of Intelligence and National Security*, (vol. 1, no. 1, January 1989,) p. 196. Bennett is the author of *Ultra and Mediterranean Strategy, 1941–45* (London, 1989).

19. Ciechanowski, J. (ed.), *Intelligence Co-operation between Poland and Great Britain during The Second World War: Vol. 2: Documents* (London, 2005) pp. 593–98. This incident is not mentioned in the English edition of Slowikowski's book.

20. Slowikowski, *op. cit.*, p. 105.

21. Stirling *et al.*, *op. cit.* In his paper, 'North Africa', Andrzej Peplonski writes (p. 254, n. 14) that the vice-consuls 'failed to do what they had promised and that Rygor's first two pouches remained in the US embassy in Lisbon for several months', and quotes documentary evidence to prove it. However, John Knox, when interviewed by John Herman in 1983, stated that all Rygor's intelligence pouches 'stopped at Tangiers'. If this is correct, the pouches probably went to the Tangiers JIC (Joint Intelligence Centre), which, after assessing their contents, disseminated their intelligence to London and Washington.

22. Ciechanowski, *op. cit.*, p. 591.

23. Slowikowski, *op. cit.*, p. 117.

24. *How Long Till Dawn*, the unpublished memoirs of Daphne Joan Tuyl Knox, Ch. 5. Her manuscript was kindly lent to the author by her son, Derek Knox.

25. *Ibid.*, Ch. 8.

26. *Ibid.*, Ch. 10.

27. Slowikowski, op. *cit.*, p. 148.

28. *Ibid.*, p. 159.

29. Vaughan, *op. cit.*, pp. 172–73.

30. TORCH had other, wider, ramifications, as the Germans broke the 1940 Armistice agreement by occupying France's free zone, which prompted the scuttling of the French fleet at Toulon to prevent it falling into their hands. Axis forces fighting to take Egypt retreated into Tunisia after the Battle of El-Alamein in October–November 1942, as the Allied forces that had landed in North Africa were slow to occupy it. There the Axis forces were caught between the two Allied forces and were forced to surrender in May 1943, and 218,000 became prisoners of war.

6

The Spies of the Double-Cross System

The Double-Cross System was run in Britain during the Second World War to exploit captured German agents. Instead of being executed – though some were – many were used to feed disinformation to the Germans, with extraordinary results. Sometimes it had amusing consequences: one double agent was decorated by both sides, receiving the MBE from the British and the Iron Cross from the Germans.

The system was one of the war's best-kept secrets. Along with its critically important partner, ULTRA intelligence – gleaned from breaking the German Enigma machine cipher – it remained unknown to the general public until the 1970s. If ever there was a looking-glass war, the Double-Cross System was it. Nothing else touched it for its complexity and its effectiveness. It did not win the war – nor did ULTRA – only the fighting men on the ground, at sea and in the air did that. But, with ULTRA, it helped shorten the war in Europe, and saved many thousands of Allied lives. It was that important.

In Britain the system was run by the Twenty Committee, or XX-Committee as it was usually called, XX being the Roman numerals for twenty, and it also spawned two similar but smaller organisations in the Middle East and North Africa, the XXX- and XXXX-committees.

The XX-Committee was, technically at least, a sub-committee of the curiously named Wireless Board; and later, when the system had expanded, it became part of the London Controlling Section which, under the chiefs of staff, had the much wider remit of co-ordinating and implementing strategic deception against Germany and Italy. The committee's most important task was to decide what intelligence, real and false, could be passed to the enemy, but it was also highly effective at counter-intelligence. As its chairman, the historian, novelist and Oxford don, J.C. Masterman, emphasised when, in 1971, he published the first factual history of the

Double-Cross System: 'We did much more than practise a large-scale deception through double agents ... by means of the double agent system *we actively ran and controlled the German espionage system in this country*.'[1]

This statement was not entirely accurate because MI5, as the official history of the service revealed in 2009, unwittingly employed two Abwehr agents during the war, something Masterman could not have known at the time his book was published. While the whole British intelligence community was constantly on its guard against agents who might still be at large and outside their control, it did not occur to anyone that within MI5 there were 'two of the Abwehr's previously most successful agents'.[2] The agents, Folkert van Koutrik and Jack Hooper, worked for the MI6 station in The Hague before moving to Britain in May 1940. When interrogated after the war, German intelligence officers revealed that both men had betrayed MI6 colleagues to the Abwehr (German Military Intelligence); and though neither seems to have communicated with the Germans during the war, they were a potential threat to the Double-Cross System.

MI5's records contain the personal files of about 120 agents who participated in the Double-Cross System, though not all operated in the UK, and the usefulness of some only lasted a few weeks. In his book Masterman lists thirty-nine of the most active and influential ones. Along with the functions and infrastructure of the Double-Cross System, the activities of four of the most daring agents are examined here, a quartet who represent the development of the system during the course of the war. They may well have had more influence on the outcome of the conflict than any number of admirals or generals.

* * * * *

The unwitting progenitor of the system, a Welsh-born electrical engineer called Arthur Owens, was a spy well before the war began. The owner of a company manufacturing batteries, and the inventor of a special electric storage cell, Owens travelled frequently to Europe, particularly to Germany, where the German Navy was one of his clients. During the mid-1930s he started to pass technical information about the German Navy to the British Naval Intelligence Division, possibly because he was having money difficulties and hoped espionage might prove lucrative. Recruitment by MI6 followed and he was given the codename SNOW,[3] a short-ened anagram of his name. However, MI5 had been monitoring his correspondence, and soon discovered he was in touch with the Abwehr, who knew him as Johnny. When challenged, SNOW did not deny his contact with the Abwehr, but vehemently denied he was acting treacherously.

MI5 gave him the benefit of the doubt but continued to moni-tor his movements and his correspondence. In an attempt to re-establish the confidence of the security services, he fed the occasional pieces of intelligence to MI6 and Special Branch, and when, in January 1939, he informed MI5 that a portable wireless transmitter was waiting for him at Victoria Station cloakroom – MI5 soon established it was there and examined it – he seemed finally to have regained some of their trust. But he was unable to make the transmitter work – his letter of complaint to the Abwehr was routinely intercepted by MI5 – and his subsequent behaviour was so suspicious that when war was declared in September 1939 he was imprisoned in Wandsworth gaol, and served with a deten-tion order.

Once SNOW was locked up, MI5 gave him his alternatives: be tried as a spy and probably hanged, or co-operate. Not surprisingly, SNOW chose the latter option. He revealed where he had hidden the transmitter after removing it from Victoria Station, and it was retrieved and repaired. Then, on 9 September 1939, under MI5 supervision, he transmitted from his prison cell his first wartime message to his German Abwehr contact, a Dr Rantzau: 'All ready. Have repaired radio. Send instructions. Now awaiting reply.'

However, the signal strength was poor and SNOW did not receive a reply. A second attempt also failed, so MI5 decided to take the risk of moving him to a better location for his radio, and he was installed – with his mistress Lily, who became adept at decoding the mes-sages he received – in a top-floor flat in Kingston-Upon-Thames. An aerial erected on the roof produced a more powerful signal and SNOW transmitted another message: 'must meet you in Holland at once. Bring weather code. Radio town and hotel. Wales ready'.

When questioned about its meaning, SNOW replied that he was supposed to meet Rantzau to collect the Abwehr code for sending details of the weather in areas of Britain that the Germans were intending to bomb. When asked about the phrase 'Wales ready', SNOW said it referred to Rantzau's plan for him to find a Welsh nationalist willing to establish a sabotage and espionage network in Wales. After a long pause, the Germans replied to the message with SNOW's call-sign, showing that communications had been established and that the meeting in Holland could take place. The Double-Cross System was born.

As it happened, the newly established British Radio Security Service, formed from amateur radio enthusiasts to scan the airwaves for any illegal transmission, picked up SNOW's signal, and direction-finding stations then traced the position of the German reply to it. It did not originate from Hamburg, as expected, but from a ship situated off the Norwegian coast. A further revelation was that those aboard the ship then enciphered SNOW's message verbatim and forwarded it to Germany. This, too, was intercepted, giving the government's code and cipher school at Bletchley Park a crib for breaking the Abwehr's hand cipher. The code Rantzau was to give SNOW for enciphering his weather messages was an added bonus.

SNOW's meeting with Rantzau in Rotterdam went well. Rantzau required intelligence on a range of matters, particularly meteorological. He suggested that next time they met, SNOW should bring with him the Welsh nationalist he was presumed to have recruited to discuss the shipment of arms and explosives by U-boat. For this role MI5 had already chosen a retired Swansea police inspector called Gwilym Williams, who was given the codename GW.

On 19 October the two men travelled to Ostend and on to Brussels to meet Rantzau. Details of where the U-boat would land explosives, the financing of the Welsh nationalists to carry out sabotage, and other similar matters, were discussed and agreed upon, and included the startling information that the Germans were to take command of the IRA – then particularly active in Ireland – and also that SNOW was to offer £50,000 to anyone who was willing to steal a modern aircraft and fly it to Germany.

The two men were given microfilmed instructions that subsequently allowed MI5 to trace the only two undetected spies resident in the country. One, Mathilde Krafft, a British citizen born in Germany, was the Abwehr's paymistress, who laundered the English banknotes she illicitly received at Selfridges store in Oxford Street. She soon ended up in Holloway gaol, but the other, a German-born British citizen called Eschborn, who was being blackmailed into co-operating with the Abwehr, was willingly turned and became the double agent codenamed CHARLIE. CHARLIE was the Abwehr's reluctant photographer, whose job, among others, was to send SNOW's reports by microfilming them for dispatch to the Abwehr's cover address in Hamburg.

After the German attack on France and Belgium in May 1940, it became impossible for SNOW to continue meeting Rantzau on the Continent. Instead, Rantzau arranged for SNOW to meet him at agreed co-ordinates in the North Sea, and to bring with him someone SNOW had suggested would make a good recruit for the Abwehr. However, this ended in failure, as the 'recruit', an MI5 agent called Sam McCarthy, codenamed BISCUIT, became convinced SNOW was a die-hard Nazi leading them into a trap, so tied him up and ordered their fishing boat to return to port.

Despite this fiasco, MI5 persevered with SNOW who continued to contact the Abwehr, receiving as well as giving intelligence. Sometimes – as when the Air Ministry asked for information about the results of a bombing attack against a German target – the information received from Rantzau was accepted as being accurate. MI5 circulated it throughout Whitehall, characterising SNOW as a trusted source. This was being somewhat economical with the truth.

More important to the development of the Double-Cross System was that SNOW became an early purveyor of disinformation. Prior to the British landings in Norway in April 1940, he was told to inform Rantzau that he had heard that the War Office urgently required photographs of the area around Bergen, when in fact the plan was to land troops over 600 kilometres north at Trondheim. It was an elaborate ruse that also involved the double agent, CHARLIE. Unfortunately, this early example of strategic deception made little difference to the outcome of the Norwegian campaign, as the British soon had to withdraw and Norway became yet another German-occupied country. However, better results were to come.

In early 1941 SNOW received a signal telling him to meet Rantzau in Lisbon, the capital of neutral Portugal and the espionage centre of Europe, and he was to bring with him another likely Abwehr recruit. This time MI5 provided a cashiered RAF officer called Walter Dicketts, codenamed CELERY. CELERY thought as little of SNOW as BISCUIT had, calling him 'an inveterate liar

[who] lies even to his wife [presumably he meant Lily, as he was separated from his wife] about everything. He is terrified of air raids and is bone idle'; SNOW was 'running with the hare and hunting with the hounds'.[4]

When CELERY reached Lisbon the Abwehr sent him to Germany, where he was interrogated to confirm his loyalty to the Third Reich, a test he passed with flying colours. However, when CELERY returned to Lisbon he found out that Rantzau had forced SNOW to confess that he was under British control. This did not stop Rantzau giving both men £10,000 and providing SNOW with explosives hidden in a soap bar and a pen, which were found when customs officers strip-searched them on their return to Britain.

In MI5's subsequent interview with SNOW about his Lisbon excursion, it was impossible, as always, to know if SNOW was telling the truth, fantasising or lying, or all three at the same time. Those interrogating him decided that as Rantzau may have forced a confession out of SNOW, the time had come to close down the case, especially as SNOW's nerve was going. Rantzau was therefore informed that SNOW was too ill to continue working, and in April 1941 he was imprisoned for the remainder of the war. It also ended the double-cross careers of CHARLIE and CELERY – though GW continued in play until 1942.

To this day no one knows for certain whose side SNOW was on – perhaps even he didn't know – but he was certainly the cornerstone on which the Double-Cross System was built and he taught MI5 an immense amount about the Abwehr, saving the Security Service, according to a future director general, Dick White, 'from absolute darkness on the subject of German espionage'.[5]

* * * * *

From the experience gained by running SNOW and his associates, it was decided to expand this method of passing disinformation to the enemy; and in January 1941 the XX-Committee was formed, and met on a weekly basis until May 1945.

The purpose of the XX-Committee was to give guidance to the MI5 section (B1) which controlled double agents; and to weigh up what intelligence could be passed to the Germans against the dangers created by doing so – a task that often involved higher authority and different departments. This alone made the committee's task a formidable one of liaison and co-ordination. It also had to make sure that the intelligence the controlled agents transmitted to their German handlers did not conflict and was reasonably consistent, while ensuring it was not too similar. The overriding rule was that no message would ever be sent to the Germans without the committee's approval. Communicating with the enemy had to be firmly controlled, since it was, as Masterman commented, like playing with dynamite.

The MI sub-section responsible for German double agents, B1(a), was run by the formidable Thomas Argyll Robertson, known as 'Tar' because of his initials. Robertson asserted that the golden rule in running an agent was to ensure that every message the agent transmitted to his Abwehr controller was indelibly stamped with his own personality. So his background, the way he expressed himself, the idiosyncrasies of his grammar and spelling, all came across loud and clear, and did not arouse any suspicions that the agent had been 'turned'. This also applied to the numerous notional sub-agents who were 'recruited', for they, too, had to be completely authentic. MI5's official historian has described Robertson as having a 'remarkable gift for selecting case officers (all previously inexperienced wartime recruits) who were capable of entering into the personalities of their double agents'.[6]

Having broken the Abwehr hand cipher, Bletchley Park was often able to give warning that an Abwehr agent was on his way: thirteen arrived in September/October 1940 alone and twenty-four in 1941. Most parachuted in and all but one were quickly rounded up and dispatched to MI5's interrogation centre, Camp 020. The exception was a Dutchman called Ter Braak who escaped detection on arrival in early November 1940. He found lodgings in Cambridge, but on 1 April 1941 his body was found in a half-built air raid shelter in the city. Probably he had been unable to contact Germany and ran out of money, and so shot himself.

Camp 020 was a vital part of the Double-Cross System's infrastructure. Located at Latchmere House near Richmond, Surrey, it was situated on a secluded estate screened from public view, and surrounded by fences and barbed wire. The building, once a hospital and rehabilitation centre, was ideally suited for housing prisoners. The camp was commanded by another of the system's formidable characters, Colonel 'Tin-Eye' Stephens, so-called because of the monocle that seemed a permanent part of his features – he was said

to even sleep in it. A talented linguist with a vile temper – largely a
façade – he ended up with a total of 480 suspects in his care, and most
saw out the war there. About fifty-five were released, eleven became
recruits for the Double-Cross System, and fourteen, including two
British citizens, were tried, found guilty of spying, and executed.

Life for a suspect in Camp 020 was harsh, and mind games were
often employed. A common tactic to encourage co-operation was
for an obdurate prisoner to be casually informed by his warder
that the man in the next cell had been shot earlier that morning,
and Tin-Eye's philosophy certainly didn't encourage familiarity
between his staff and their captives. 'The penalty for espionage is
death,' he later wrote:

> If the spy tells the truth he may live. There is no guarantee; it is
> a hope no more. The quicker the spy realises that fundamen-
> tal position the better … Arrest must be efficient. The less said
> the better. The quicker the handcuffs are slipped on the more
> pronounced is the effect of stark reality. The quicker the ill fit-
> ting and shabby prison garb take the place of sartorial elegance
> the more profound and depressing is the effect. No exceptions.
> No chivalry. No gossip. No cigarettes. Incommunicado is the
> watchword … Figuratively, a spy in war should be at the point
> of a bayonet.[7]

The routine was harsh but never brutal. Only on one occasion
was violence employed on a prisoner – when an MI19 intelligence
officer called Scotland became enraged by the answers being given
by one suspect, and was later found punching him after he had
been returned to his cell. Scotland was banned from entering the
premises again.[8] In fact, decorum seemed to be the norm, with the
camp dentist on one occasion obtaining a prisoner's written con-
sent before removing a hollow molar which contained a capsule of
secret ink.

The first objective of Camp 020 was to establish if the suspect
really was a spy. On his arrival he was strip-searched and then given
prison clothing that had a diamond-shaped white mark sewn on
the jacket. His old clothes were closely examined for identification marks and to see if any chemicals for invisible writing were
impregnated into the cloth or in the seams, and his teeth were
also examined for hidden capsules. He was then given a medical

examination by the camp doctor, a well-known criminologist who was also a trained psychiatrist.

Interrogation commenced as soon as possible while the suspect was still uncertain of his fate and confused by his sudden capture. He was taken before a board of officers who sat at a table in front of a window, and his belongings and papers were placed on the table for the officers to examine. The suspect remained standing to attention throughout the interview and could not speak unless ordered to do so. He was told his life depended on the answers he gave and questions were fired at him remorselessly, often without him having time to answer them.

If at this first interrogation the suspect did not break down, other methods were used, such as 'stool pigeons' and the 'hard guy–soft guy' approach. Rumours were also spread amongst the prisoners that anyone about to be shot was put in cells 13 or 14. Telling a suspect he was about to be put in one of them often produced the desired results. Tin-Eye would conclude an unsatisfactory interview thus:

> You will now be taken to Cell Fourteen. In time of peace it was a padded cell, so protected that raving maniacs could not bash out their brains against the wall. Some recovered. Some committed suicide. Some died from natural causes. The mortuary is conveniently opposite ... perhaps it [the cell] is remote, and cold and a little dark ... Some spies have told the truth and have been transferred. Some have committed suicide. Some have passed out for the last time to their judicial hanging – their rich desert [sic]. I shall not see you again. I do not know how long you will be there. Petitions will be ignored ...[9]

* * * * *

The first agent the interrogators at Camp 020 turned was Wulf Schmidt, a Dane by birth who spoke fluent English, though he had a distinct accent. After studying agronomy at the University of Berlin, he had been employed on a banana plantation in the Cameroon, but by 1940 he had found himself stranded and penniless in Hamburg, a situation the Abwehr had probably arranged in order to recruit him. On his uppers, Schmidt, already known to be a Nazi sympathiser, had little alternative but to accept whatever employment was offered him. This seems hardly the best way to recruit a spy but, as will be seen, the Abwehr's methods of recruitment and training were somewhat amateur to say the least.

Wulf's first mission was to his homeland, but this ended in failure. It was then suggested he go to England. As he had no money, He accepted reluctantly. While on a communications course to learn Morse code and how to encipher and decipher messages, he met another would-be agent, a Swede called Gösta Caroli, who was to play a significant part in Schmidt's immediate future. The invasion of Britain was expected at any moment and they were required to find out as much as possible about the defences to stop it. Information about troop movements, new air bases, equipment, the position of A-A batteries and fuel dumps, and the strengths and positions of troops defending the country, was therefore urgently required.

After some confusion and several false starts, Caroli was dropped by parachute near Nottingham on the night of 5 September 1940, and Wulf, whose espionage area was bordered by London–Bedford–Cambridge–Chelmsford, followed on the night of 19 September. Both had their radio transmitters and receivers strapped to their bodies, and their equipment included a shovel to bury their parachutes, a pistol and ammunition, amphetamine pills, and some English and American currency. Wulf had his genuine Danish passport – with a page removed that showed he had been in Germany – and a forged identity card and ration book in the name of Harry Williamson.

As SNOW had supplied the Abwehr with the details necessary for forging identity cards and ration books, Wulf's documents had gross errors that any alert policeman could spot. In any case, the spies' missions were doomed from the start as neither had had any parachute training and both were injured on landing. Wulf broke a wrist on jumping from the aircraft and then sprained his ankle when he hit the ground near the village of Willingham some miles north-west of Cambridge. His behaviour of bathing his ankle at the village pump, and then ordering breakfast in the local café with a foreign accent, not surprisingly aroused suspicion. By lunchtime he was locked up in Cambridge police station and he was transferred to Camp 020 the next day.

Even if he had landed uninjured, Wulf would not have survived long because MI5, thanks to Caroli, were expecting him. Caroli had been knocked unconscious when landing and was found soon afterwards lying on his parachute in a ditch. At Camp 020 he quickly confessed and told his captors two more agents were expected, Wulf Schmidt and Kurt Goose.[10]

Caroli had been especially reluctant to betray his friend Schmidt, but did so after being reassured that Schmidt's life would be spared, the first and last time a promise was given by Camp 020 interrogators to a prisoner. After expressing his willingness to co-operate, Caroli was codenamed SUMMER and housed, with other early agents employed in the Double-Cross System, at an MI5 safe house at Hinxton in Cambridgeshire, which had been commandeered officially as a home for incurables. In January 1941 he tried to make a run for it. He attacked his guard, stole a motorbike and a canoe from a nearby barn, and set off for the coast. However, he fell off his bike at Newmarket and gave himself up.

This was a good example of how the delicate and precarious workings of the Double-Cross System were always in danger of being exposed by unforeseen events. In this case SUMMER was promptly locked up. However, a plausible explanation for his disappearance had to be invented if the Double-Cross System wasn't to unravel before it had even really got started. It was decided BISCUIT would report that SUMMER was on the run, but that he had managed to put his wireless in the cloakroom at Cambridge Station, and had sent the key to BISCUIT. The Germans would then be informed that SUMMER had been picked up by the police for not registering for war service and that SNOW would suggest a candidate from his group of notional agents for using SUMMER's wireless.

SUMMER proved to be a dead end, but his friend Wulf Schmidt became one of the system's most successful agents. Codenamed TATE by the British and LEONHARD by the Germans, the Dane soon confessed after his interrogators told him his friend had already given away his impending arrival, and where he would land. Schmidt was also persuaded to change sides when he realised the propaganda that the Abwehr had fed him – that London was in ruins and the population starving – was nonsense, as he had been driven through London on his way to Camp 020. He showed his captors where he had hidden his wireless and managed to make contact with his German controller. He was then moved to a safe house near Watford and, though closely guarded, lived reasonably well. He was paid £1 – invested in National Saving certificates which he received after the war – was given a holiday in the Lake District, and was eventually allowed to work in a local photographic shop.

TATE's case was managed by 'Tar' Robertson, though the Dane was looked after on a day-to-day basis by his guards and his MI5 case officer. He also had a skilled radio operator working with him who, once he had learnt TATE's 'fist', often sent TATE's reports himself. During the last quarter of 1940 TATE sent about thirty-eight reports to the Abwehr. Most of the intelligence he supplied was disinformation, but sometimes he was allowed to report accurately the population's morale as well as the damage caused by air raids. Doubtless, this added authenticity to TATE's messages, for the Germans came to have a high regard for the information he sent.

So involved did TATE become in this work that he began making his own suggestions as to what should and should not be transmitted, particularly details of the damage caused by bombing raids. He then demanded from his German controller a wider geographical area to cover, and shortly afterwards received orders to move about the country and report on factories and airfields. An awkward problem arose from this wider remit when TATE was asked to go to Coventry and report on the aftermath of the devastating raid of 14/15 November 1940, which had been followed by a smaller one in April 1941.

The XX-Committee had the difficult task of deciding what TATE should say, which would be enough to satisfy his case officer but not enough to encourage yet another attack. Eventually, TATE reported that the police presence had been too heavy for him to make an accurate assessment, and was deliberately vague about the damage, which, he said, was only based on rumours he had heard. Then, to dissuade the Germans from attacking again, he added that the surviving factories had been relocated and were now widely scattered. However, unlike some of TATE's later reports, this one had no effect as the Germans bombed the city again in 1942.

* * * * *

In January 1941, TATE complained to his German controller that he was running short of money. SNOW was ordered to send him £100 by mail, but all the other attempts to get money to him failed. Then, in May 1941, he managed to receive some via the Japanese assistant naval attaché in London, who, on a bus, handed him a wad of notes wrapped in a copy of *The Times*. But his funding was not finally resolved until another double agent, TRICYCLE – of whom more later – hoodwinked the Abwehr into depositing nearly £20,000 in a New York bank in an operation MI5 code-named MIDAS.[11] This was notionally passed to TATE, who was instructed by the Abwehr to use some of it to fund any future agents – a useful additional check on any new arrivals.

The first agents he supplied with cash were two Norwegians, who MI5 codenamed MUTT and JEFF. They were delivered to the Moray Firth by seaplane in April 1941 with the brief to undertake sabotage and report back on bomb damage, civilian morale and troop movements. They immediately gave themselves up, and were easily turned. To their German controller they proved adept at sabotage[12] – in reality this was faked by MI5 – and were able to wring extra equipment and money out of him, before JEFF became unreliable and had to be locked up, with the usual excuses about his absence being made to his Abwehr controller.

One of the Abwehr's early attempts to send TATE money was via an agent called Karel Richter, who was dropped by parachute in April 1941 between Cambridge and Bury St Edmunds. Although uninjured, Richter was quickly captured and the large sum of money he was to deliver to TATE was found on him. He was promptly dispatched to Camp 020 where another German agent, Josef Jakobs, who had who had arrived the previous January by parachute, positively identified him.

Richter was a committed Nazi and a tough nut to crack, and it took many hours of interrogation to break him. But he eventually admitted his mission was espionage – and that he had also been sent not just to give TATE money, but to check if he was genuine or not. He was then to return to Germany and report to the same case officer who had earlier called TATE 'our finest pearl. If he is a fake, then the whole necklace is false.'

As neither Jakobs nor Richter co-operated – at least not until it was too late – they were put on trial and executed. Richter was hanged; Jakobs was shot in the Tower of London. Having broken his ankle on landing, he was executed sitting on a chair.

Richter's mission to investigate TATE's loyalty naturally alarmed MI5 but the signs were that the Abwehr still considered him loyal.[13] Indeed, so satisfied were they with their 'pearl' that in May 1941 TATE was awarded the Iron Cross, both First Class and

Second Class. However, from MI5's point of view the quality of the intelligence he was receiving didn't match what he was giving to the Germans. It was therefore decided he must be made less available, and he told his controller that, having been exempted from conscription, he was now employed in war work on a farm, and that this would restrict his travels. But to keep him in play, the XX-Committee gave him two new notional contacts: an over-talkative girl called Mary who worked in the Admiralty's cipher department; and a friend of TATE's employer who occasionally needed an extra hand on his Kent farm.

Both these acquaintances were preliminaries for TATE's partici-pation in the greatest strategic deception of the war, codenamed FORTITUDE SOUTH.[14] This aimed to fool the Germans into believing that the main Allied landings would be in the Pas de Calais area, spearheaded by an entirely fictional formation, the First United States Army Group (FUSAG). To deceive the Germans into believing that a massive build-up of troops and equipment was being concentrated in south-east England prior to carrying out the landings, false wireless signals filled the air, and dummy tanks and fake landing craft and airfields turned the countryside into an armed camp.

* * * * *

In early June 1944, TATE's Abwehr controller requested he move to the farm in Kent to report the build-up for the impending invasion. In case the Germans were able to take bearings on his transmitter's position, TATE's signals were passed by cable from his safe house near Watford, and then transmitted from the area in Kent where he was supposed to be staying. His loose-tongued notional friend Mary, having returned from Washington where she had been temporarily seconded, was now working as a secretary at Eisenhower's invasion headquarters at Norfolk House in London, and remained a useful conduit of false intelligence.

Even after the Normandy landings of 6 June, the Double-Cross System continued to delude the Germans into believing that these were just a feint and that the main ones were still to come in the Pas de Calais area. So impressed were the Germans by what TATE was now providing that on 10 June one MI5 officer noted in his diary: 'A very encouraging message has been received by TATE. The enemy say that his reports can even decide the outcome of the

war'; and in early July he noted that 'TATE, through his connection with a railway clerk at Ashford, has seen a schedule of troop
movements [which] indicated the movement of FUSAG formations from concentration to embarkation ...'[15]

TATE played his part in FORTITUDE SOUTH but a number
of other double agents were also employed to maintain the deception, notably GARBO (see below), and each had his, or her, role
to play. For instance, it was sometimes as effective to send a nega-
tive report, as it was to signal the movement of fictional forces.
TREASURE,[16] whom the Germans thought lived in Bath, did
this very effectively by signalling the absence of any troop movements in the area when in fact it was swarming with Allied forces
waiting to embark for Normandy.

The agent who played the major role in FORTITUDE
SOUTH was GARBO, but TATE's chance to shine came during
the last year of the war when he fed inaccurate intelligence to the
Germans about the fall of the V-weapons (the V-1 flying bomb
and the V-2 rocket) that they launched against London from June
1944 onwards. The Germans wanted TATE to tell them where and
when these weapons landed, to ensure they were targeting central
London. To counter this it was decided to encourage the Germans
to shorten their range so that the weapons fell relatively harmlessly
into the countryside to the south. TATE did this by exaggerat-
ing the number falling in northern and western parts of London
and underestimating the number falling to the south and east. He
would also report correctly the time a weapon exploded, but give
the landing site of an earlier one that had exploded further north.

There was a twist to this particular tale that showed, again, just
how lucky the Double-Cross System was to remain undetected.
When the German headquarters controlling the V-weapons was
overrun during the Allied advance, it was found that some of the
bombs had been fitted with radio transmitters, so that the time and
place of impact could be plotted exactly by radio signals. However,
the Germans, thinking there was some technical fault with their
calculations, preferred to believe TATE!

But perhaps TATE's biggest single achievement during the last
months of the war was to persuade the Germans that large anti-
U-boat minefields had been laid off southern Ireland. By then
U-boat bases had been relocated to Norway, so the U-boats had
to cover much longer distances to reach their hunting grounds in

the South-West Approaches, and much of that distance had to be covered underwater to avoid detection. TATE's minefield would therefore be yet another major obstacle. On 15 November 1944 he reported that he had met a sailor who had told him how a certain U-boat had been sunk by a minefield off southern Ireland, and that a new type of minefield had been laid both south and north of Ireland. In fact the U-boat had been sunk by depth charges elsewhere, but at the time the Germans only knew that it had been lost. This ruse proved effective, for the next day German U-Boat Command ordered two other U-boats operating in the vicinity to stay out of the area, thus disrupting their hunt for Allied shipping.

In the following months TATE's deception and U-Boat Command's response to it were closely monitored by Bletchley Park. At first it looked as if the deception might not succeed, for on 24 November 1944, when TATE gave more details of the minefields that had been laid off the north coast of Ireland as well as the south, U-Boat Command signalled to its U-boats that the report was doubtful, 'since there is no evidence that the agent is still credible. He has already spent three years in England. He is also suspected of working for the enemy.'[17]

However, when TATE reported a new minefield south-east of the Fastnet Rock off southern Ireland, a signal Bletchley Park intercepted from U-Boat Command on 1 January 1945 confirmed that the bait had been swallowed after all: 'An agent reports a deep-set minefield 30 miles south-east of Fastnet Rock south Ireland. Size not known. Avoid this area. Channel boats [i.e. those directed to attack Channel shipping] would do best to haul off to southward.'[18] Further intercepts also confirmed that U-Boat Command had accepted his information was reliable.

Then, on 12 March 1945, a U-boat was mined very near TATE's fictional minefield. It reported its position, and that it would have to be scuttled, and the next day U-Boat Command issued a further warning: 'Hereby confirmation of agent's report concerning suspected mining southeast of Ireland.'[19] U-boats were also ordered to avoid a huge area of 3,600 square miles south-east of the Fastnet Rock, and were advised to travel at a shallower depth, which of course increased their vulnerability to detection and attack.

TATE's last deception operation gave Allied convoys a virtually trouble-free voyage in the South-West Approaches. It had saved a lot of valuable cargo and even more valuable lives, and he must have ended the war on a high. The Germans had had doubts about him, but he had continued to persuade them of his loyalty, and between October 1940 and July 1944 – there is no record of the number of transmissions he sent after that date – he dispatched over a thousand intelligence reports to his German controllers. It was a notable achievement for the Double-Cross System's longest-serving agent. After the war, he settled in Britain, married and had a daughter. He called himself Harry Williamson, the name the Germans had used for his forged identity and ration books.

* * * * *

MI6 was also involved in the Double-Cross System, as it assisted its agents when they travelled out of Britain. It also recruited new ones outside the British Isles, whom it then usually – and sometimes not without argument – passed on to MI5. Its first important recruit was a 29-year-old Yugoslav commercial lawyer, Dusko Popov. Educated in Paris and Belgrade before studying for his doctorate at Freiburg University, Popov was from a well-to-do Dubrovnik family and had the lifestyle of a rich playboy, in which fast cars and fast girls played the most prominent part. He was quite extraordinarily extravagant and to the consternation of the intelligence services that employed him (German and British, not to mention the Americans) ran up debts that they then had to pay.

Soon after war started, he met an old university friend, Johnny Jebsen, who lived the same high-flying lifestyle as Popov. Despite being anti-Nazi, Jebsen had become an Abwehr researcher, as this gave him the freedom to travel and attend to his business interests. He introduced Popov to a senior Abwehr officer who suggested he should join the Abwehr. Although Popov was also strongly anti-Nazi, he agreed to do so, but he then contacted the head of Belgrade's MI6 station, who saw the possibilities of a pro-British Yugoslav being recruited by German Military Intelligence. It was agreed that Popov should play along with his contacts, and that it would be a good idea to start an import-export business between Britain and Yugoslavia – then governed by a prince regent desperately trying to keep his country neutral – as it would give him the cover he needed to travel abroad.

In November 1940, Popov travelled to Lisbon to meet his future controller, Major Ludovico Von Karsthoff' (real name Kremer Von Auenrode). Von Karsthoff, who worked under diplomatic cover, was no Nazi and he enjoyed the fun-loving atmosphere of the neutral country's capital, and introduced his new recruit to it with relish. The two got along famously with Von Karsthoff instructing Popov on the basics of espionage: how to use a camera and secret ink, how to code and decode, how to throw off a tail, and so on.

His training completed, Popov flew to London in December 1940 with $400 in cash in his pocket, and a list of questions he was required to answer to help the Germans assess the morale of a Britain on the verge of invasion (it was this questionnaire that prompted the formation of the XX-Committee the following month). He was told to bring back the answers personally, and Von Karsthoff then added that, if Popov happened to still be in England when the Germans invaded, he should demand to see a senior officer and give him Von Karsthoff's name. 'He will know who I am'!

In London, Popov was closely questioned by MI5, and his inter-rogators soon agreed they had acquired a double agent of the highest calibre who could cause the Germans untold mischief. Initially, MI5 codenamed him SKOOT, but once he had acquired two notional sub-agents for his non-existent espionage network, he was given the codename TRICYCLE as the three of them would be working together. The rumour that he acquired the codename because he enjoyed three-in-a-bed sex was probably spread to reinforce his image of a playboy.

In January, TRICYCLE returned to Lisbon with the answers to the Abwehr's questionnaire compiled by MI5. Satisfied, Von Karsthoff dispatched TRICYCLE again to London with another questionnaire. This time he was given a phial of invisible ink crys-tals and instructed to dissolve them in a wineglass three-quarters full of water, and to send his answers in the ink on the back of three ordinary letters which he was to write to three cover addresses in Lisbon. Communicating by secret writing was laborious, as each word had to be printed in capital letters. The water had to be free of chlorine to prevent the paper from being discoloured, and not a speck of dirt could contaminate the pen nib. To make the invisible message readable, the paper was ironed until it turned brown.

Initially impressed with TRICYCLE, the XX-Committee now began to have doubts. For instance, he claimed to own a yacht, but on questioning him, the committee's naval representative, Commander Ewen Montagu, found he seemed to know little about the sport – though Montagu admitted this might have been because TRICYCLE did not sail the yacht himself. His case officer also had doubts: 'I have just the general feeling that he may be a most accomplished liar. In fact, if he was able to persuade the Germans that he had influential English connections, whereas the truth is that he only knows three rather insignificant people in the whole country, he must be a good liar.'[20]

However, after a trip to Scotland, during which TRICYCLE was discreetly quizzed by various people, his case officer wrote: 'I have come to the conclusion that he is definitely working for us and not the Germans', and after writing a favourable analysis of his character, added: 'He is fond of the society of attractive women, who are apparently plentiful in Dubrovnik … He has personality and charm and would feel at home, I should think, in society circles in any European or American capital, being much the usual type of international playboy.'[21]

The XX-Committee agreed and set about composing plausible responses to the many Abwehr questions TRICYCLE had brought with him, supplied him with the necessary documents to trade between Yugoslavia and the UK, and arranged for him to rent an office in Regent Street. Two suitable candidates were also found for his British espionage network. The network was notional, but the sub-agents were real enough as the XX-Committee knew the Germans might want to meet them. An obvious choice, as the two men had similar tastes and interests, was Dickie Metcalfe, an ex-army officer who had already been involved in intelligence work. Codenamed BALLOON, Metcalfe was to be presented to the Abwehr as an embittered officer who had been cashiered for passing dud cheques and who was in desperate need of money. He was told by MI5 that if the Abwehr employed him they would pay him well, though it 'was made clear to him of course that we would regard any money which he might receive as being our property, although he would receive a proportion of it'.[22]

The other recruit was the beautiful Friedl Gaertner, a future lover of TRICYCLE's who mixed in the highest social circles and to whom he had already taken a great liking. Codenamed GELATINE, Gaertner was a part-time informer for MI5, and as some of her family lived in Germany, the Abwehr would think her a logical choice for TRICYCLE to make.

* * * * *

On 14 March 1941, TRICYCLE flew back to Lisbon, carrying with him a number of ordinary letters from his two recruits. On the back of these was written in secret ink the answers to the questions he had been sent to England to obtain. Von Karsthoff was delighted with TRICYCLE's information, and that he had acquired two promising sub-agents. However, the Abwehr had other plans for him, for it had been decided to send him to the still neutral United States to create a new espionage network there.

This news was received unenthusiastically by MI5, as the warmth of TRICYCLE's reception in Lisbon convinced them that the Yugoslav was now trusted by the Germans and could become an important part of the Double-Cross System. However, if TRICYCLE was to retain German confidence, it seemed best to play along with their plans, and it was suggested to the American Federal Bureau of Investigation (FBI), the country's domestic intelligence agency, that it would be a good idea to run TRICYCLE as a double agent from the United States. The FBI agreed to co-operate – or at least seemed to do so – and to obtain a diplomatic visa, which would give him complete freedom of movement, TRICYCLE was appointed as 'Delegate of the Yugoslav Ministry of Information'[23] to co-ordinate propaganda in the United States and the Americas. When TRICYCLE asked exactly how he was to organise his network, Von Karsthoff replied:

> Organise nothing. We don't want an organization *per se*. We had that and it collapsed because there were too many links between agents. Do as you did in England. Make your own contacts and when you find someone likely, rely on your own judgment. If you are absolutely sure of a man, you have the authority to appoint him a sub-agent. Run each agent separately and concentrate on quality, not quantity. A compact reliable group will do better than a horde of amateurs like we had. And above all, Ivan [TRICYCLE's German codename], don't risk your life or your position. If you have the slightest doubt about anyone, let him drop.[24]

He was then handed yet another questionnaire to answer when he reached America. TRICYCLE groaned and made a remark about having to go back to school, but promised to start memorising its contents. Von Karsthoff laughed. 'No, no,' he said. He took

TRICYCLE into his study and pointed to a microscope on a table. TRICYCLE peered into it and saw a dot on a piece of paper. He adjusted the lens and saw the first page of his multi-page question-naire appear in sharp focus. That, Von Karsthoff stated proudly, was a *Mikropunkt*. It was the future of espionage, and had just been perfected by German scientists for the Abwehr to communicate with its agents.

TRICYCLE immediately made a report of this ingenious tech-nology to London:

> Very often during recent months the Germans do not write any more to their first class agents in secret ink. They employ full stop marks. These are diminutive photographs of letters reduced to about this size. It is possible to read the whole letter with a microscope. I received 6 for my trip to America. I will show them to J. [Captain Ralph Jarvis, the MI6 representative in Lisbon]. I am doing what I can to arrange for the future correspondence with Ivan II [the Germans' codename for BALLOON] with these full stops … My six full stops have been stuck on an old telegram and in the letter which I shall receive at New York they will be inside the envelope.[25]

What astonished TRICYCLE even more were the contents of the questionnaire, as many questions required information relat-ing to the US naval base at Pearl Harbor[26] on the island of Hawaii. When he queried the relevance of this information to Germany, Von Karsthoff was non-committal. But he was adamant that it was essential for TRICYCLE to visit Hawaii to find answers to these questions.

On 10 August 1941 TRICYCLE flew by clipper flying boat to New York. In his briefcase he carried $70,000 in notes; eleven microdots concealed in four telegrams; a novel by Virginia Woolf which he was to use for encoding his radio messages; half a busi-ness card, the other half being in the possession of a New York contact who was to hand him a wireless transmitter; a phial of white crystals with which to make invisible ink; and ten addresses for mail drops.

Shortly after his arrival, TRICYCLE was summoned to the New York office of the FBI, which MI5 understood would co-operate in running him as a double agent. However, his story was met with great scepticism. In vain did TRICYCLE explain how he had acquired the Pearl Harbor questionnaire, and it was not until he showed the FBI officers present how the microdots worked that they showed any interest in what he had to say. But it was the technology that interested them, not what the microdots contained, and when examples were forwarded to the president they did not include the questions about Pearl Harbor.

TRICYCLE was equally infuriated by the head of the FBI, J. Edgar Hoover, when they eventually met, as Hoover obviously regarded him with the deepest suspicion and distrust. He did not disguise his disgust at the Yugoslav's high living, which at that time included a passionate affair with the film actress, Simone Simon. Hoover knew all about TRICYCLE's lifestyle, as his men monitored his every move, bugged his apartment – which interfered with TRICYCLE's love life – and tried to dictate what he could and could not do. The low-level intelligence he was allowed to feed to the Abwehr by letter – the radio had not materialised – reduced him, so he thought, almost to the level of a gossip columnist. To make matters worse he was forbidden to go to Hawaii.

In an effort to improve the situation – and the intelligence TRICYCLE was providing – Ewen Montagu flew to New York to form a small XX-Committee, but without Hoover's co-operation nothing was achieved, and he refused to give it. However, as Montagu wrote later, he felt his trip had not been entirely wasted because it boosted TRICYCLE's morale and 'persuaded him that there were people who still believed in him'. To Montagu, Hoover's attitude was quite extraordinary:

> He couldn't, or wouldn't, see the value of deception of the enemy. I suppose it was because he was really just a policeman and just good at catching people. There was, of course, also his reported pathological jealousy of, and reluctance to share [intelligence] with other services – and double-cross deception can only be done with some form of XX-Committee bringing complete co-operation of all services.[27]

When the FBI did eventually come round to feeding disinformation to the Germans, TRICYCLE was not allowed any input into the signals being sent by an FBI transmitter, or even to know what was being sent; and he soon realised that the Americans were only establishing a radio link to obtain leads to any German agents at work in the United States.

Inevitably, the poor intelligence TRICYCLE was providing, and his inability to visit Hawaii, had adverse consequences: in March, Bletchley Park intercepted a signal from Berlin warning Lisbon that TRICYCLE could be playing a double game and that he should be treated with 'extreme caution'. This was a serious blow for the British, who still had high expectations of TRICYCLE's work in America; and though the FBI did begin to answer the stream of questions TRICYCLE was receiving, another intercept revealed that Berlin had decided TRICYCLE was under British control and had been ever since arriving in the United States.

By now TRICYCLE had run through most of the money he had arrived with and began demanding more from Lisbon, which was not forthcoming. He had already borrowed considerable sums from the FBI, who were now thoroughly disenchanted with him; and, as he had entirely failed to be a lure for any German agents who might be at liberty in the country, they considered him of no value to them, and recommended he be returned to Britain immediately. In this situation the British could only suggest to TRICYCLE that he could either bow out gracefully, and with their gratitude, or return to Britain via Lisbon and try and extricate himself from the mess the Americans had put him in. To their astonishment and admiration, TRICYCLE chose the latter course.

'How was he to explain his complete failure in America, in spite of having spent the large sum that they [the Abwehr] had given him?' Ewen Montagu wrote.

Even more difficult – how to explain his complete failure to do any of the things that he had been told to do? Worst of all, how to cover up his complete ignorance of anything that he had [allegedly] sent on the radio? The odds must be at least two to one that he was blown. And, if he was, it was pretty certain that he would be tortured to squeeze him dry of information about our system, and there was equally probable death awaiting him at the end.

For TRICYCLE to return to Lisbon, he added, 'remains for me the greatest instance of cold-blooded courage that I have ever been in contact with'.[28]

* * * * *

TRICYCLE arrived in the Portuguese capital on 14 October 1942, and with his usual mixture of charm, bluster and bluff – and the judicious gift of nylon stockings to Von Karsthoff's secretary-girlfriend – he persuaded his interrogators of his continuing loyalty and that it was all Berlin's fault for not providing him with sufficient funds. His fury knew no bounds, and being a natural gambler he then threatened to resign. The gamble paid off and Von Karsthoff agreed that Berlin had been at fault. It was, of course, in the German's interests to be persuaded. To have his most valuable asset exposed as a double agent would almost certainly have resulted in him being posted to the horrors of the Eastern Front, if not worse. To London's delight – and astonishment – on 17 October, Bletchley Park intercepted a signal to Berlin exonerating TRICYCLE from any duplicity.

However, Von Karsthoff warned TRICYCLE that if he wanted to remain on the Abwehr's pay roll he would have to work a lot harder. The only intelligence now required was military, particularly information regarding Allied plans to land in Europe, and how they were preparing for it. TRICYCLE was then issued with the latest technique for invisible writing, where the crystals were no longer mixed separately, but were contained in the head of a 'pen' shaped like a matchstick. To create an invisible message he was to attach a matchstick to an ordinary pencil, write lightly in capital letters on one side of smooth airmail paper, and then write a normal letter over it in pen and ink. Five of these matches were wrapped in cotton wool and sewn into the shoulders of TRICYCLE's overcoat.

There was one last argument about money – 'I had the very strong impression,' TRICYCLE wrote in his report to MI5, 'that Berlin was sending them more money than they gave me'[29] – before TRICYCLE flew to London on 21 October, where he found a comfortable house near Hyde Park. But he was soon in debt again, in America as well as in Britain, ordering such extravagances as nylon stockings and expensive chocolate from New York for his latest conquest. MI5 did its best to bring him under some sort of financial control, but it never really succeeded.

TRICYCLE spent the following months passing intelligence to Lisbon supplied to him by the XX-Committee, much of it groundwork for FORTITUDE SOUTH. This passive role did not suit TRICYCLE at all, and in the spring of 1943, when he heard that the Yugoslav government-in-exile wanted some Yugoslav officers stranded in Switzerland brought back to Britain, he offered to arrange this by organising an escape line for them. This would give him the cover he needed to return to Lisbon, where he knew Von Karsthoff would be only too willing to help him, as he could then infiltrate the escape line with his own agents.

TRICYCLE's plan was approved and the Yugoslav government appointed him an assistant military attaché and gave him a diplomatic passport. He left for Lisbon in July 1943, and in the diplomatic bag that accompanied him was a package of deception material that MI5 had carefully compiled. In Lisbon he found Von Karsthoff receptive to the idea of creating an escape line, and he also had long talks with Jebsen. Officially Jebsen, who was now his case officer, urged TRICYCLE to work harder, but unofficially he told his friend he was in trouble with the Gestapo over foreign currency dealings, and might need help to escape. He then began to speak freely about the Abwehr's organisation and operations, and who ran them. All this made TRICYCLE certain that Jebsen knew he was a double agent working for the British, and that he, Jebsen, was ready to switch sides.

TRICYCLE returned to Britain in September 1943 with a brief to discover everything he could about Allied plans for the invasion of Europe. He brought with him in the diplomatic bag a wireless transmitter, a Leica camera, the considerable wages he had negotiated, and a pile of nylon stockings. But what really interested 'Tar' Robertson when TRICYCLE arrived home was that Jebsen, now codenamed ARTIST by MI5, had warned TRICYCLE to get out of the capital as a new kind of weapon would shortly start bombarding it.

MI5 now decided the time had come to formally recruit ARTIST, and on 10 November 1943 a representative from MI5 and one from MI6 flew to Lisbon to meet him. TRICYCLE was aboard the same plane, carrying more intelligence material in his diplomatic bag, and was again travelling on behalf of the Yugoslav government-in-exile to oversee the escape line that the Abwehr had now agreed to fund. In due course, ARTIST held a series of secret meetings with the two British secret service officers and gave them invaluable intelligence about the Abwehr. To their consternation he then named GARBO as an Abwehr spy and gave them sufficient evidence to arrest him. He also gave them useful feedback about Berlin's opinion of TRICYCLE's network, which now included the two Yugoslav escapees. GELATINE, for instance, was thought lazy and produced a lot of nonsense, but occasionally she sent useful material and one day could, perhaps, come across something really important.

By early January 1944, TRICYCLE was back in England with yet another lengthy questionnaire. By this time the XX-Committee was devoting all its energies to implementing the FORTITUDE deception plans, but initially TRICYCLE was not allowed to be involved for fear that ARTIST – whose troubles with the Gestapo fluctuated almost on a daily basis – would be arrested and under torture would reveal what he knew about TRICYCLE, which was quite a lot. But the counter-argument within MI5 ran that the Abwehr regarded TRICYCLE so highly – the head of its espionage department (Amt I) said he was the best spy they had in England – that he could not be kept on the sidelines at such a critical time, and that the danger ARTIST posed was exaggerated.

With some misgivings the XX-Committee agreed TRICYCLE could return to Lisbon once more, again using the escape line as cover. He left on 26 February 1944, taking with him deception material comprising doctored documents and a bogus order of battle that included the fictional FUSAG now assembling in south-east England. However, in the interim the Abwehr had been subsumed into the Nazis' intelligence service, the *Sicherheitsdienst* (SD), and an SD officer called Alois Schreiber had replaced Von Karsthoff. Schreiber's debriefing methods were somewhat different to Von Karsthoff's fireside chats, and TRICYCLE had to endure an intensive interrogation lasting over forty-eight hours. But his ability to bluff served him well and the XX-Committee was delighted when on 9 March Bletchley Park intercepted a signal to the German High Command which confirmed that TRICYCLE's deception material had been accepted as genuine.

All seemed to be going well when, on 30 April, shortly after TRICYCLE had returned from Portugal, Schreiber was ordered to abduct ARTIST and have him flown to Berlin. When they heard this the XX-Committee knew they had miscalculated. However, Masterman believed that, while the committee had to assume TRICYCLE's network might be blown, he did not believe 'that even a lengthy and exhaustive study' by the Germans 'would sift the truth from the falsehood',[30] and therefore he was confident that the secret of the deception plan remained safe.

It was, of course, the end of TRICYCLE's career as a double agent, but FORTITUDE SOUTH proved more successful than some had thought possible, as did the landings when they took place on 6 June 1944. The lack of German reinforcements to the Normandy beachheads from the Pas de Calais was proof enough that the Germans had been totally deceived.

Later the same month a celebration dinner was held in TRICYCLE's honour. He later wrote in his memoirs:

> It would be false modesty to say I wasn't gratified, although I did squirm in my seat at the exaggerations of some of the feats attributed to me. I felt like Horatio at the bridge when General Petrie [MI5's director general, but he was not a general] described me as the man who by himself had held up seven of the fifteen German divisions during the invasion. Then to top it all came the announcement that I was getting an OBE. It would have been a splendid evening if I could have kept my thoughts on the festivities and not on Johnny.[31]

But TRICYCLE never saw his friend again. ARTIST was sent to a concentration camp, and was later shot by an SD officer called Salzer. When TRICYCLE discovered this, he tracked Salzer down in Germany. He intended to kill him, but when he eventually found him, he felt too disgusted to shoot the grovelling wreck, who fell to his knees begging for mercy. Instead, he vented his rage on Jebsen's murderer with his fists. But Salzer refused to fight back; he just whimpered and sobbed until TRICYCLE, thoroughly sickened, drove off.

After the war TRICYCLE settled in Paris and started a publishing business. He even married, not once but twice. He continued to have fierce clashes with Hoover, who after the war claimed all the credit for discovering the microdots; and he remained convinced that the FBI director had been guilty of negligence when he failed to pass on the Pearl Harbor questionnaire to President Roosevelt. However, the CIA's official historian, Thomas Troy, mounted a strong defence of Hoover after Popov published his memoirs in 1974. He suggested the questionnaire could have been for German intelligence, which just wanted to update its intelligence on US naval bases.

Perhaps; but perhaps not.

* * * * *

With TRICYCLE out of play, the success of FORTITUDE
SOUTH depended largely on the work of another double agent,
whose consummate skill in acting his part, combined with a fertile imagination, earned him the codename GARBO after the
famous film actress, Greta Garbo. Masterman, a lifelong cricket
devotee, wrote that 'If in the double-cross world SNOW was the
W.G. Grace of the early period, then GARBO was certainly the
Bradman of the later years.'[32]

GARBO was a Spaniard called Juan Pujol who, like
TRICYCLE, was recruited by MI6. A small businessman from
Barcelona, he had somehow managed to fight for both the
Nationalists and the Republicans in the Spanish Civil War, though
he said he had not fired a single bullet for either side. When the
Second World War broke out, the 27-year-old's detestation of the
Nazis grew in proportion to the admiration he felt for the British,
whom he saw as the only European barrier against Hitler's totali-
tarian regime; and it occurred to him that, as a deserter from the
Republican side during the Civil War, it should be possible for him
to acquire work in Germany or Italy, which could be a useful first
move to becoming a spy for the British. In January 1941, he therefore got his wife, whom he later also used as an intermediary with
the Germans, to offer his services in either country to the British
legation in Madrid.

It was not a propitious time for such an approach, as the British
ambassador, Sir Samuel Hoare, was determined to keep Spain neutral. He had therefore given orders to restrict intelligence activities
to a minimum to prevent any diplomatic incidents, so GARBO's
offer was turned down out of hand. Rebuffed, but not deterred,
he decided to become a spy on behalf of the British whether they
liked it or not, and what better way to do this, he reasoned, than to
join the ranks of the enemy. He therefore approached the Germans,
and offered to spy for them, either in Lisbon or in Britain. The
Germans were hardly more enthusiastic than the British, but after
some persuasion said that they might possibly be interested in
using him in Britain, provided – and it was a large proviso – he
could get himself there.

This half-hearted offer gave GARBO the chance he needed and
he jumped at it. He was a convincing liar, and a persistent one, and

eventually, with the Germans' grudging approval and a thousand pesetas, he travelled to Lisbon where by devious means – at which he was obviously adept – he acquired both a residency permit and a visa to enter Britain. On returning to his German contacts in Madrid, he was met by two new faces: Friedrich Knappe-Ratey (codename FEDERICO), and his superior, Karl Erich Kuehlanthal (codenames CARLOS and FELIPE). They, too, succumbed to his ingenious story, backed by telegrams from his alleged contacts in Lisbon, and eventually they agreed to recruit him, and gave him the codename ARABEL.

Equipped with secret ink,[33] four questionnaires reduced to a miniature size, and $3,000 – which he hid in tubes of toothpaste and shaving cream – GARBO returned to Lisbon, taking his wife and child with him. After another abortive attempt to be recruited by British intelligence, he came up with the idea of pretending to have reached his destination, and on 19 July 1941 he posted a letter to his German controllers telling them he had arrived safely in England. He said that the letter had been posted in Lisbon by a courier who worked for a civil airline, and that the courier had agreed to perform this task on a regular basis for $1 a time. In the letter GARBO also gave them a name and *poste restante* address in Lisbon, which he had previously arranged, saying that the recipient would pass their correspondence on to the airline courier, who would deliver it to him in London.

GARBO's German controllers accepted this explanation, for a few weeks later FEDERICO replied, approving his method of communication and reported that the secret ink in his letter had developed well. He told him that they awaited any further news with interest, and that he wasn't to forget to number his letters. Now armed with hard evidence that he really was in contact with the Germans, he returned to the British embassy. This time someone in the military attaché's office agreed to see him, but then failed to make the rendezvous. A further meeting convinced him that his only hope was the MI6 station at the Madrid embassy, and that to get a hearing there he would need a bundle of correspondence filled with intelligence the Germans had accepted as genuine.

Creating such reports from scratch must have seemed an almost impossible task, for GARBO spoke no English and had never been to England. Initially, he concentrated on creating a network of agents as his German controllers instructed him to do, reasoning that if he made an error in his intelligence he could blame it on one of them. He therefore reported in his second letter that he had recruited a Portuguese resident of South Wales who would watch and record shipping in the Bristol Channel, and take note of their cargoes if they docked in the area; and a Swiss he codenamed GERBERS, who would perform the same task at Liverpool docks.

This accomplished, he set about creating the kind of intelligence his controllers required. He purchased a map of Great Britain, a Blue Guide to England, a Portuguese book called *The British Fleet*, and an English/French vocabulary of military terms. Equipped with these and some relevant reference books and magazines from the Lisbon library, he started work. Especially useful were the advertisements he found in the library material, as these provided him with the names and addresses of firms that could have been connected with the British war effort, and one of his reports showed how he employed them to excellent effect:

> The firm of SMITH & COVENTRY LTD, of Glasgow who before the war made machinery have recently enlarged their factory and are now producing munitions, aerial bombs of heavy calibre … the same agent informs me that on the 2nd instant part of a convoy amounting to five ships of about 2,000 tons each unloaded large cases in the port of Glasgow addressed to HERBERT ALFREND LTD., of Birmingham which had arrived from New York.[34]

He also made good use of daily press reports and the British newsreels he saw in the cinema, and sometimes he made up an entire report, based on information from the Blue Guide:

> All along the Windermere–Barness road and along the road which follows the shores of the lake to where it crosses the Windermere–Ambleside road (at a point called the Wood where there is a small chapel of Santa Catalina) there are camps full of troops. These forces are excellently equipped and have modern weapons. They carry out intensive training exercises daily. They practise landings on Lake Windermere. They are equipped with numerous amphibious tanks manufactured in North America … etc., etc.[35]

He was also astute enough to vary his method of communication and to use whatever resources were available to him in Portugal. For instance, when his German controllers requested some publications published by the Institute of Statistics at Oxford, he went to the British Propaganda Department in Lisbon, claimed he was studying statistics, and asked if the department could obtain the documents for him. They not only willingly obliged, but did not charge him for them.

So plausible were the reports that GARBO devised, as were the notional agents who supplied him with the 'intelligence' he used, that they fooled not only the Germans, but MI5 as well when Bletchley Park intercepted Abwehr signals about them. 'Substantial and Plausible' was their initial reaction, though on closer examination they revealed flaws obvious to any Englishman. There were workers in Glasgow, GARBO wrote in one report, who would do anything to get their hands on a litre of wine.

This egregious error was not questioned by his controllers – perhaps they thought the inhabitants of Glasgow enjoyed their wine as much as the average Spaniard – but another mistake GARBO made might well have betrayed him if he had not bluffed his way out of trouble. Having received a letter from his controllers in which British regiments were numbered instead of named – perhaps they were perpetuating an error made by an earlier agent – GARBO, knowing nothing about the British Army, not unnaturally copied this method of identification in a later report he devised. This was nearly his undoing, for shortly before he was due to leave for England his controllers posed him a very awkward question: he had told them about the numbers of the infantry regiments he had seen on his way to Guildford, but that infantry regiments had names not numbers, so his message was of no use, and would he please clarify.

GARBO may not have had much military knowledge, but he knew the military dictum that attack was the best form of defence. He replied by saying that he was surprised at the remarks about the numbering of regiments and had his controllers never heard of the organisations known at the War Office and the General Staff? Almost a year ago, to avoid espionage, these organisations had begun referring to fighting units by numbers, though they were not as well known as the names. As his controllers had already used numbers and not names in their correspondence, he had assumed they were aware of this fact, and he had proof of it. Which did they require, the numbers or the names?

The Germans swallowed GARBO's mendacious explanation hook, line and sinker, and were suitably contrite. If he could provide both, well and good; if not, one or the other would do, but it wasn't necessary to send any proof as they trusted him completely. His work in England was most important and it was important for him to stay as long as possible, and they concluded by saying they were more than happy with how he was collaborating. In short, it was all of a bit of a climb-down which GARBO must have enjoyed reading; and, as GARBO's case officer later commented, it showed how important it was to be firm with the Germans. They were obviously keen to hang on to GARBO at any cost and 'The more we dictated our terms the more they co-operated; the more arrogant and temperamental GARBO became the more considerate they were in return.'[36]

* * * * *

By November GARBO was getting desperate, as he knew his reports, however cleverly devised, would not fool the Germans indefinitely. His ingenious wife, as a last resort, had already contacted the Americans and spun her own convincing tale, and in January 1942 she managed to obtain an interview for her husband. The Americans, perhaps less cynical than their British counterparts, accepted GARBO was genuine, but it was not until February that he was eventually introduced to a member of MI6 in Lisbon, and the following month the station recruited him as a double agent.

When MI5 had finally been informed of GARBO's existence there followed one of those not infrequent spats between the two intelligence services: MI5 wanted to run him in England, MI6 thought he should be run by them in the Iberian Peninsula. Eventually, common sense prevailed for it was obvious GARBO could not maintain his charade indefinitely, and in April 1942 it was arranged for him to fly to England after being smuggled out of Portugal to Gibraltar by sea. Soon afterwards he requested that his family be allowed to join him. The British agreed, but as his wife did not have a passport, mother and child had to be smuggled out of Portugal, too. GARBO's Abwehr controllers had already agreed that they should join him, if he could arrange it. As GARBO explained to them, living as a family man in England would give him excellent cover for his espionage.

Before leaving Lisbon, GARBO had sent a report about a notional Malta-bound convoy from Liverpool, details of which had then been passed to Berlin by FELIPE as coming from one of his informers, V-Mann (agent) 372. The message was deciphered by Bletchley Park, and when it was found to tally exactly with information GARBO had sent to his German controllers in one of his letters – copies of which he had handed over to MI5 when he reached England – it was established beyond doubt that GARBO was V-Mann 372, and MI5 realised they had an ideal candidate for the Double-Cross System. However, at that time only the XX-Committee's naval and MI6 representatives knew about Bletchley Park's ULTRA intelligence – the uninitiated simply knew it as MSS (Most Secret Sources) – and some of the committee expressed their doubts about GARBO's authenticity, as well they might. This led to giving the entire committee security clearance on ULTRA, and GARBO was duly recruited, and given a remarkable case officer, Tomas Harris. They hit it off immediately – helped no doubt by the fact that Harris's mother was Spanish – and they soon formed the most formidable duo within the system. A report prepared for the Prime Minister on GARBO's activities gives a glimpse of how they worked:

> Apart from the case officer, who spends his entire time in controlling, organising and developing the case, living GARBO's life and thinking GARBO's thoughts, GARBO himself works on average from six to eight hours a day – drafting secret letters, enciphering, composing cover texts, writing them and planning for the future. Fortunately he has a facile and lurid style, great ingenuity and a passionate quixotic zeal for his task.[37]

The first step was for GARBO and Harris to expand the notional network of sub-agents – they eventually created twenty-eight, some of whom went overseas – and for the Spaniard to establish in the Germans' eyes that he was a freelancer working for the BBC on propaganda programmes. This gave him good cover, and accounted for his ability to move around the country. It was a large, complicated enterprise that had to be carefully synchronised and controlled, and several MI5 officers were employed composing and checking the intelligence they were supplying to the Germans.

One of the XX-Committee's early conundrums created by GARBO's network was the convoy build-up at Liverpool which would occur in preparation for the Allied North African landings of November 1942. The committee reasoned that this concentration of ships would probably not escape the notice of the Germans, who would then be bound to seek information from GERBERS, GARBO's notional agent there, and would be suspicious if he failed to provide it.

As it was impossible to pass anything about the convoys without endangering them, the committee decided to pre-empt a potentially dangerous situation by eliminating GERBERS before the Germans had a chance to request intelligence from him. So it was decided that GARBO should inform his controllers that, having not heard from GERBERS, he had gone to Liverpool and found the Swiss gravely ill in hospital. Once the North African landings had taken place, he conveniently died and an obituary notice was placed by MI5 in a Liverpool newspaper, which GARBO cut out and sent to his German controllers as confirmation of the sad event. In another ploy, GARBO sent factually correct details of the convoys, though MI5 ensured these were delayed until after the convoy had sailed and was safe from German attack. The Germans were disappointed that GARBO's reports were too late to be of operational use, but expressed delight at their accuracy.

By 1943 GARBO's network had become so large, better communications had to be established with Madrid. The Spaniard had already informed his controllers that he could obtain a transmitter and operator, but needed the correct code in which to send his messages. In March 1943 this was provided for him – and was of great help to Bletchley Park, no doubt – and by the autumn an MI5 transmitter was sending nearly all his messages.

It was this extensive network that played such a crucial part in deceiving the Germans when FORTITUDE SOUTH was launched. But it also helped to deceive the Germans into believing that Chislehurst caves in Kent were part of an underground network of factories and arms dumps which they were invited to sabotage. However, the Germans on this occasion did not take the bait, and as the deception planners were unable to incorporate that particular ruse into their overall strategy, PLAN BODEGA, as it was called, was quietly dropped.

FORTITUDE SOUTH's notional formation, FUSAG, was commanded by the American General George S. Patton. Patton had blotted his copy-book in Italy – he had struck a soldier for alleged cowardice – and had been denied the chance to take part in the initial phase of the invasion. But this was not the only reason he was given his phony appointment, as intelligence sources had indicated that the Germans believed Patton – the most aggressive general of his day – would command the Allied invasion when it was launched. Patton even made his own personal contribution to this fiction: allegedly, some days before D-Day, he shouted across a crowded room at the Ritz Hotel to the paratroop commander General Jim Gavin, 'I'll see you in the Pas de Calais, Gavin!'

GARBO'S contribution to FORTITUDE SOUTH was pivotal. During the first half of 1944 he sent over 500 messages to his controllers in Madrid, many of which, as Bletchley Park intercepts verified, were forwarded to Berlin marked 'urgent'. In them GARBO played down the advanced state of the invasion forces and emphasised the importance of FUSAG to the Allies' strategy.

However, the risk of discovery was always present, just as the incident about ARTIST shows how narrow the margin was between success and failure. Indeed, Harris was so concerned that ARTIST might bring down the whole Double-Cross System that he recommended GARBO's work be discontinued. The XX-Committee decided against such a drastic step, as they had with TRICYCLE, but they did consider the possibility of having ARTIST assassinated.

When the invasion was launched GARBO's good fortune still held. The message he sent announcing it was imminent was, of course, deliberately delayed by MI5. As it was a ploy that had been used before, this was risky and could have roused German suspicions at a time when their complete trust in GARBO was essential for the next phase of FORTITUDE SOUTH. In fact, GARBO's signal was genuinely delayed because the German wireless operator in Madrid was not available to receive it. So GARBO sent a second message giving the operator's absence as the excuse for the delay of his original message. This arrived just as the first troops were landing at dawn on 6 June.

GARBO's most important contribution to FORTITUDE SOUTH was still to come, for in the ensuing weeks he helped dupe the Germans into believing that the Normandy landings were just a feint and that the main ones would be in the Pas de Calais. This resulted in the German High Command retaining formations in northern France when they were badly needed to stem the advance of the Allied armies in Normandy. The deception had been expected to last for no more than ten days, but intercepts, and the capture of a German map of England accurately marked with FUSAG formations, indicated that the German High Command remained convinced of a second landing in the Pas de Calais. GARBO therefore continued to inform Madrid of the massive Allied build-up of FUSAG forces there, and at the end of June there were still twenty-two German divisions waiting to drive them back into the sea. However, at the end of July the headquarters of Field Marshal von Rundstedt, C-in-C West, concluded that the further the Allied armies advanced into Normandy, the less likely it became that a second landing would be launched elsewhere.

Like TATE and other double agents, GARBO also passed disinformation about the V-1 flying bomb campaign against London that started on 13 June, a week after the Normandy landings. His first message was typical of the aggressive stance he took with his controllers, complaining furiously that though they knew he was a London resident he had been given no warning of the attack. After receiving profuse apologies from Madrid, he then proceeded, in a series of messages, to play down the effectiveness of the flying bombs and to manipulate the statistics of where they were falling.

However, the XX-Committee soon concluded that this disinformation might jeopardise GARBO's credibility, so on 5 July his notional deputy reported that GARBO had disappeared. Two days later he signalled that GARBO had been arrested while examining V-1 bomb damage in the East End. This caused great consternation in Madrid and then equally great relief when GARBO's controllers heard that he had been released without charge. GARBO then sent them by courier a detailed report of what had happened, copies of his arrest warrant and a letter from the Home Office to the Ministry of Information (GARBO's supposed employer) apologising for the over-zealousness of the police. Further apologies from Madrid followed, along with orders not to continue reporting V-1 damage as it was too risky. Shortly afterwards, GARBO received a message that Hitler had approved the award to him of the Iron Cross, Second Class – though it had been hard to obtain Berlin's agreement, his controllers said, as GARBO was a civilian.

His award of a British decoration, the MBE, that December met no such resistance.

Though the war was nearing its end, GARBO's deception role remained a secret closely guarded by the British, for they considered him well placed to discover if any German underground resistance was being formed to continue fighting after their country surrendered. To this end GARBO returned to Madrid after Germany capitulated and met up with his German controllers. He found both of them practically destitute, and neither gave any indication that any underground resistance had been formed. He could have returned to England, where he had been offered a job. Instead, he emigrated to Venezuela with the £15,000 gratuity MI5 gave him for his outstanding contribution to the war effort.

* * * * *

Finally, it is worth recording that, apart from the double agents run by the XXX-Committee (in Cairo) and the XXXX-Committee (based in Algiers and later Caserta), at least one operative of the Double-Cross System lived in Berlin and fed his intelligence to the MI6 Stockholm head of station, Harry Carr. This was OUTCAST, a Russian émigré who worked for the Abwehr's Russian section. He was also in touch with Swedish military intelligence, and was therefore able to pass information to Carr, not from one source but two. In May 1942, he became part of the Double-Cross System when, at Carr's suggestion, he told the Abwehr that he could obtain useful intelligence from his Swedish contacts in Britain. This 'foodstuff', as MI6 called the false intelligence passed by OUTCAST, was supplied by 'Tar' Robertson and was the usual mix of half-truths, facts and pure imagination. Impressed by it, the Abwehr allowed OUTCAST more frequent visits to Stockholm, where Carr had the advantage of debriefing him personally. Most valued by MI6 were the details OUTCAST provided of the damage caused by the Allied bombing raids on Berlin and the political struggle between the Abwehr and its Nazi secret service rival, the *Sicherheitsdienst*. So useful was his intelligence that in early 1943 MI6 called him 'the best source for information on the German interior produced so far in the war', and later described him 'as one of the most successful spies against Germany that the 1939–45 war produced'.[38]

NOTES

1. Masterman, J., *The Double-Cross System in the War of 1939 to 1945* (New Haven, CT, 1971) p. 3. The book was originally a report Masterman had written on the Double-Cross System in 1945. However, he had made public the principles on which the system worked many years earlier in a novel, *The Case of Four Friends*, which was published in 1957.

2. Andrew, C., *The Defence of the Realm: The Authorised History of MI5* (London, 2009) pp. 256–57.

3. The MI5 files on SNOW are in The National Archives, Kew. See KV2/444–453. For the other early double-cross agents he was associated with, see KV2/468 (GW), 454 (CHARLIE) and 674 (CELERY).

4. West, N. and Roberts, M., SNOW: *The Double Life of a World War II Spy* (London, 2011) p. 108.

5. Andrew, *op. cit.*, p. 249.

6. *Ibid.*, p. 249.

7. From *A Digest of Ham* by 'Tin-Eye' Stephens, published in Hoare, O., *Camp 020: MI5 and the Nazi Spies – The Official History of MI5's Wartime Interrogation Centre* (Kew, 2000, pp. 114 and 117). See KV4/13, KV4/14, and KV4/15 in The National Archives, Kew.

8. 'It was quite clear to me that we cannot have this sort of thing going on in our establishment,' one MI5 officer confided to his diary. 'Apart from the moral aspect of the whole thing, I am quite convinced that these Gestapo methods do not work in the long run.' See West, N. (ed.), *The Guy Liddell Diaries: Vol. 1, 1939–42* (Taylor & Francis, 2005) p. 98.

9. Hoare, *op. cit.* pp. 126–27.

10. One of the half-dozen German-born agents sent to England, Goose was quickly turned at Camp 020. But his time as a double agent only lasted a few weeks, as he was unable to contact his controller.

11. The Double-Cross System was largely funded by the money the Abwehr sent its agents to fund their espionage. In his book, Masterman calculates that the Abwehr provided about £85,000, a small fortune at that time when the average annual salary in Britain was around £320.

12. Another sabotage agent working for the Double-Cross System was Eddie Chapman, codenamed ZIG ZAG, a colourful character who had been jailed in Jersey for burglary. His MI5 files are in TNA KV2/456–463. See also Macintyre, B., *Agent Zig Zag* (London, 2007).

13. Even post-war interrogations of those involved in running TATE could not clarify whether the Abwehr believed TATE loyal or not. However, it was generally known that Abwehr case officers lived very well on the reflected glory of their agents and were notoriously reluctant to admit they were not as loyal or as competent as they seemed.

14. Another deception operation, FORTITUDE NORTH, was conceived to convince the Germans that the Allies would invade Norway. Both were part of an overall deception plan, codenamed BODYGUARD. The codename came from Churchill's remark that 'In war-time, truth is so precious that she should always be attended by a bodyguard of lies.'

15. West, N. (ed.), *The Guy Liddell Diaries, Vol. II, 1942–45* (Taylor & Francis, 2005) pp. 209 and 216.

16. TREASURE was a French woman of Russian descent called Nathalie Sergueiew. When France fell she was recruited and trained by the Abwehr, but once in England she defected. Though she was a competent double agent, her codename proved to be misplaced as she was temperamental and extremely difficult to handle; and when MI5 failed to bring her beloved dog to England without being quarantined, as had been promised, she went on strike. The split with the service when it came was acrimonious.

17. Jonason, T. and Olsson, S., *Agent Tate: The Wartime Story of Harry Williamson* (Stroud, 2011) p. 188.

18. *Ibid.*, p. 189.

19. *Ibid.*, pp. 191–92.

20. TNA KV2/845.

21. *Ibid.*

22. TNA KV2/846.

23. Popov, D., *Spy/Counterspy* (London, 1974) p. 121. However, a document (KV2/847) in The National Archive, Kew, records that the Yugoslav Legation in London refused to co-operate in this subterfuge. According to another source – see n. 29 below, p. 79 – TRICYCLE obtained a visa that June 'with the discreet assistance of MI5'.

24. *Ibid.*, p. 121.

25. TNA KV2/849.

26. The Japanese attack on Pearl Harbor on 7 December 1941 remains one of the most controversial incidents of the Second World War, and many historians have voiced their opinions on how and why it succeeded. TRICYCLE's questionnaire was just one of a number of early warnings which, with hindsight, could have alerted the authorities to the raid. The questionnaire can be read in full in Masterman, *op. cit.*, pp. 196–98.

27. Montagu, E., *Beyond Top Secret Ultra* (London, 1977) p. 80.

28. *Ibid.*, p. 81.

29. Miller, R., *Codename Tricycle: The True Story of the Second World War's Most Extraordinary Double Agent* (London, 1977) pp. 159–60.

30. TNA KV2/858.

31. Popov, *op. cit.*, p. 249.

32. Masterman, *op. cit.*, p. 114.

33. Cotton-wool pellets were impregnated with the secret ink, and GARBO could hide them in his ears before passing through British customs.

34. *Garbo: The Spy Who Saved D-Day*, introduction by Mark Seaman (Kew, 2004) p. 56. See TNA KV2/41.

35. *Ibid.*, p. 58.

36. *Ibid.*, p. 86.

37. Andrew, *op. cit.*, p. 294.

38. Jeffery, K., *MI6: The History of the Secret Intelligence Service, 1909–1949* (London, 2010) pp. 516–17. The author does not reveal the real name of OUTCAST, who died of TB in London in 1944 after MI6 had managed to get him and his family to London.

7

Decoding America's Soviet Spy Rings

Spies, or HUMINT (human intelligence), are not the only means of obtaining another country's secrets; SIGINT (signals intelligence) also plays a vital part – as did ULTRA intelligence during the Second World War – and sometimes a predominant one.

In February 1943 work began in the United States to break the complex cipher in which the Soviet People's Commissariat of Foreign Affairs – the Soviet Union's Foreign Office – communicated with its diplomatic staff overseas. Colonel Carter Clarke of the US War Department's Military Intelligence Division tasked the Signals Intelligence Service – which became the Signals Security Agency (SSA) in July 1943 – to break this cipher, as he suspected Stalin might be attempting to negotiate a separate peace with Nazi Germany, which would have been calamitous for the Allies. If the cipher could be cracked, the decrypted messages, he reasoned, would surely give an indication of the Soviet leader's intentions.

Clarke's initiative was given several codenames before eventually becoming known as VENONA.[1] It started with a single cryptographer, but the numbers gradually increased and when the war ended many other cryptographic experts, who had been working on the notoriously difficult Japanese ciphers, joined the programme which was based at the SSA's headquarters at Arlington Hall, Virginia. However, so secure was the Soviet cipher, and so painstaking were the methods necessary to break it, that it took until mid-1946 for the signals to begin yielding up their secrets. Once they did so, it became clear there was no evidence of a wartime Soviet–German peace deal. What they did reveal was a lot more startling: the signals, or deciphered fragments of them, concerned espionage, not diplomacy. The very first signal, partly decrypted on 31 July 1946 by the brilliant cryptographer Meredith Gardner, was sent to Moscow by Soviet agents in New York on 10 August 1944, and was found to relate to Soviet intelligence undercover work in Latin America.

This put the programme on an entirely different footing, as the SSA was an agency that specialised in cryptology, not in hunting down spies whose identities were concealed by cover names in the text of the messages. Carter Clarke, now a general, therefore requested the aid of the FBI, and in September 1948 Special Agent Robert Lamphere[2] was attached to the SSA to liaise full time with those working on the project. Eventually, the FBI provided the probable cover names for 200 individuals it suspected of espionage. Right from the start it was like fitting together a very complicated, and incomplete, puzzle. Decrypting the signals was, as one of the agency's cryptographers later remarked,

> [an] agonizingly slow and difficult process in which sometimes only one or two words at a time were wrenched grudgingly from the code. Each new recovery came with the elation akin to finding a pearl in an oyster. But each recovery also led to renewed work as each message had to be reviewed so see if that code group was present and, if it was, then the enlarged context was checked and scrutinised to see if it provided clues to other unrecovered code groups. Similarly, as counterintelligence information based on the decrypts was passed to the FBI and the FBI investigated the leads, new information was developed which sometimes enabled new breaks into the code. Then the process would begin all over again.[3]

The first part of the Soviet cipher's two-part system was the virtually unbreakable 'one-time pad'.[4] However, the Arlington Hall cryptanalysts found a flaw in how it had been used by their Soviet counterparts. It is conjecture how this flaw occurred, but one book on the subject gives a convincing scenario of what happened:

> The Soviets, who had a well-deserved reputation for obsession with secrecy, chose to do things the hard way, using one-time pads and paying the price of employing a small army of codemakers. For a while, though, Soviet cryptographers were unable to produce new key pages[5] fast enough to meet demand. In June 1941 Adolf Hitler broke his alliance with Joseph Stalin and invaded the USSR. Overnight the production of ciphered messages by Soviet diplomatic and intelligence offices skyrocketed. It is not known for certain, but it appears that the existing stock

of one-time pads began to melt away, and the Soviet cryptographic office in Moscow faced an emergency. Individuals who
failed to meet military production quotas faced severe, sometimes mortal consequences, so the crisis was not only national
but also personal. The solution, in early 1942, was to produce
duplicate key pages. Whether this expedient was introduced
intentionally, by a panicky senior official or a desperately overworked staff of cryptographers, is not known. In any case, tens of
thousands of duplicate key pages were bound in one-time pads
during 1942 ...[6]

Thus turning the one-time pad into a two-time one. Even so, this
only degraded the system marginally and those responsible must
have thought it a low-risk stratagem. They probably reasoned that
only someone with extensive resources and the time to employ
them would even consider tackling the task: unfortunately for the
Soviet cryptographers, the Americans possessed both.

Once the key had been identified and its random numbers
stripped from the four-digit groups, the second part of the cipher
came into play as the groups themselves had to be deciphered.
This meant recreating the Soviet codebook with which the groups
had been originally enciphered. This was made possible after five
variants of the one-time pad cipher had been identified and large
numbers of four-digit groups, where duplicate key pages had been
used, had been extracted from two of them: trade and the Soviet
foreign intelligence service. The latter was renamed a number of
times over the years – NKGB, NKVD, MGB, etc. – but for the sake
of simplicity it will be known in this chapter as the NKVD until
it was finally renamed the KGB in 1954, just as from this point the
Signals Security Agency and its multifarious successors will simply
be called Arlington Hall.

When the codebook for the NKVD variant began to be recon-
structed in July 1946, it was found to cover the period between
November 1943 and early 1946, but an earlier codebook had been
used for 1942 and most of 1943. Little progress was made on recon-
structing the codebook for this earlier period until there was a
breakthrough in late 1952, but even so it was never as complete as
that achieved by the reconstruction of the later codebook. Initially,
this reconstruction was done without computers, but cryptanalysts were later aided by partially burnt copies of the Soviet

codebook that the Finns had captured at Petsamo when they and the Germans had launched their invasion of the Soviet Union on 22 June 1941. The copies were then acquired by the Germans, and in May 1945 were discovered in a signals intelligence archive in Saxony by a US Army intelligence team, who removed them just a day before the Red Army occupied the area.

A breakthrough of another of the system's five variants, the one used by Soviet diplomats, came in 1950, which two years later led to the GRU (Soviet Military Intelligence) variant partially yielding to computer analysis, as it also did to British cryptanalysts who were working with the Americans on breaking the ciphers. Work continued on the programme throughout the 1970s, finally ceasing on 1 October 1980, but complete success with any of the five variants remained elusive.

More than 2,900 signals, sent and received between 1940 and 1948, produced over 5,000 pages of deciphered text. But this included only 49 per cent of the 1944 messages sent between the NKVD station in New York and its Moscow headquarters, 15 per cent of those sent in 1943, and only 1.8 per cent sent in 1942. An even smaller percentage – 1.5 per cent – of the 1945 signals between the NKVD's Washington station and Moscow were deciphered, and though about half of the naval GRU's 1943 messages were eventually broken, no other year yielded anything at all. Decryption in real time was never possible.

* * * * *

From the start of the European war in September 1939, the US government kept copies of all international cables to and from the United States. Unlike the British, who had agreed to the Soviet embassy communicating with Moscow by radio, Soviet staff in the USA used encrypted cable messages, copies of which the cable companies then passed, as required by a wartime law, to the American censors. Soviet encrypted messages were also acquired from a number of other nations to help break the cipher. Australia was one of these and in 1947 Meredith Gardner discovered that the Soviet foreign intelligence service in Moscow was still reusing one-time pads to communicate with its *rezidentura* in Canberra, and its cables were therefore vulnerable.

At the request of Arlington Hall, the British Government Communications Headquarters (GCHQ), the peacetime successor of Bletchley Park but still part of MI5, sent a liaison officer to work on decrypting the Moscow–Canberra messages, though he was not informed about the other VENONA traffic the Americans were working on. However, the few MI5 officers in the know about VENONA soon suspected that the Americans were also attempting to decrypt wartime signals between Moscow and its American *rezidentura*. But they only learnt this for certain when they were informed in early 1949 that VENONA indicated there had been a Soviet spy in Britain's Washington embassy in 1945. MI5's assistance was requested to help identify him, and led to the unmasking in April 1951 of Donald Maclean, one of The Cambridge Five (see Chapter 3).

On 24 November 1947, MI5's deputy director general was informed that a two-year-old Soviet cable showed that there had been a leakage of highly confidential British material from an Australian government department. MI5's director general at the time, Percy Sillitoe, therefore had to brief Attlee, the British Prime Minister, about VENONA and tell him that decrypts showed that Soviet agents had acquired confidential documents 'on post-war strategic planning from "friends" in the Australian Department of External Affairs'[7] – 'friends' in intelligence terminology meant spies. Attlee then dispatched Sillitoe to Australia to brief the Australian Prime Minister, Ben Chifley, on what had happened, but not on how it had been revealed.

Chifley and Sillitoe did not hit it off – 'There is a fellow here with a bloody silly name – Sillitoe,' Chifley telephoned Sir Frederick Snedden, secretary of the Department of Defence. 'As far as I can make out he is the chief bloody spy – you had better have a look at him and find out what he wants.'[8] Nor did the cover story spun by Sillitoe to protect VENONA deceive the hard-nosed Australians. The result of this debacle was that Sillitoe had to go cap in hand to Washington to obtain permission to brief Chifley on VENONA. This was granted but in the meantime the Americans had put an embargo on sending any classified material to Canberra, which caused further ructions. The suspects were eventually identified – but were never prosecuted as Australia at the time had no laws against spying in peacetime – and the furore led to the formation of the Australian Security Intelligence Organisation (ASIO).

From all this arose an extraordinary situation: the British and Australians were now privy to a highly secret American source which the FBI had gone to extreme lengths to keep from their own people, as not even President Truman or the CIA (Central Intelligence Agency, roughly the American equivalent of MI6), knew about the VENONA programme. In July 1949 the new head of Arlington Hall was outraged to discover, on taking up his post, that while previously serving on the United States Communications Intelligence Board he had not been informed about VENONA; and was even more outraged to hear that neither the CIA nor the President had been briefed on it. He demanded that Carter Clarke, the previous head, inform both immediately. Carter Clarke refused and the dispute was put before the chairman of the Joint Chiefs of Staff, General Omar Bradley.

Bradley sided with Carter Clarke. It was, as MI5's official historian commented, 'an extraordinary act of insubordination'[9] against Truman, who was his commander-in-chief, though Bradley did say he would take personal responsibility for passing the President any crucial intelligence VENONA might divulge, if it was absolutely essential to do so. Even then, Bradley assured Carter Clarke, its origin would be disguised. Both men took this drastic step because they feared the CIA would hear about VENONA from Truman, who had a daily briefing with its director. Both agreed the CIA could not be trusted, as VENONA had already revealed that its wartime predecessor, the OSS, had been penetrated by Soviet agents, who could well have joined the CIA when the OSS was disbanded at the end of the war. It turned out they may have been right, as the NKVD agent, Vitaly Pavlov, later wrote that when the CIA was formed in 1947, some Soviet agents within the OSS were able to transfer to the new organisation.[10]

Once GCHQ was made privy to VENONA, it began work on decrypting Soviet radio signals that Bletchley Park had intercepted and recorded during the war. However, recordings had had to be abandoned in August 1941 (April 1942 for the signals of Soviet Military Intelligence, the GRU) so as to concentrate limited resources on the more important ULTRA intelligence traffic. They were, therefore, far fewer in number than the cables transmitted between the United States and the Soviet Union, but despite only having this patchy intelligence to work on, the British did not draw a total blank as recording the Soviet radio traffic had been resumed in June 1945, and all but one of the signals sent from Moscow to London between 15 and 21 September 1945 were deciphered. These apart, only five others were even partially decrypted, a meagre haul indeed, and only twelve of the twenty-four cover names mentioned in the signals were ever identified. It is not surprising, therefore, that by the mid-1950s MI5 had lost interest, though GCHQ continued to work on trying to crack the remaining signals.

Then in 1960 there were two unexpected breakthroughs. One of the cables deciphered in September 1945 had revealed that what Moscow called 'a valuable network of agents' had penetrated British intelligence, and this was now identified by a KGB defector called Anatoli Golitsyn as being some of the members of The Cambridge Five. Then the same year Sweden began supplying GCHQ with wartime GRU signals sent between Stockholm and Moscow. Some of these had been encrypted with the same one-time pads that had been used to encrypt the London–Moscow GRU signals that GCHQ had been unable to break. As a result, nearly 180 of these signals, from the period March 1940 to April 1942, were wholly or partly decrypted, and later another 110 were decrypted from the period September 1945 to March 1947.

These decrypts uncovered the presence of a GRU network in Britain, codenamed the 'X Group', which had certainly been active by 1940 and perhaps before then. Its probable leader had the cover name INTELLIGENTSIA, and in a signal to Moscow from his handler, dated 25 July 1940, he was revealed as the Honourable Ivor Montagu, a committed member of the Communist Party of Great Britain (CPGB) and the brother of Commander Ewen Montagu RNVR, a member of the XX-Committee (see Chapter 6).

From the decrypted signals INTELLIGENTSIA seems to have been rather a disappointment to his Soviet masters. However, he did obtain certain classified material from his friend, Professor J.B.S. Haldane, a fellow Communist and a scientist of international repute whose wartime work included time at the Royal Navy's secret underwater research establishment on the south coast near Portsmouth.

The identity of the others in the group remains uncertain, or at least unrevealed by the authorities, and in the early 1970s those working on it were obliged to report that they had not been able to establish who or what the X Group was. It did not appear to be the Communist Party but could be a faction of it. Moscow must have seen the group's role as gathering military intelligence, 'but it is difficult to trace the connection between Ivor Montagu (whose interests were largely in Film Production, Jewish affairs, International Table Tennis etc.), a Colonel in the R[oyal] A[rtillery], a girl in a Government Department and NOBILITY, a journalist'.[11] And there the matter rested.

* * * * *

Once the war had been won, and there were early signs of the Cold War, American perceptions of the Soviet Union began to change, from one of a wartime ally to a potentially hostile adversary, a perception championed by the virulently anti-Communist Senator Joseph McCarthy, whose influence in the immediate post-war years seems to have penetrated every nook and cranny of American society. However, in 1945 the Democratic administration still had its Soviet sympathisers, who accused the Republican right of 'red baiting', but its mood quickly changed to hostility when, in the autumn of 1945, Igor Gouzenko, a GRU code clerk in the Soviet embassy in Ottawa, and an American-born Soviet agent, Elizabeth Bentley, defected and uncovered the startling extent of the Soviet spy networks in the United States.

Gouzenko's motives for defecting were simple. Although he later said it was because he was disillusioned with Communism and the Soviet Union, almost certainly his real reason was to escape retribution for some minor administrative matter that had resulted in his recall to Moscow. Instead of complying, he decamped one night in September 1945, taking with him certain crucial files from the embassy's cipher room that he had carefully preselected for such an eventuality. These contained original plain text messages and pages from the GRU *rezident*'s daily diary. The messages did not match any of the VENONA material, but Gouzenko's knowledge of the GRU's cipher system was to prove invaluable to the Americans, as did his information about how Soviet agents had penetrated, among other organisations, the top-secret MANHATTAN PROJECT, the codename given by the Allies for the development of the atomic bomb at Los Alamos.

The defection of Bentley, later known as 'The Red Spy Queen', was more complex. Sexually promiscuous and prone to alcoholism, she was, wrote her biographer,

... much less of an idealist than her sources. She had only the vaguest grasp of Communist doctrine, which of course made it all the easier for her to abandon it later. For her, spying offered the chance to take risks and break the rules, all while earning a good income. Most important her supervisor loved her and kept her bed warm at night.[12]

While taking a master's degree at Columbia University in the 1930s, she had joined the university's branch of the Communist Party of the United States of America (CPUSA). There she was introduced to Jacob Golos (real name Jacob Rasin, cover name SOUND), an NKVD operative and a member of the CPUSA's Central Control Commission, who had helped arrange Trotsky's assassination in Mexico. Despite the strict rules (*konspiratsiya*) governing the lives of all agents, Bentley soon became his mistress, and by the time he died of a heart attack in November 1943, he had taught her all he knew about espionage, and employed her as an intermediary with his various networks. She had therefore encountered many of the agents he controlled for the CPUSA, and indeed controlled some herself, and after his death was determined to take over his role. However, her Soviet NKVD handler, Iskhak Akhmerov (ALBERT), wanted to remove her, and this eventually caused her defection.

Bentley gave the FBI details of spies in a number of government agencies, including the State and Treasury departments, the Pentagon and the White House. Among those whose espionage was uncovered were over two dozen government employees, including senior officials such as White House aides, Laughlin Currie and Alger Hiss, and assistant secretary of the Treasury, Harry Dexter White. According to her biographer, Bentley described and identified 'the most powerful Soviet spymasters in the United States, as well as the American government officials who served as their agents. Her defection would effectively shut down Soviet espionage in the United States for a period of years.'[13]

Dexter White was one of the few agents Bentley had never met and this must have told in his favour when he was investigated during and after the war. However, she knew all about him:

Harry had access to almost all the Treasury's top-secret material. In addition, because of [secretary of the Treasury] Morgenthau's policy of exchanging information with other Government agencies, we also received 'hush-hush' data from many other strategic departments. Harry was also one of our friends at court: he pulled strings to help any of our agents who were in difficulties.[14]

VENONA decrypts appear to confirm Dexter White's involvement with Soviet intelligence, and the autobiography[15] of one American-based NKVD agent, Vitaly Pavlov, records how, in May 1941, he met Dexter White and passed on to him a brief to persuade the White House to take a more aggressive line against Japan to divert Japanese military pressure from the Soviet Union's eastern borders.

The trouble for the authorities at the time was that Bentley had not a scrap of evidence to prove her accusations, and this is where VENONA eventually proved vital, once a series of cryptological breakthroughs had been achieved. Several decrypts also mention Bentley, using her cover name of CLEVER GIRL and later MYRNA, and these helped verify her statements to the FBI. The first cable, dated 11 December 1943, did no more than connect her to Earl Browder, the CPUSA's general secretary, because only fragments of it could be decrypted. But the next one, dated 23 February 1944, though only partly decrypted as well, did show she was an important intermediary between the New York *rezidentura* and another extensive Soviet network in Washington DC headed by Nathan Gregory Silvermaster.

Silvermaster (PAL and ROBERT) was one of the NKVD's most important spies in the United States. This is borne out by the fact that sixty-one VENONA cables – that is, 3 per cent of those decrypted or partly decrypted – referred to his activities and to those who were members of his spy ring. They included various summaries, copies and reports of diplomatic and governmental importance; details from the War Production Board on the manufacture of armour, guns, aircraft and ships; and data from the Board of Economic Warfare on raw material, manpower and food.

Born in Odessa in 1898, Silvermaster's family moved to China where, apparently, he learnt to speak English with an English accent. After the First World War the family emigrated to California, where Silvermaster gained a doctorate in economics at the University of California. Though always politically active – he played an important part in the general strike in San Francisco in 1933 – he was never an open member of CPUSA. After finishing his studies he became a teacher before moving to the State Labor Department and then to the Department of Agriculture's Farm Security Administration in Washington. Although he nominally remained in the Department of Agriculture, in 1942 he moved to the Board of Economic Warfare. His affiliations were well known within the American intelligence community but, though recommendations were made to remove him from such a sensitive department, he was protected by fellow agents within the Roosevelt administration.

So well regarded was Silvermaster by the Soviet intelligence community that later VENONA signals revealed he had received a regular income from Moscow, a bonus of $3,000 in 1944, and apparently – the deciphered signal is not entirely clear – a decoration as well, which his NKVD handler, Akhmerov (ALBERT), reported that Silvermaster was overjoyed to receive. Moscow certainly thought highly of him, as at one time Silvermaster was the only American citizen in the KGB's secret Hall of Fame.

* * * * *

The decrypts on the VENONA website[16] have been annotated by cryptanalysts as follows: where groups in a signal could not be deciphered this has been shown by the words 'unrecovered' or 'unrecoverable', or (very rarely) 'garbled', which is self-explanatory. 'Unrecovered' indicates that the original Russian language text could theoretically be obtained, but the cryptanalysts did not have sufficient text to work on. 'Unrecoverable' indicates groups that were not affected by the original cryptographic error caused by Soviet cipher staff, and were therefore not vulnerable to attack.

In the deciphered texts, the cryptanalysts occasionally added in brackets a letter followed by a percentage followed by a word or words. This indicates how the decrypted words were rated for accuracy, from a scale of A% to D%, the latter being the least reliable, and sometimes a transliteration of the original Russian word was also added in brackets. Words in capitals were cover names, with the person's real identity being added in brackets, though if someone did not have a cover name, his name was put in capitals without a bracket. For a better understanding of the decrypts, the cryptologists' explanatory notes accompanying them have been added in square brackets in the appropriate place.

A cable sent on 31 August 1944 by Vladimir Pravdin (SERGEI), an NKVD officer whose cover was working for the TASS news agency in New York, showed the extent of Silvermaster's network. Unusually most of it was able to be decrypted:

Your proposal about using AILERON (ELERON) [Abraham G. Silverman] as a group leader (GRUPPOVOD) cannot be realised for the time being, as the management has decided on the transfer of AILERON's and DONALD's [William Ludwig Ullman] branch (OTDEL) to a provincial (B% town) which will make it all but impossible to use them. In order to stay in CARTHAGE (KARFAGEN) [Washingon DC], A[E] proposes to resign (C% and get from) ROBERT [Nathan GREGORY Silvermaster] a situation in his establishment. Although PAGE (PAZH) [possibly Laughlin B. Currie], who is practically master of the establishment, is in strained relations with A. and will evidently be against taking him on, ROBERT hopes to influence PAGE through PEAK (PIK) [possibly Virginius Frank Coe]. ROBERT admits that the concentration of people in one establishment is inadvisable, but thinks that this is the only thing to do. For DONALD who is on military service, postponement is impossible. He and A. are making an attempt to stay in the old institution but to transfer to another branch that is remaining in CARTHAGE, but hopes for success (21 groups unrecoverable) about 'MIKHAILOV' [Engineer Petr A. BELYAEV] no communication was made. The workers of the OFFICE (KONTORA) [i.e. the MGB office in the Soviet Consulate General in New York] do not know about the MIKHAILOV you mention. Please be more specific.

The most important spy mentioned in this decrypt was Abraham Silverman (AILERON), who worked during the war as a civilian for the US Army Air Corps at the Pentagon. In July 1943, via Silvermaster, he supplied Moscow with details about the personnel strength of the Air Corps both in the United States and overseas, highly secret intelligence that must have been vital in helping Moscow estimate the Americans' order of battle. However, according to Bentley, he was a reluctant spy, being, she said,

… frightened of his own shadow. He saw FBI men behind every bush, and he would arrive at an appointment dripping with cold sweat, yet somehow – I could never figure out how – he kept on going. Periodically he would threaten to resign, and wearily the Silvermasters would invite him over for a meal of his favourite broiled lobster. Then, when he was well fed and at peace with the world, they would argue him into continuing.[17]

Another important member of Silvermaster's group mentioned in this decrypt was William Ludwig Ullman (DONALD, also PILOT and POLO). He shared a house with Silvermaster – and also Silvermaster's wife. Despite apparently being unable to work on his own initiative for any length of time, and requiring constant encouragement, Ullman was, according to Bentley, 'one of the best agents we ever had'.[18]

After being drafted into the US Army Air Corps from the Treasury, the Harvard-educated Ullman was posted to the Pentagon where he was able to pick up interesting intelligence from all the combat areas. For instance, on 29 December 1944 his NKVD handler in New York, Stepan Apresyan (MAY), cabled Moscow about the situation in China, where Allied forces, including those loyal to the Chinese leader, Chiang Kai-shek, were fighting the Japanese. In its first paragraph the decrypt says that the British had withdrawn from the fighting for the winter months, and part of the second paragraph makes it clear that the Chinese weren't doing anything either:

> Colonel of the Air Force of the COUNTRY [USA] ROSENBLAT saw in China caves and concrete buildings where they keep cargoes which have arrived from the COUNTRY in the course of the last few years but which have not been used. In his words the whole army of the COUNTRY in China is disgusted with CHIANG KAI-CHEK and with the fact what while not waging war on the Japanese he is nevertheless taking and stockpiling materials from the COUNTRY.

The third paragraph concerns the activities of the OSS, to which Soviet intelligence had given the cover name IZBA, a type of log cabin for peasants and which the VENONA cryptanalysts translated simply as the HUT. Part of this paragraph reads: 'One of the strongest and most evil of the COUNTRY's forces in China is IZBA that is closely connected with the secret police.'

VENONA shows that apart from ENORMOZ, the Soviet codename for the atomic bomb project, Moscow's greatest interest concerned the American intelligence agencies, particularly the OSS and its immediate predecessor, the Office of the Co-ordinator of Information, to which it gave the same cover name, and the NKVD took considerable trouble to penetrate it. One decrypt of a message from Moscow, dated 17 May 1942, said explicitly: 'We are interested in the Russian Section [SEKTsIYa] of the HUT', to which Vasili Zubilin (MAXIM) in the New York *rezidentura* responded by sending a list of everyone who worked in it.

One of the NKVD's most important assets within the OSS was Duncan Lee (KOCH), despite Bentley assessing him as 'one of the most nervous people with whom I had to deal. His innate fear had been greatly heightened by the "cloak and dagger" attitude that was then rampant in the OSS.'[19] Lee was a graduate of Yale and a Rhodes scholar whose time at Oxford coincided with an era when many of the students were active Communists. In 1939 he joined a Wall Street law firm, one of whose senior partners was William Donovan, the man later picked to head the OSS.

It is therefore not surprising that once the United States entered the war Lee was commissioned into the OSS after it was formed in June 1942. Initially he acted as Donovan's adviser and aide before being appointed head of the China section of the OSS's secret intelligence branch. As Lee had been involved in Russian War Relief and similar organisations, his political sympathies must have been known to Donovan. However, Donovan himself was relaxed about having Communists in his organisation and once joked that he would have employed Stalin himself if it meant defeating the Nazis. It would never have occurred to him that Lee, the epitome of an Ivy League American gentleman, would betray his country.

A cable Zubilin (MAXIM) sent to Moscow on 26 May 1943 gives an indication of the intelligence Lee was able to provide:

'KOCH' (KOKh) [Duncan C. Lee] reports that at the CAPTAIN [Franklin Delano Roosevelt]–BOAR [Winston Leonard Spencer Churchill] conference (1 group garbled) (16 groups unrecovered) known, 'IZBA' [Office of Strategic Services] has no (40 groups unrecoverable) information from ISTANBUL (8 groups unrecovered) (D% known to the Romanian ambassador but in the situation after) (53 groups unrecovered) thousand

dollars in support of an underground (B% diversion and) espionage group in France ... We discussed with KOCH the question
of his removing documents for photographing. KOCH said that
in some cases he (B% agrees) to do this, but as a rule he considers
it inexpedient. He promised to think (6 groups unrecovered).

Another decrypt, dated 8 June 1943, showed that Lee was far from
being the only spy in what was the most secret of America's wartime intelligence agencies:

(20 groups unrecovered) about the 'IZBA' and 'RATsIYa'
(RADIO STATION) [The Office of War Information] (24
groups unrecovered) PROBATIONERS (STAZhERY)
[agents] ZAYaTs [i.e. HARE; Maurice Halperin], KOKh
[Duncan Chaplin Lee], OSTOROZhNYJ [i.e. CAUTIOUS;
Julius J. Joseph] (he works in the Far Eastern Section of the
IZBA on the question of the maritime resources of JAPAN)
[or naval reserves]. KOLLEGA (COLLEAGUE), [unidenti-
fied;[20] sole occurrence] (he works in the Photographic Section
PICTURIAL DEVISION [probably the Pictures Division
of the News and Features Bureau of the Office of War
Information], ERSh [RUFF) [unidentified],[21] and UCN/19
[unidentified] (9 groups unrecovered) COMPETITORS
(KONKURENTY) [members of a non-Soviet intelligence
organisation] (49 groups unrecovered) with which we are now
occupying ourselves. On receipt of full information about the
people (1 group unrecovered) [the unrecovered group probably
represents either 'we will report further' or 'we will report by
postal dispatch'].

Halperin (HARE) in particular must have been an important
source if, as Bentley alleged, he had 'access to the OSS secret
cable room and the reports from their undercover men abroad,
but because of an exchange agreement he was also able to secure
confidential State Department cables and reports'.[22] He certainly
seems to have been one of the few agents Bentley didn't damn as
being nervous or frightened of his own shadow, saying Halperin
seemed a stable personality who didn't have a nerve in his body.

In due course VENONA also confirmed the existence of
another spy ring that Bentley described to the FBI, though she

failed to mention in her autobiography one of its more important members, Harold Glasser (RUBLE), a vice-chairman of the War Production Board, and only publicly named one of them, Charles Kramer, who worked in Congress on a number of Senate committees, including a sub-committee on War Mobilisation. Glasser, described in one VENONA decrypt sent in 1944 as an 'old fellow COUNTRYMAN' – the Soviet cover name for the CPUSA – admitted interest in Communism in the early 1930s when he was questioned by the FBI in 1947. But he strongly denied being a spy, though when questioned later on oath about his espionage activities he refused to answer. In fact, he had been working for Soviet intelligence since May 1937, usually for the NKVD but also for the GRU, as several VENONA decrypts made clear. One sent in March 1945 indicated he was a talent-spotter for Soviet intelligence, and others sent in June 1945 say he handed 'over a State Department analysis of Soviet war losses, a State Department report on a Finnish company that was believed to be hiding Nazi financial assets, and an OSS report on the movement of Nazi gold through Swiss banks'.[23]

Though no VENONA decrypts mentioned him until 1945, the leader of the ring to which Glasser and Kramer, and several others, belonged was Victor Perlo (RAIDER), a statistician working in the War Production Board. However, as he had been recruited by Bentley's lover, Jacob Golos, he must have been active before Golos died in November 1943. RAIDER's importance to Soviet intelligence on military matters is shown by the details he supplied about the introduction of jet engines, which his Soviet handler in Washington cabled Moscow on 29 June 1945:

Colonel BANKER of the American Army Air Forces, on the 8th June of this year at a meeting in the 'DEPOT' [War Production Board] on the work of the aviation industry, told me:
1. The motor for the new propellerless planes of which the most important is the 'P-80' is still (3 groups unrecovered) perfected at this time. In the factory they operate only 25 hours. (1 group unrecovered) in the Pacific Ocean theatre, at present, mainly are being used the fighters 'P-47' and 'P-51' 'MUSTANG'. The P-51 is the standard fighter but the P-47 is considered especially valuable for spotting targets with support taking into account its flight and analogous work at

low altitudes. The production of P-47 planes, possibly, will be considered in (10 groups unrecoverable) (5 groups unrecovered) 'ISLAND (OSTROV),' [England] used high-grade fuel – '115–145,' (1 group unrecovered), in the Pacific Ocean theatre fuel '100–130' is still being used. Fuel '115–145' will be introduced there only after 1 January 1946, when in the Pacific Ocean will be (13 groups unrecovered) fuel, changes are need in the cooling systems of the motors. (12 groups unrecovered).

To preserve the secrecy of the VENONA programme, Perlo and his group were not prosecuted. But this did not mean they escaped retribution, and those who were still working for the government were obliged to resign or retire, or their posts were simply abolished. Perlo, who was forced to leave his job at the Division of Monetary Research, refused to admit his guilt for many years. However, in 1981 he acknowledged his role in the leadership of the CPUSA; and when this split in 1991, following Gorbachev's attempts at political reform, Perlo sided with the hardliners, calling Gorbachev's new policies 'treachery' and a betrayal of Communist ideals.

To ensure that the top-secret VENONA project was not compromised, none of the other Soviet agents Bentley informed on were imprisoned for espionage, though two, William W. Remington of the War Production Board, and the White House aide, Alger Hiss, were gaoled for perjury. Golos had recruited the former to supply him with classified aircraft production data, and when Bentley revealed his treachery Remington was forced to resign his naval commission, and in 1953 was given a three-year prison term on two counts of perjury. He never made it out of prison, as another prisoner murdered him shortly before he was due to be released.

If Remington was a relatively minor player, Hiss definitely was not and his case caused a sensation when the US Congress's House Un-American Activities Committee began investigating Bentley's claims in 1948. The journalist Whittaker Chambers, who had been part of a pre-war CPUSA–GRU network and who had already admitted being a Soviet courier, took the stand and accused both Hiss and Dexter White of being Communists; and, later in the hearings, claimed that Hiss had passed confidential documents to him. In August 1948 Dexter White, who had heart problems, went before the committee at his own request and denied he was a Communist. He did not come out of the hearing very well, and a few days later he died of a heart attack, caused by an accidental overdose of digitalis that had been prescribed to help his heart, though others have said it was no accident and that he had committed suicide.

Hiss, a member of the Washington establishment, vehemently denied the charge, and sued Chambers. But America was now strongly anti-Communist and a member of the committee, the future President Nixon, who was a Republican Representative in Congress at the time, adroitly used the case to further his career. 'We won the Hiss case in the papers,' he boasted twenty-five years later. 'I had Hiss convicted before he ever got to the grand jury.'[24]

Hiss could not be charged with spying, as the statute of limitations had expired, but in January 1950, after two trials, a grand jury found him guilty of perjury and he was sentenced to five years' imprisonment, the maximum penalty. By June 1950 the FBI seemed to have confirmation of his guilt from a VENONA decrypt, numbered 1822, which appeared to identify him as having the cover name of ALES. Dated 30 March 1945, it had been sent to Moscow from the *Rezident* in Washington, Anatoli Gromov (alias Anatoli Gorsky, cover name VADIM), and read:

As a result of '(D% A.'s)'[25] [A.: 'A.' seems the most likely garble here, although 'A.' has not been confirmed elsewhere in the WASHINGTON TRAFFIC] *chat with ALES* [probably Alger Hiss] *the following was being ascertained:*
1. ALES has been working with the NEIGHBOURS (SOSEDI) [member of another Soviet intelligence organisation, here probably the GRU] *continuously since 1935.*
2. For some years he has been the leader of a small group of the NEIGHBOURS' PROBATIONERS (STAZHERY), for the most part consisting of his relations.
3. The group and ALES himself work on obtaining military informa-tion only. Material on the BANK [US State Department] *allegedly interest the NEIGHBOURS very little and he does not produce them regularly.*
4. All the last few years ALES has been working with 'POL' [i.e. 'PAUL,' unidentified cover-name] *who also meets other members of the group occasionally.*
5. Recently ALES and his whole group were awarded Soviet decorations.

6. After the YALTA conference, when he had gone on to Moscow, a Soviet personage in a very responsible position (ALES gave to understand that it was Comrade VYSHINSKIJ) allegedly got in touch with ALES and at the behest of the military NEIGHBOURS passed on to him their gratitude and so on.

Only Hiss appeared to fit the description in paragraph 6, for as a senior assistant to the US secretary of state he had accompanied Roosevelt to the Allied conference at Yalta in the Crimea, held in early February 1945, where future strategy and the division of post-war Germany were discussed by the great powers. But the evidence appeared far from being conclusive and in 2000 the historian John Lowenthal, a law professor, wrote a persuasive article[26] asserting Hiss's innocence. He and others put different interpretations on message 1822 after the VENONA decrypts were made public in 1995–96, and pointed out that the original Russian texts had not been released, making an independent assessment of the decrypts impossible. Subsequently, the original Russian text of the message was made available, without solving the argument one way or the other. In his autobiography Vitaly Pavlov asserts unequivocally that Hiss was not a Soviet agent; and when, in the early 1990s, the Russian archives, at Hiss's request, were searched for any evidence that he had been a Soviet agent, none was found. However, John Earl Haynes and Harvey Klehr make it clear in their book, *Spies: The Rise and Fall of the KGB in America* (Yale University Press, 2009), that the weight of evidence now shows that Hiss was guilty of espionage. It is the sort of situation in which conspiracy theorists revel.[27]

Soviet intelligence, of course, knew all about Gouzenko's defection. But it knew nothing about Bentley's betrayal, and the head of the FBI, J. Edgar Hoover, ordered total secrecy to surround Bentley so that any further contacts she made with other Soviet agents could be monitored by the agency. However, Moscow suddenly ordered all contact with her to cease because Hoover, as a matter of routine Allied co-operation, had informed the head of British Security Coordination[28] in New York of Bentley's defection, and this had been passed to MI6's Section IX in London. This was the section that specialised in counter-intelligence against Soviet espionage, but as its head was the Soviet agent Kim Philby, one of The Cambridge Five, it did not take long for Moscow to hear about Bentley's change of allegiance.

When Lamphere began the long job of comparing the information gleaned from the VENONA decrypts – where the cover names were and on what dates, their jobs, their family circumstances, and so on – with individuals in the FBI's investigative files, many of the cover names were eventually identified. They included the atomic bomb spy Julius Rosenberg, whose cover name was revealed in 1950 as ANTENNA/LIBERAL. This was successfully traced after a VENONA message decrypted in 1944 reported that ANTENNA/LIBERAL's 29-year-old wife had been married to him for five years and was named Ethel, a description that only fitted Rosenberg's wife, the sister of another atomic bomb spy called David Greenglass. Traced by the same method was the real identity of HOMER when it was deduced that the only British Foreign Office employee to visit his pregnant wife in New York had been Donald Maclean.

* * * * *

The first spy to be arrested and brought to trial purely on evidence provided by VENONA came in March 1949, when the FBI identified a Soviet agent with the cover name of SIMA as Judith Coplon. Coplon was an analyst in the Economic Warfare Section of the Justice Department who had joined a Communist student group at Barnard College, from where she had graduated in 1943. In 1944 she had been recruited by a young Communist friend, Flora Wovschin (ZORA), who was already working for the NKVD. It might be thought that the routine security check on new personnel would have alerted Coplon's future employers to her political sympathies; but it must be remembered that the Soviet Union was America's ally during the war, and that being a Communist supporter would not have disqualified her from government employment, as would have been the case with anyone linked to any Nazi organisation.

On 4 January 1945 the NKVD officer Vladimir Pravdin (SERGEI) met Coplon, and was impressed by her. Their meeting was reported to Moscow on 8 January by the head of the Washington *Rezidentura*, Stepan Apresyan (MAY), in a message that the VENONA programme was later largely able to decipher in 1948. A more recent version of it read:

SERGEJ's [Vladimir Sergesvich PRAVDIN] conversation with SIMA [Judith Coplon] took place on (B% 4 January).

SIMA gives the impression of being a serious person who is politically well developed and there is no doubt of her sincere desire to help us. She had no doubts about whom she is working for and said that the nature of the materials in which we are interested pointed to the fact that it was our country that was in question. She was very satisfied that she was dealing with us and said that she deeply appreciated the confidence shown in her and understood the importance of our work.

SIMA's transfer to a new job was made at the insistence of her (D% superiors) (64 groups unrecoverable) generalizing materials from all departments (OTDELY). SIMA will probably start work on 15 February.

On the basis of this preliminary information there is reason to assume that in her new job SIMA will be able to carry out very important work for us throwing light on the activities of the KhATA [the Federal Bureau of Investigation]. The fruitfulness of her work will be to a considerable extent dependent upon our ability to organise correct and constant direction. It should be remembered that SIMA from an operational point of view is quite undeveloped and she will need time to learn conspiracy and to correctly gain an understanding of the questions which interest us.

A final decision on the question of direction and liaison can be taken (B% only) after she has moved to CARTHAGE (CARTHAGEN) [Washington DC] when it will be ascertained (B% specifically) what her new job consists of.

This gave the FBI its first clue that the Justice Department harboured a spy. Another message reported that she was learning Russian, and this gave her access to FBI files on suspected Russian agents that enabled her to forewarn Moscow of any FBI counter-intelligence operations. However, it was the date for the commencement of SIMA's job in Washington, 15 February 1945, which gave Robert Lamphere the evidence he needed to track her down, for he soon ascertained she was the only person on that date to move from the Justice Department's Economic Warfare section in New York to the Department's Foreign Agents Registration section in Washington.

Lamphere knew Coplon's new posting would increase her potential value to Moscow, and she was therefore placed under observation.

This revealed, *inter alia*, that she was having an affair with a Justice Department attorney and that she travelled to New York twice a month to visit her parents. On 14 January 1949 she dined with a man in Manhattan, later identified as Valentin A. Gubitchev, who worked for the United Nations Secretariat, and she met him twice more in the following months. On the last occasion both were arrested and, when Coplon's handbag was searched, she was found to be carrying classified material, including some that had been deliberately planted in her department by the FBI as bait.

At her trial Coplon asserted that her only connection with Gubitchev was a romantic one and that the papers she was carrying in her handbag were just notes for a novel she was writing. The prosecution, by revealing her affair with the attorney, had no trouble in destroying her story of her romantic attachment to Gubitchev, but the FBI had been forbidden from introducing the VENONA decrypts as evidence. Instead, the court was told the evidence had come from a wiretap on Coplon's telephone, and both she and Gubitchev were found guilty. However, her prison sentence was overturned on appeal on a technicality.

Incidentally, Coplon's recruiter, Flora Wovschin (ZORA), who had worked for the Office of War Information, was also implicated in spying by VENONA decrypts. But by the time the FBI had managed to trace her, she had married someone who worked for Amtorg, the Soviet Union's foreign trade agency, and had moved to Moscow where the CIA said she took part in anti-American propaganda during the Korean War.

During the late 1940s Meredith Gardner, and those working with him on VENONA, collaborated with Lamphere in hunting down a number of other Soviet agents. They included the British physicist, Klaus Fuchs (cover names REST and CHARLES), who had worked on the MANHATTAN PROJECT. He was identified in September 1949 when a VENONA decrypt quoted from a scientific paper and referred to Fuchs as the author. British authorities interrogated him at the end of 1949 and he confessed, and the information elicited from him led the FBI to Harry Gold (codename GOOSE, later ARNOLD), who was arrested in Philadelphia in May 1950.

Gold's career as a Soviet agent was mainly devoted to industrial espionage and was a typical example of the success that Soviet intelligence, abetted by Elizabeth Bentley and her lover Golos, achieved in penetrating the American industrial complex before and during the war. Born in Switzerland in 1912 of Russian Jewish parents who moved to the United States when he was 2 years old, Gold's early working life was blighted by the Great Depression. He worked as a laboratory assistant for a sugar company before enrolling in the University of Pennsylvania. However, money problems prevented him from completing his studies, and his firm then made him redundant.

These events led him to become interested in Communism and the more just society it seemed to represent. He was even considering emigrating to an autonomous Jewish region in the Soviet Union (Birobidzhan). Instead, a fellow chemist and Communist sympathiser, Thomas Black, found him another laboratory job, and eventually he was re-employed by the sugar company. Black also tried to recruit Gold into the CPUSA, but Gold thought the organisation dull and refused to join. Later, Black approached Gold again, saying he had left the CPUSA and was employed in secret work for Amtorg. Helping the economic success of a more just society by pilfering the capitalists' scientific secrets appealed to Gold much more than the CPUSA, and he soon moved on from stealing what was being developed at his sugar firm's laboratories to being the courier for a network of industrial spies. He obviously found this no easy task, as his FBI interrogation made clear:

> The planning of a meeting with a Soviet agent; the careful preparation for obtaining data from Penn Sugar [his employer], the writing of technical reports and the filching of blueprints for copying (and then returning them); the meetings with Paul Smith or Ruga or Fred [Soviet intelligence officers] or Semenov [Gold's handler], in New York or Cincinnati ... the cajoling of Brothman [a chemist and industrial spy, a close associate of Gold's, who passed to his Soviet masters the processes for producing synthetic rubber and developing industrial aerosols] to do work and the outright blackmailing of Ben Smilg [a potential recruit for the network] for the same purpose; and the many lies I had to tell at home, and to my friends, to explain my whereabouts during these absences from home ... the hours of waiting on street corners, waiting dubiously and fearfully in strange towns where I had no business to be, and the uneasy killing of time in cheap movies.[29]

Despite these difficulties, Gold persevered and in 1943 Semenov rewarded him with more important work: that of acting as the middleman for a group of highly placed scientists, including Klaus Fuchs and Julius Rosenberg, who were working on the top-secret MANHATTAN PROJECT. It was to be Gold's undoing, for in 1949, three years after Fuchs had returned to England to work on the British Atomic Bomb project, the FBI gave MI5 evidence that he was a Soviet spy, including a VENONA decrypt dated 9 February 1944. Sent from New York to Moscow, it was marked personal for VIKTOR [Lieutenant-General Fitin], the Soviet chief of intelligence:

On 5th February a meeting took place between GUS (GOOSE) [Harry Gold] and REST [Klaus Fuchs]. Beforehand GUS was given a detailed briefing by us. REST greeted him pleasantly but was rather cautious at first, (1 group unrecovered) the discussion on GUS satisfied himself that REST was aware of whom he was working with. R. [Fuchs] arrived in the COUNTRY[STRANA] [USA] in September as a member of the ISLAND (OSTROV) [British] mission on ENORMOUS (ENORMOZ) [US atomic energy project]. According to him the work on ENORMOUS in the COUNTRY is being carried out under the direct control of the COUNTRY's army represented by General SOMERVELL (SOMERVILL) [US Commanding General Army Service Forces, US War Department] and STIMSON [US Secretary of War]: at the head of the group of ISLANDERS (OSTROVITYANE) [British] is a Labour Member of Parliament, Ben SMITH [Minister Resident in WASHINGTON for Supply from 1943]. The whole operation amounts to the working out of the process for the separation of isotopes of ENORMOUS. The work is proceeding in two directions: the electron method developed by LAWRENCE (LAURENS) [Professor Ernest Orlando LAWRENCE] (17 groups unrecoverable) separation of isotopes by the combined method, using the diffusion method for preliminary and the electron method for final separation. The work (46 groups unrecovered) 18th February, we shall report the results. Anton [Leonid Romanovich KVASNIKOV]

When Fuchs was interrogated in London by, among others, MI5's top interrogator, Jim Skardon, he implicated Gold, and when the FBI arrested Gold he in turn implicated David Greenglass. Greenglass then readily confessed all he knew about not only Julius Rosenberg but also his own wife, Ruth, whom Rosenberg had also recruited. Later the Greenglasses also implicated Rosenberg's wife, Ethel. Rosenberg's act of recruiting Ruth Greenglass led to his downfall and is documented in the first part of a VENONA decrypt dated 21 September 1944:

> To VIKTOR [Lt-General Fitin], Lately the development of new people (D% has been in progress). LIBERAL [Julius Rosenberg] recommended the wife of his wife's brother, Ruth Greenglass [later given the cover name OSA, but in clear text here so that Moscow would know who she was], with a safe flat in view. She is 21 years old, a TOWNSWOMAN (GOROZhANKA) [American citizen], a GYMNAST (FIZKUL'TURNITsA) [probably a member of the Young Communist League] since 1942. She lives on STANTON (STANTAUN) Street. LIBERAL and his wife recommend her as an intelligent and clever girl. (15 groups unrecoverable) (C% Ruth) learned that her husband [i.e. David Greenglass] was called up by the army but he was not sent to the front. He is a mechanical engineer and is now working at the ENORMOUS (ENORMOZ) [atomic energy project] plant in SANTA FE, New Mexico.

Gold, who was sentenced to 30 years' imprisonment, received parole in 1966 while Fuchs received a fourteen-year prison sentence but was released in 1959 and went to Communist East Germany to live. The Rosenbergs were not so lucky. Their prosecution for conspiracy to pass atomic bomb secrets to the Soviet Union led to their execution in 1953. It was a rare case of Soviet spies being brought to justice for spying – if justice it could be called, as Ethel Rosenberg's execution, especially, is still viewed by many as a travesty. Apparently, the authorities never expected the sentence to be carried out, as they thought Rosenberg, on being condemned to death, would confess, and then the death sentence would be commuted. But Rosenberg refused to confess and so did his wife.

* * * * *

Another cover name the FBI and the VENONA programme were able to identify was NICK, a Spanish Civil War veteran called

Amadeo Sabatini, whose cover name was mentioned in no fewer than fourteen decrypts. Sabatini was a long-time member of the CPUSA who during the war had worked for a Californian company that made aircraft parts. This had given him the opportunity for espionage by developing contacts with industrial and technical aircraft personnel. But he was also involved in a much more sinister affair when he helped shadow a high-level GRU officer, Walter Krivitsky, who had defected to the west in 1937 and was found shot in the head in a Washington hotel room in February 1941. Although he left three suicide notes beside him, the suspicion remains that the NKVD murdered Krivitsky, just as they had assassinated Trotsky in Mexico in 1940.

When interrogated in 1949, Sabatini implicated Jones Orin York, an aeronautical engineer and pilot with the Douglas Aircraft Corporation in California. The FBI caught up with York the following year and he admitted he had been recruited as an NKVD agent during a Soviet delegation's visit to the Douglas Plant in 1935. He also confessed that he had been paid to take photographs of classified Douglas aircraft plans, and had passed aircraft specifications belonging to the Northrop Aircraft Company's plant at Hawthorne, California.

York's cover name, NEEDLE, was mentioned in four VENONA decrypts. The earliest cable was dated 31 October 1943 and was sent to Moscow by the Soviet vice-consul in San Francisco:

'NEEDLE (IGLA)' [Jones Orin York] has handed over 5 films of material on the 'XP-58'[30] and the new motors for it. (3 groups unrecovered) will be sent by the next post. 'NICK (NIK)' [Amadeo Sabatini] has received the impression that 'NEEDLE' at present is doing all he can to (1 group unrecovered) and to pass on to us the most essential material. NEEDLE (C% considers that) all material on (17 groups unrecovered) nevertheless complains of difficulties. NEEDLE is in desperate need of funds for buying a house and his (3 groups unrecovered) 800 dollars. (1 group unrecovered) giving of this sum.

When questioned further about his Soviet contacts, York recalled that his last was a man called Bill who had given him money for a very expensive camera, with which he had photographed technical documents concerning a night fighter developed by Northrop

Aircraft. York said he had met Bill on a number of occasions, some
of them in his, (York's) house. The FBI suspected who Bill was and
one day they positioned York in a street so that he could observe a
man walking down it, and York immediately identified him as the
man he knew as Bill.

Bill was in fact William Weisband, an NKVD agent who had
been recruited in the 1930s. Born in Odessa in 1908, he had emigrated with his family to the United States in 1924. A fluent Russian
speaker, he attended the American University in Washington DC
and was drafted into the army in 1942. He was commissioned the
following year and, after taking a course in Italian at Arlington Hall,
went to London in the summer of 1943 before serving in signals
intelligence in North Africa. A shortage of fluent Russian speakers
led to him being posted back to Arlington Hall, where he began
working in the Russian section early in 1945. Though he was not
directly involved with VENONA, his work as a roving adviser on
the Russian language often brought him in contact with Meredith
Gardner and other cryptanalysts working on the programme.
A convivial man who got on well with all his colleagues, he would
have had plenty of opportunities to pick up gossip and information about the latest developments. Decades later, in 1998, Gardner
recalled in an interview on BBC Radio 4 that at the end of 1946
he remembered Weisband looking over his shoulder while he was
in the process of decrypting an NKVD cable which revealed how
the MANHATTAN PROJECT had been penetrated by its agents.

Weisband's importance to the VENONA story lies in the fact
that he almost certainly became the first person Soviet intelligence
took seriously when he informed Moscow in early 1947[31] that the
Americans were working on breaking their code. 'Considering
his position inside America's chief cryptologic agency,' one source
commented, 'there is every reason to assume that he did significant
damage to American security. Weisband certainly was in a position
to tell the KGB a good deal about the success of the National
Security Agency (NSA), which Arlington Hall became part of in
1952, against the KGB system used for most of 1944 and 1945. He
was exposed, however, before any breakthrough on earlier KGB
traffic or on GRU and Naval GRU cables, and the Soviets may
have thought those still immune.'[32]

Moscow had had earlier indications that its code might not
be totally secure. For instance, in late 1941 a Soviet agent warned

Moscow that a copy of the Petsamo codebook was in German hands, but so confident were Soviet intelligence that the code was unbreakable that they failed to replace it until 1943. The same year, 1943, the White House aide, Laughlin Currie, told Bentley that the Soviet code was about to be broken. In Bentley's original statement to the FBI in November 1945, she stated that she had heard rumours that the Americans were attempting to break the Soviet code, though she had no direct knowledge of the programme. More importantly, she mentioned relaying a message to this effect to Moscow from Laughlin Currie, who 'rushed over to Silverman's office and breathlessly informed him that the United States was about to break the Soviet code'.[33] This was a gross exaggeration, but as Currie and Dexter White were almost certainly behind White House pressure to put a stop to the VENONA programme, Bentley's recollection sounds plausible. Though the intelligence must have been too vague for Moscow to act upon decisively, it took the warning sufficiently seriously to make minor changes to the method of encryption in April 1944. Ironically, this only helped those at Arlington Hall to identify more easily the cables enciphered with the duplicated one-time pads.

Of course, the mere suggestion that the Soviet code might have been broken posed a real threat to those still working in the United States for the Soviet Union, or who had done so during the war, and Moscow had little idea of the extent to which it had been broken, or who was at risk. As one of the handlers of The Cambridge Five, Yuri Modin, later commented: 'This caused a ripple of alarm at the Centre. We had no idea what the Americans might uncover, and this information hung over us like a sword of Damocles.'[34]

* * * * *

What led the FBI to suspect Weisband in the first place is not known, although they would surely have closely monitored any Soviet-born citizen working in as sensitive a place as Arlington Hall. Once York had identified Weisband, the FBI interrogated him repeatedly. His reactions were not those of an innocent man. He vehemently denied committing espionage, but refused to sign a statement to that effect. He also refused to respond to a grand jury subpoena, which resulted in him being imprisoned for a year for contempt of court, and he lost his job. However, he remained obdurate, admitting to knowing York, but refusing to explain the circumstances.

Weisband was unmasked by York's evidence, and then condemned by his own behaviour, but much later, in 1979, VENONA played its part in proving his guilt, when the FBI concluded that his cover name was probably LINK. Only three decrypts refer to LINK, and the first was the only significant one. Dated 23 June 1943, it was sent by Pavel Klarin (LUKA), a senior NKVD officer working in the New York consulate. It read:

> The last 4 weeks 'ZVENO' [i.e. 'LINK'; unidentified] has spent (1 group unrecovered) school (4 groups unrecovered) … INGTON [there is some evidence that this may be Arlington Hall], where he underwent a course of instruction in Italian. At the moment he has been given leave until the 27th of June (12 groups unrecovered) the ISLAND [Great Britain]. By his calculations he will leave the COUNTRY [United States of America] in the first half of July and will arrive on the ISLAND at the end of July. We are setting up the following arrangements with ZVENO: the password for (1 group unrecovered) contact in any place in Russian or in English: our man: 'Hullo, Bill. Greetings from Gregorij.' He: '(7 groups unrecovered) on the west coast.' Starting from 24 July Z. will wait for our man in LONDON on Sundays on the (1 group unrecovered) at the entrance to Leicester galleries, Leicester Square and on (C% Wednesdays) (3 groups unrecovered) on the (1 group unrecovered) on the (1 group unrecovered) east corner of Orchard [this portion of the message was later repeated as ORCHARD and WIGMORE] (41 groups unrecoverable) Rush the telephone number and your instructions before (1 group unrecovered) June.

Even if Weisband, who died in 1967, had been caught earlier, the VENONA secret would not have been kept for much longer from Soviet intelligence, as Kim Philby started his tour of duty in Washington in October 1949, and he regularly received decryptions of Soviet cables and analyses of them.

Bentley died in 1963, aged 55, having been subjected to many years of vilification by those who hotly denied her accusations of their espionage, and by others who were just violently anti-Communist. She had continued to be in contact with the FBI, and to correspond with its director, and towards the end of her life agents noted the high esteem, indeed affection, in which she held the bureau. As her biographer has pointed out, her newspaper obituaries misunderstood the importance of her role in the Cold War, in helping to destroy much of the infrastructure of Soviet espionage in the United States. She was also at least partially responsible for setting the political tone of American life in the 1950s, which 'helped define the partisan warfare of the early period of the Cold War'[35]. Sadly, it was this warfare that discredited the radical and liberal causes that she had always espoused.

Despite the very large gaps remaining in our knowledge of what the VENONA messages contain, the programme must be acknowledged as a coup for western intelligence and a brilliant technological achievement. But the most exciting prospect is what the programme might still reveal when a Russian government, in the name of scholarship and historical accuracy, releases the key that enables western cryptanalysts to decipher all the VENONA messages.

NOTES

1. The word has no special meaning. There are at least two good summaries of the VENONA programme on the web: 'The Venona Story' by Robert L. Benson, which can be found on www.nsa.gov/about/_files/cryptologic_heritage/.../venona_story.pdf and on the CIA website: www.cia.gov: 'Venona: Soviet Espionage and the American Response 1939–1957'.

2. Lamphere describes his role in the VENONA programme in his memoir *The FBI-KGB War: A Special Agent's Story* (Macon, GA, 1995, new edn).

3. From a recollection of the project by Mr William P. Crowell, deputy director of the National Security Agency when the declassification of the VENONA project was announced at CIA headquarters on 11 July 1995. Courtesy of the National Security Agency. See http://www.nsa.gov then search for VENONA, then 'Remembrances of Venona'.

4. One-time pads, or OTPs, were used for enciphering and deciphering messages. Those employed in sending these messages and in receiving them used sheets of identical numbers and letters. The sheets were then destroyed, preventing any possibility of the message being deciphered by unauthorised individuals.

5. After the original text had been converted into four-digit code groups by means of a code book – a kind of dictionary – random numbers, known as the 'key', were added to each of the digits of the four-digit code groups for additional security. The key was known to both the sender and receiver as the numbers were printed on the pages of the one-time pads that were distributed to Soviet embassies, consulates, etc. on a regular basis.

6. Haynes, J. and Klehr, H., *Venona: Decoding Soviet Espionage in America* (New Haven, CT, 1999) p. 29.

7. Andrew, C., *The Defence of the Realm: The Authorised History of MI5* (London, 2009) p. 369. His source is the unpublished parts of Guy Liddell's diary, now in The National Archives, Kew.

8. *Ibid.*, p. 369.

9. *Ibid.*, p. 375.

10. A translated extract from Pavlov's autobiography *Operation SNOW* can be found on https://files.nyu.edu/th15/public/pavlov.html. As of 2013 there is no English edition of this book.

11. Andrew, *op. cit.*, p. 381. For a different take on the British VENONA programme, see Nigel West's 'Venona: The British Dimension' in *Journal of Intelligence and National Security*, (vol. 17, no. 1, Spring 2002,) pp. 117–34.

12. Olmsted, K., *Red Spy Queen: A Biography of Elizabeth Bentley* (Chapel Hill, NC, 2002) p. 54.

13. *Ibid*, p. ix.

14. Bentley, E., *Out of Bondage* (London, 1952) p. 136. *Treasonable Doubt: The Harry Dexter White Spy Case* (Lawrence, KS, 2004) by Bruce Craig covers Dexter White's life and the accusations levelled against him.

15. Pavlov, V., *Operation SNOW* (Moscow, 1996). See also n. 10 above and Koster, J., *Operation SNOW: How a Soviet Mole in FDR's White House Triggered Pearl Harbor* (Washington DC, 2012).

16. The translated signals, with accompanying explanatory footnotes, can be found at http://www.nsa.gov then search for VENONA.

17. Bentley, *op. cit.*, p. 137.

18. *Ibid.*, p. 139.

19. *Ibid.*, p. 151.

20. West, N., *VENONA: The Greatest Secret of the Cold War* (London, 1999) p. 252, names him as Carl Marzani. He was an OSS officer who worked in its Analysis Branch.

21. *Ibid.*, p. 252. West says he was Franz L. Neumann. He was a German-born left-wing political scientist who moved to the USA in 1942. The explanatory notes to the signals record that RUFF is mentioned no fewer than five times in other VENONA signals between June and August 1943.

22. Bentley, *op. cit.*, p. 218.

23. Haynes and Klehr, *op. cit.*, pp. 127–28.

24. Quoted in Lowenthal, J., 'Venona and Alger Hiss' in *Journal of Intelligence and National Security*, (vol. 15, no. 3, 2000) pp. 98–130. Lowenthal cites Kutler, S. (ed.), *The Abuse of Power: The New Nixon Tapes* (Free Press/Simon & Schuster, NY, 1997) pp. 7 and 9, as the source for Nixon's remarks.

25. West, *op. cit.*, p. 234, names 'A.' as Iskhak Akhmerov (ALBERT), Bentley's one-time NKVD handler.

26. See *Journal of Intelligence and National Security*, vol. 13, no. 3, pp. 98–130.

27. The website https://files.nyu.edu/th15/public/home.html, is dedicated to proving Hiss's innocence and has a lot of information on this controversial case.

28. A British intelligence organisation established in New York in August 1940 by the Canadian-born William Stephenson. Early on it represented MI6 and SOE (Special Operations Executive) in the Western Hemisphere and, until 1943, MI5 in Canada and the Caribbean. After the USA entered the war it was the liaison office between SOE and MI6 and the Office of Strategic Services (OSS). When the OSS and the FBI took over many of BSC's intelligence-gathering and counter-espionage activities, it became the intelligence channel

between these organisations and Whitehall. It also administered Camp X, a training camp for SOE personnel situated near Oshawa, Ontario, Canada.

29. Radosh, R. and Milton, J., *The Rosenberg File: A Search for the Truth* (New Haven, CT, 1997) p. 30.

30. A development of a heavier, improved Lockheed Lightning twin-boom P38 fighter, but there were constant problems with fitting it with adequate engines. In its final version it became a high-altitude fighter, using large-bore cannon firing high-explosive shells to break up bomber formations. Only one was ever built.

31. Andrew, C. and Mitrokhin, V., *The Mitrokhin Archive* (London, 1999) p. 718. As they point out, Stalin therefore knew about VENONA some five years before the president or the CIA.

32. Haynes and Klehr, *op. cit.*, p. 51.

33. Olmsted, *op. cit.*, p. 49.

34. Modin, Y., *My Five Cambridge Friends* (New York, 1994) p. 189.

35. Olmsted, *op. cit.*, p. 203.

BIBLIOGRAPHY

Andrew, C., *The Defence of the Realm: The Authorised History of MI5* (London, 2009)

Andrew, C. and Gordievsky, O., *KGB: The Inside Story of Its Foreign Operations from Lenin to Gorbachev* (London, 1990)

Andrew. C. and Mitrokhin, V., *The Mitrokhin Archive* (London, 2000)

Bagnold, R., *Libyan Sands: Travels in a Dead World* (London, 2010)

Bazna, E., *I was Cicero* (London, 1962)

Bentley, E., *Out of Bondage* (London, 1952)

Bierman, J., *The Secret Life of Laszlo Almasy* (London, 2004)

Borovik, G., *The Philby Files* (Boston, 1994)

Bristow, D., *A Game of Moles* (London, 1993)

Cairncross, J., *The Enigma Spy* (London, 1997)

Carré, M., *I was the Cat* (London, 1960)

Carter, M., *Anthony Blunt: His Lives* (London, 2001)

Cecil, R., *A Divided Life: A Personal Portrait of the Spy Donald Maclean* (London, 1989)

Ciechanowski, J. (ed.), *Intelligence Co-operation between Poland and Great Britain during the Second World War: Vol. 2: Documents* (Warsaw, 2005)

Connolly, C., *The Missing Diplomats* (London, 1952)

Costello, J. and Tsarev, O., *Deadly Illusions* (London, 1993)

Damaskin, I. with Elliott, G., *Kitty Harris: The Spy with Seventeen Names* (London, 2001)

Dear, I.C.B. (ed.), *Oxford Companion to World War II* (rev. edn, Oxford, 2005)

Delattre, L., *A Spy at the Heart of the Third Reich* (London, 2003)

Denniston, R., *Churchill's Secret War* (London, 1997)

Doerries, R., *Hitler's Last Chief of Foreign Intelligence: Allied Interrogations of Walter Schellenberg* (Portland, OR, 2003)

Douglas, W. and Wright, R., *Combat and Command: The Story of an Airman in Two World Wars* (London, 1966)

Elliott, N., *Never Judge a Man by his Umbrella* (Salisbury, 1991)

Elliott, N., *With My Little Eye* (London, 1993)

Eppler, J., *Operation Condor* (London, 1977)

Haggett, P. (ed.), *Encyclopedia of World Geography*, vol. 8 (London, 2001)

Harris, J., *Goronwy Rees* (Cardiff, 2001)

Haynes, J. and Klehr, H., *Venona: Decoding Soviet Espionage in America* (New Haven, CT, 1999)

Haynes, J. and Klehr, H., *Spies: The Rise and Fall of the KGB in America* (New Haven, CT, 2009)

Hennessey, T. and Thomas, C., *Spooks – The Unofficial History of MI5* (Stroud, 2009)

Hinsley, F.H. *et al.*, *British Intelligence in the Second World War*, 4 Vols (London, 1978–90)

Hoare, O., *Camp 020: MI5 and the Nazi Spies – The Official History of MI5's Wartime Interrogation Centre* (Kew, 2000)

Jeffery, K., *MI6: The History of the Secret Intelligence Service, 1909–1949* (London, 2010)

Johnson, C., *An Instance of Treason: Ozaki Hotsumi and the Sorge Spy Ring* (expanded edn, Stanford, CA, 1990)

Jonason, T. and Olsson, S., *Agent Tate: The Wartime Story of Harry Williamson* (Stroud, 2011)

Kitson, S., *The Hunt for Nazi Spies: Fighting Espionage in Vichy France* (Chicago, IL, 2008)

Koster, J., *Operation SNOW: How a Soviet Mole in FDR's White House Triggered Pearl Harbor* (Washington DC, 2012)

Kotani, K., *Japanese Intelligence in World War II* (Oxford, 2009)

Lamphere, R., *The FBI–KGB War: A Special Agent's Story* (new edn, Macon, GA, 1995)

Macintyre, B., *Agent Zig Zag* (London, 2007)

MacKinnon, J. and MacKinnon, S., *Agnes Smedley: The Life and Times of an American Radical* (London, 1988)

Masterman, J., *The Double-Cross System in the War of 1939 to 1945* (New Haven, CT, 1971)

Miller, R., *Codename Tricycle* (London, 2005)

Modin, Y., *My Five Cambridge Friends* (New York, 1994)

Montagu, E., *Beyond Top Secret Ultra* (London, 1977)

Mosley, L., *The Cat and the Mice* (London, 1958)

Moyzisch, L., *Operation Cicero* (London, 1950)

Murphy, R., *Diplomat Among Warriors* (New York, 1964)

Obi Toshito (ed.), *Gendai-shi Shiryo, Zoruge Jiken (Collection of Source Materials Relating to Modern Japanese History)*, 4 Vols (Tokyo, 1962, 1971).

Olmsted, K., *Red Spy Queen: A Biography of Elizabeth Bentley* (Chapel Hill, NC, 2002).

Philby, K., *My Silent War* (London, 1968).

Philby, R., Peake, H. and Lyubimov, M., *The Private Life of Kim Philby: The Moscow Years* (London, 2000)

Popov, D., *Spy/Counterspy* (London, 1974)

Prange, G.W., *Target Tokyo* (New York, 1985)

Radosh, R. and Milton, J., *The Rosenberg File: A Search for the Truth* (New Haven, 1997)

Rees, J., *Looking for Mr Nobody: The Secret Life of Goronwy Rees* (London, 1994)

Rimer, J. (ed.), *Patriots and Traitors: Sorge and Ozaki* (Portland, ME, 1963)

Roosevelt, K. (intro.), *The Secret War Report of the OSS* (New York, 1976)

Rose, K., *Elusive Rothschild* (London, 2003)

Sadat, A., *Revolt on the Nile* (London, 1947)

Sansom, A., *I Spied Spies* (London, 1965)

Schellenberg, W., *The Schellenberg Memoirs* (London, 1956)

Seaman, M. (intro.) *Garbo: The Spy Who Saved D-Day* (Kew, 2004)

Shillony, B.-A., *Politics and Culture in Wartime Japan* (Oxford, 1991)

Slowikowski, R., *In The Secret Service: The Lighting of the Torch* (London, 1988)

Stirling, T. *et al.* (ed.), *Intelligence Co-operation between Poland and Great Britain during the Second World War: Vol. 1: The Report of the Anglo-Polish Historical Committee* (London, 2005)

Vaughan, H., *FDR's 12 Apostles* (Guilford, CT, 2006)

Von Papen, F., *Memoirs* (London, 1952)

West, N., *Unreliable Witness* (London, 1984). Published in the United States as *A Thread of Deceit*

West, N., *Counterfeit Spies* (London, 1998)

West, N., *VENONA: The Greatest Secret of the Cold War* (London, 1999)

West, N., *Historical Dictionary of Cold War Counterintelligence* (Lanham, MD, 2007)

West, N. (ed.), *The Guy Liddell Diaries, Vol. I: 1939–42* (London, 2005)

West, N. (ed.), *The Guy Liddell Diaries, Vol. II: 1942–45* (London, 2005)

West, N. and Pujol, J., *Operation Garbo* (London, 2011)

West, N. and Roberts, M., *SNOW: The Double Life of a World War II Spy* (London, 2011)

West, N. and Tsarev, O., *The Crown Jewels* (London, 1998)

West, N. and Tsarev, O., *Triplex* (London, 2009)

Whymant, R., *Stalin's Spy* (London, 1996)

Wires, R., *The Cicero Spy Affair* (London, 1999)

Wright, P., *Spycatcher* (New York, 1987)

Index